$45.00

Bloom's Modern Critical Views

Bloom's Modern Critical Views

Bloom's Modern Critical Views

ERNEST HEMINGWAY

Edited and with an introduction by
Harold Bloom
Sterling Professor of the Humanities
Yale University

CHELSEA HOUSE
PUBLISHERS
A Haights Cross Communications Company

Philadelphia

©2005 by Chelsea House Publishers, a subsidiary of
Haights Cross Communications.

A Haights Cross Communications ⬥ Company

Introduction © 2005 by Harold Bloom.

Printed and bound in the United States of America.
10 9 8 7 6 5 4 3 2 1

Library of Congress Cataloging-in-Publication Data applied for.

Ernest Hemingway / Harold Bloom, ed.
    p. cm. — (Bloom's modern critical views)
  Includes bibliographical references and index.
  ISBN 0-7910-8135-4 (alk. paper)
  1. Hemingway, Ernest, 1899-1961—Criticism and interpretation.   I. Bloom, Harold.
II. Series.
PS3515.E37Z58655 2004
813'.52—dc21

                                        2004012644

Contributing Editor: Grace Kim

Cover designed by Keith Trego

Cover photo: © Hulton/Archive by Getty Images, Inc.

Layout by EJB Publishing Services

All links and web addresses were checked and verified to be correct at the time of
publication. Because of the dynamic nature of the web, some addresses and links may
have changed since publication and may no longer be valid.

Contents

The Disabled Able Body and White Heteromasculinity   179
    Debra A. Moddelmog

Santiago and the Eternal Feminine:
Gendering *La Mar* in *The Old Man and the Sea*   193
    Susan F. Beegel

Editor's Note

My Introduction acknowledges Hemingway's genius at composing the short story, while questioning his achievement as a novelist.

The distinguished poet-novelist Robert Penn Warren commends Hemingway as a lyric writer, while the major critic Edmund Wilson measures Hemingway's criticism of society as being unique in its sensibility.

Hemingway's biographer, Carlos Baker, admires the beauty of his subject's prose, after which the grand poet John Hollander examines the "poetics of extraordinary actuality" in some of the best stories.

Earl Rovit and Gerry Bremer give us Hemingway as a writer of romances, while Edwin Stanton vividly describes *Death In the Afternoon*, and Mark Spilka powerfully muses upon the writer's androgyny, remarkably memorialized by the posthumously published *The Garden of Eden*.

Aspects of Hemingway's implied reader are explained by Hubert Zapf, after which Earl Rovit returns with a wise meditation upon the psychic, social, and aesthetic *exclusion* that centers the narrative art.

The wound and its meanings in Hemingway are the matter on which Debra A. Moddelmog ruminates, while Susan F. Beegel studies aspects of gendering in *The Old Man and the Sea*, which I myself read as involuntary self-parody.

HAROLD BLOOM

Introduction

I

Hemingway freely proclaimed his relationship to *Huckleberry Finn*, and there is some basis for the assertion, except that there is little in common between the rhetorical stances of Twain and of Hemingway. Kipling's *Kim*, in style and mode, is far closer to *Huckleberry Finn* than anything Hemingway wrote. The true accent of Hemingway's admirable style is to be found in an even greater and more surprising precursor:

> This grass is very dark to be from the white heads of old
>   mothers,
> Darker than the colorless beards of old men,
> Dark to come from under the faint red roofs of mouths.

Or again:

> I clutch the rails of the fence, my gore drips, thinn'd with
>   the ooze of my skin,
> I fall on the weeds and stones,
> The riders spur their unwilling horses, haul close,
> Taunt my dizzy ears and beat me violently over the head
>   with whip-stocks.
> Agonies are one of my changes of garments,
> I do not ask the wounded person how he feels, I myself
>   become the wounded person,
> My hurts turn livid upon me as I lean on a cane and observe.

1

Hemingway is scarcely unique in not acknowledging the paternity of Walt Whitman; T.S. Eliot and Wallace Stevens are far closer to Whitman than William Carlos Williams and Hart Crane were, but literary influence is a paradoxical and antithetical process, about which we continue to know all too little. The profound affinities between Hemingway, Eliot, and Stevens are not accidental, but are family resemblances due to the repressed but crucial relation each had to Whitman's work. Hemingway characteristically boasted (in a letter to Sara Murphy, February 27, 1936) that he had knocked Stevens down quite handily: "... for statistics sake Mr. Stevens is 6 feet 2 weighs 225 lbs. and ... when he hits the ground it is highly spectaculous." Since this match between the two writers took place in Key West on February 19, 1936, I am moved, as a loyal Stevensian, for statistics' sake to point out that the victorious Hemingway was born in 1899, and the defeated Stevens in 1879, so that the novelist was then going on thirty-seven, and the poet verging on fifty-seven. The two men doubtless despised one another, but in the letter celebrating his victory, Hemingway calls Stevens "a damned fine poet" and Stevens always affirmed that Hemingway was essentially a poet, a judgment concurred in by Robert Penn Warren when he wrote that Hemingway "is essentially a lyric rather than a dramatic writer." Warren compared Hemingway to Wordsworth, which is feasible, but the resemblance to Whitman is far closer. Wordsworth would not have written: "I am the man, I suffer'd, I was there," but Hemingway almost persuades us he would have achieved that line had not Whitman set it down first.

II

It is now more than twenty years since Hemingway's suicide, and some aspects of his permanent canonical status seem beyond doubt. Only a few modern American novels seem certain to endure: *The Sun Also Rises, The Great Gatsby, Miss Lonelyhearts, The Crying of Lot 49* and at least several by Faulkner, including *As I Lay Dying, Sanctuary, Light in August, The Sound and the Fury, Absalom, Absalom!* Two dozen stories by Hemingway could be added to the group, indeed perhaps all of *The First Forty-Nine Stories*. Faulkner is an eminence apart, but critics agree that Hemingway and Fitzgerald are his nearest rivals, largely on the strength of their shorter fiction. What seems unique is that Hemingway is the only American writer of prose fiction in this century who, as a stylist, rivals the principal poets: Stevens, Eliot, Frost, Hart Crane, aspects of Pound, W.C. Williams, Robert Penn Warren, and Elizabeth Bishop. This is hardly to say that Hemingway, at his best, fails at narrative or the representation of character. Rather, his peculiar excellence is closer to Whitman than to Twain, closer to Stevens than to Faulkner, and even closer to Eliot than to Fitzgerald, who was his friend and rival. He is an elegiac poet who mourns the self, who celebrates the self (rather less effectively) and who suffers divisions in the self. In the broadest tradition of American literature, he stems ultimately from the Emersonian reliance on the god within, which is the line of Whitman, Thoreau, and Dickinson. He arrives late and dark in this tradition, and is one of its negative theologians, as it were, but as in Stevens the negations, the cancellings, are never final. Even the most ferocious of his stories, say "God Rest You Merry, Gentlemen" or "A Natural History of the Dead," can be said to celebrate what we might call the Real Absence. Doc Fischer, in "God Rest You Merry, Gentlemen," is a precursor of Nathanael West's Shrike in *Miss Lonelyhearts*, and his savage, implicit religiosity prophesies not only Shrike's Satanic stance but the entire demonic world of Pynchon's explicitly paranoid or Luddite visions. Perhaps there was a nostalgia for a Catholic order always abiding in Hemingway's consciousness, but the cosmos of his fiction, early and late, is American Gnostic, as it was in Melville, who first developed so strongly the negative side of the Emersonian religion of self-reliance.

III

Hemingway notoriously and splendidly was given to overtly agonistic images whenever he described his relationship to canonical writers, including Melville, a habit of description in which he has been followed by his true ephebe, Norman Mailer. In a grand letter (September 6–7, 1949) to his publisher, Charles Scribner, he charmingly confessed: "Am a man without any ambition, except to be champion of the world, I wouldn't fight Dr. Tolstoi in a 20 round bout because I know he would knock my ears off." This modesty passed quickly, to be followed by: "If I can live to 60 I can beat him. (MAYBE)" Since the rest of the letter counts Turgenev, De Maupassant, Henry James, even Cervantes, as well as Melville and Dostoevsky, among the defeated, we can join Hemingway, himself, in admiring his extraordinary self-confidence. How justified was it, in terms of his ambitions?

It could be argued persuasively that Hemingway is the best short-story writer in the English language from Joyce's *Dubliners* until the present. The aesthetic dignity of the short story need not be questioned, and yet we seem to ask more of a canonical writer. Hemingway wrote *The Sun Also Rises* and not *Ulysses*, which is only to say that his true genius was for very short stories, and hardly at all for extended narrative. Had he been primarily a poet, his lyrical gifts would have sufficed: we do not hold it against Yeats that his poems, not his plays, are his principal glory. Alas, neither Turgenev nor Henry James, neither Melville nor Mark Twain provide true agonists for Hemingway. Instead, De Maupassant is the apter rival. Of Hemingway's intensity of style in the briefer compass, there is no question, but even *The Sun Also Rises* reads now as a series of epiphanies, of brilliant and memorable vignettes.

Much that has been harshly criticized in Hemingway, particularly in *For Whom the Bell Tolls*, results from his difficulty in adjusting his gifts to the demands of the novel. Robert Penn Warren suggests that Hemingway is successful when his "system of ironies and understatements is coherent." When incoherent, then Hemingway's rhetoric fails as persuasion, which is to say, we read *To Have and Have Not* or *For Whom the Bell Tolls* and we are all too aware that the system of tropes is primarily what we are offered. Warren believes this not to be true of *A Farewell to Arms*, yet even the celebrated close of the novel seems now a worn understatement:

> But after I had got them out and shut the door and turned off the light it wasn't any good. It was like saying good-by to a statue. After a while I went out and left the hospital and walked back to the hotel in the rain.

Contrast this to the close of "Old Man at the Bridge," a story only two and a half pages long:

> There was nothing to do about him. It was Easter Sunday and the Fascists were advancing toward the Ebro. It was a gray overcast day with a low ceiling so their planes were not up. That and the fact that cats know how to look after themselves was all the good luck that old man would ever have.

The understatement continues to persuade here because the stoicism remains coherent, and is admirably fitted by the rhetoric. A very short story concludes itself by permanently troping the mood of a particular moment in history. Vignette is Hemingway's natural mode, or call it hard-edged vignette: a literary sketch that somehow seems to be the beginning or end of something longer, yet truly is complete in itself. Hemingway's style encloses what ought to be unenclosed, so that the genre remains subtle yet trades its charm for punch. But a novel of three hundred and forty pages (*A Farewell to Arms*) which I have just finished reading again (after twenty years away from it) cannot sustain itself upon the rhetoric of vignette. After many understatements, too many, the reader begins to believe that he is reading a Hemingway imitator, like the accomplished John O'Hara, rather than the master himself. Hemingway's notorious fault is the monotony of repetition, which becomes a dulling litany in a somewhat less accomplished imitator like Nelson Algren, and sometimes seems self-parody when we must confront it in Hemingway.

Nothing is got for nothing, and a great style generates defenses in us, particularly when it sets the style of an age, as the Byronic Hemingway did. As with Byron, the color and variety of the artist's life becomes something of a veil between the work and our aesthetic apprehension of it. Hemingway's career included four marriages (and three divorces); service as an ambulance driver for the Italians in World War I (with an honorable wound); activity as a war correspondent in the Greek-Turkish War (1922), the Spanish Civil War (1937–39), the Chinese-Japanese War (1941) and the War against Hitler in Europe (1944–45). Add big-game hunting and fishing, safaris, expatriation in France and Cuba, bullfighting, the Nobel prize, and ultimate suicide in Idaho, and you have an absurdly implausible life, apparently lived in imitation of Hemingway's own fiction. The final effect of the work and the life together is not less than mythological, as it was with Byron, and with Whitman and with Oscar Wilde. Hemingway now is myth, and so is permanent as an image of American heroism, or perhaps more ruefully the American illusion of heroism. The best of Hemingway's work, the stories and *The Sun Also Rises*, are also a permanent part of the American mythology. Faulkner, Stevens, Frost, perhaps Eliot, and Hart Crane were stronger writers than Hemingway, but he alone in this American century has achieved the enduring status of myth.

EDMUND WILSON

Hemingway: Gauge of Morale

Ernest Hemingway's *In Our Time* was an odd and original book. It had the appearance of a miscellany of stories and fragments; but actually the parts hung together and produced a definite effect. There were two distinct series of pieces which alternated with one another: one a set of brief and brutal sketches of police shootings, bullfight crises, hangings of criminals, and incidents of the war; and the other a set of short stories dealing in its principal sequence with the growing-up of an American boy against a landscape of idyllic Michigan, but interspersed also with glimpses of American soldiers returning home. It seems to have been Hemingway's intention—'*In Our Time*'—that the war should set the key for the whole. The cold-bloodedness of the battles and executions strikes a discord with the sensitiveness and candor of the boy at home in the States; and presently the boy turns up in Europe in one of the intermediate vignettes as a soldier in the Italian army, hit in the spine by machine-gun fire and trying to talk to a dying Italian: '*Senta*, Rinaldi. *Senta*,' he says, 'you and me, we've made a separate peace.'

But there is a more fundamental relationship between the pieces of the two series. The shooting of Nick in the war does not really connect two different worlds: has he not found in the butchery abroad the same world that he knew back in Michigan? Was not life in the Michigan woods equally

---

From *The Wound and the Bow: Seven Studies in the Literature*. © 1941 by Edmund Wilson. New printing with corrections, 1947.

destructive and cruel? He had gone once with his father, the doctor, when he had performed a Caesarean operation on an Indian squaw with a jackknife and no anaesthetic and had sewed her up with fishing leaders, while the Indian hadn't been able to bear it and had cut his throat in his bunk. Another time, when the doctor had saved the life of a squaw, her Indian had picked a quarrel with him rather than pay him in work. And Nick himself had sent his girl about her business when he had found out how terrible her mother was. Even fishing in Big Two-Hearted River—away and free in the woods—he had been conscious in a curious way of the cruelty inflicted on the fish, even of the silent agonies endured by the live bait, the grasshoppers kicking on the hook.

Not that life isn't enjoyable. Talking and drinking with one's friends is great fun; fishing in Big Two-Hearted River is a tranquil exhilaration. But the brutality of life is always there, and it is somehow bound up with the enjoyment. Bullfights are especially enjoyable. It is even exhilarating to build a simply priceless barricade and pot the enemy as they are trying to get over it. The condition of life is pain; and the joys of the most innocent surface are somehow tied to its stifled pangs.

The resolution of this dissonance in art made the beauty of Hemingway's stories. He had in the process tuned a marvelous prose. Out of the colloquial American speech, with its simple declarative sentences and its strings of Nordic monosyllables, he got effects of the utmost subtlety. F.M. Ford has found the perfect simile for the impression produced by this writing: 'Hemingway's words strike you, each one, as if they were pebbles fetched fresh from a brook. They live and shine, each in its place. So one of his pages has the effect of a brook-bottom into which you look down through the flowing water. The words form a tesellation, each in order beside the other.'

Looking back, we can see how this style was already being refined and developed at a time—fifty years before—when it was regarded in most literary quarters as hopelessly non-literary and vulgar. Had there not been the nineteenth chapter of *Huckleberry Finn?*—'Two or three nights went by; I reckon I might say they swum by; they slid along so quick and smooth and lovely. Here is the way we put in the time. It was a monstrous big river down there—sometimes a mile and a half wide,' and so forth. These pages, when we happen to meet them in Carl Van Doren's anthology of world literature, stand up in a striking way beside a passage of description from Turgenev; and the pages which Hemingway was later to write about American wood and water are equivalents to the transcriptions by Turgenev—the *Sportsman's Notebook* is much admired by Hemingway—of Russian forests and fields.

Each has brought to an immense and wild country the freshness of a new speech and a sensibility not yet conventionalized by literary associations. Yet it *is* the European sensibility which has come to Big Two-Hearted River, where the Indians are now obsolescent; in those solitudes it feels for the first time the cold current, the hot morning sun, sees the pine stumps, smells the sweet fern. And along with the mottled trout, with its 'clear water-over-gravel color,' the boy from the American Middle West fishes up a nice little masterpiece.

In the meantime there had been also Ring Lardner, Sherwood Anderson, Gertrude Stein, using this American language for irony, lyric poetry or psychological insight. Hemingway seems to have learned from them all. But he is now able to charge this naïve accent with a new complexity of emotion, a new shade of emotion: a malaise. The wholesale shattering of human beings in which he has taken part has given the boy a touch of panic.

II

The next fishing trip is strikingly different. Perhaps the first had been an idealization. Is it possible to attain to such sensuous bliss merely through going alone into the woods: smoking, fishing, and eating, with no thought about anyone else or about anything one has ever done or will ever be obliged to do? At any rate, today, in *The Sun Also Rises*, all the things that are wrong with human life are there on the holiday, too—though one tries to keep them back out of the foreground and to occupy one's mind with the trout, caught now in a stream of the Pyrenees, and with the kidding of the friend from the States. The feeling of insecurity has deepened. The young American now appears in a seriously damaged condition: he has somehow been incapacitated sexually through wounds received in the war. He is in love with one of those international sirens who flourished in the cafés of the post-war period and whose ruthless and uncontrollable infidelities, in such a circle as that depicted by Hemingway, have made any sort of security impossible for the relations between women and men. The lovers of such a woman turn upon and rend one another because they are powerless to make themselves felt by *her*.

The casualties of the bullfight at Pamplona, to which these young people have gone for the *fiesta*, only reflect the blows and betrayals of demoralized human beings out of hand. What is the tiresome lover with whom the lady has just been off on a casual escapade, and who is unable to understand that he has been discarded, but the man who, on his way to the bull ring, has been accidentally gored by the bull? The young American who tells the story is the only character who keeps up standards of conduct, and he is prevented by his disability from dominating and directing the woman, who otherwise, it is intimated, might love him. Here the membrane of the style has been stretched taut to convey the vibrations of these qualms. The dry sunlight and the green summer landscapes have been invested with a sinister quality which must be new in literature. One enjoys the sun and the green as one enjoys suckling pigs and Spanish wine, but the uneasiness and apprehension are undruggable.

Yet one can catch hold of a code in all the drunkenness and the social chaos. 'Perhaps as you went along you did learn something,' Jake, the hero, reflects at one point. 'I did not care what it was all about. All I wanted to know was how to live in it. Maybe if you found out how to live in it you learned from that what it was all about.' 'Everybody behaves badly. Give them the proper chance,' he says later to Lady Brett.

'"You wouldn't behave badly." Brett looked at me.' In the end, she sends for Jake, who finds her alone in a hotel. She has left her regular lover for a young bullfighter, and this boy has for the first time inspired her with a respect which has restrained her from 'ruining' him: 'You know it makes one feel rather good deciding not to be a bitch.' We suffer and we make suffer, and everybody loses out in the long run; but in the meantime we can lose with honor.

This code still markedly figures, still supplies a dependable moral backbone, in Hemingway's next book of short stories, *Men Without Women*. Here Hemingway has mastered his method of economy in apparent casualness and relevance in apparent indirection, and has turned his sense of what happens and the way in which it happens into something as hard and clear as a crystal but as disturbing as a great lyric. Yet it is usually some principle of courage, of honor, of pity—that is, some principle of sportsmanship in its largest human sense—upon which the drama hinges. The old bullfighter in *The Undefeated* is defeated in everything except the spirit which will not accept defeat. You get the bull or he gets you: if you die, you can die game; there are certain things you cannot do. The burlesque show manager in *A Pursuit Race* refrains from waking his advance publicity agent when he overtakes him and realizes that the man has just lost a long struggle against whatever anguish it is that has driven him to drink and dope. 'They got a cure for that,' the manager had said to him before he went to sleep; '"No," William Campbell said, "they haven't got a cure for anything."' The burned major in *A Simple Enquiry*—that strange picture of the bedrock stoicism compatible with the abasement of war—has the decency not to dismiss the orderly who has rejected his proposition. The brutalized Alpine peasant who has been in the habit of hanging a lantern in the jaws of the stiffened corpse of his wife, stood in the corner of the woodshed till the spring will make it possible to bury her, is ashamed to drink with the sexton after the latter has found out what he has done. And there is a little sketch of Roman soldiers just after the Crucifixion: 'You see me slip the old spear into him?—You'll get into trouble doing that some day.—It was the least I could do for him. I'll tell you he looked pretty good to me in there today.'

This Hemingway of the middle twenties—*The Sun Also Rises* came out in '26—expressed the romantic disillusion and set the favorite pose for the period. It was the moment of gallantry in heartbreak, grim and nonchalant banter, and heroic dissipation. The great watchword was 'Have a drink', and in the bars of New York and Paris the young people were getting to talk like Hemingway.

III

The novel, *A Farewell to Arms*, which followed *Men Without Women*, is in a sense not so serious an affair. Beautifully written and quite moving of course it is. Probably no other book has caught so well the strangeness of life in the army for an American in Europe during the war. The new places to which one was sent of which one had never heard, and the things that turned out to be in them; the ordinary people of foreign countries as one saw them when one was quartered among them or obliged to perform some common work with them; the pleasures of which one managed to cheat the war, intensified by the uncertainty and horror—and the uncertainty, nevertheless, almost become a constant, the horror almost taken for granted; the love affairs, always subject to being suddenly broken up and yet carried on while they lasted in a spirit of irresponsible freedom which derived from one's having forfeited control of all one's other actions—this Hemingway got into his book, written long enough after the events for them to present themselves under an aspect fully idyllic.

But *A Farewell to Arms* is a tragedy, and the lovers are shown as innocent victims with no relation to the forces that torment them. They themselves are not tormented within by that dissonance between personal satisfaction and the suffering one shares with others which it has been Hemingway's triumph to handle. *A Farewell to Arms*, as the author once said, is a *Romeo and Juliet*. And when Catherine and her lover emerge from the stream of action—the account of the Caporetto retreat is Hemingway's best sustained piece of narrative—when they escape from the alien necessities of which their romance has been merely an accident, which have been writing their story for them, then we see that they are not in themselves convincing as human personalities. And we are confronted with the paradox that Hemingway, who possesses so remarkable a mimetic gift in getting the tone of social and national types and in making his people talk appropriately, has not shown any very solid sense of character, or, indeed, any real interest in it. The people in his short stories are satisfactory because he has only to hit them off: the point of the story does not lie in personalities, but in the emotion to which a situation gives rise. This is true even in *The Sun Also Rises*, where the characters are sketched with wonderful cleverness. But in *A Farewell to Arms*, as soon as we are brought into real intimacy with the lovers, as soon as the author is obliged to see them through a searching personal experience, we find merely an idealized relationship, the abstractions of a lyric emotion.

With *Death in the Afternoon*, three years later, a new development for Hemingway commences. He writes a book not merely in the first person, but in the first person in his own character as Hemingway, and the results are unexpected and disconcerting. *Death in the Afternoon* has its value as an exposition of bullfighting; and Hemingway is able to use the subject as a text for an explicit statement of his conception of man eternally pitting himself— he thinks the bullfight a ritual of this—against animal force and the odds of death. But the book is partly infected by a queer kind of maudlin emotion, which sounds at once neurotic and drunken. He overdoes his glorification of the bravery and martyrdom of the bullfighter. No doubt the professional expert at risking his life single-handed is impressive in contrast to the flatness and unreality of much of the business of the modern world; but this admirable miniaturist in prose has already made the point perhaps more tellingly in the little prose poem called *Banal Story*. Now he offsets the virility of the bullfighters by anecdotes of the male homosexuals that frequent the Paris cafés, at the same time that he puts his chief celebration of the voluptuous excitement of the spectacle into the mouth of an imaginary old lady. The whole thing becomes a little hysterical.

The master of that precise and clean style now indulges in purple patches which go on spreading for pages. I am not one of those who admire the last chapter of *Death in the Afternoon*, with its rich, all too rich, unrollings of memories of good times in Spain, and with its what seem to me irrelevant reminiscences of the soliloquy of Mrs. Bloom in *Ulysses*. Also, there are interludes of kidding of a kind which Hemingway handles with skill when he assigns them to characters in his stories, but in connection with which he seems to become incapable of exercising good sense or good taste as soon as he undertakes them in his own person (the burlesque *Torrents of Spring* was an early omen of this). In short, we are compelled to recognize that, as soon as Hemingway drops the burning-glass of the disciplined and objective art with which he has learned to concentrate in a story the light of the emotions that flood in on him, he straightway becomes befuddled, slops over.

This befuddlement is later to go further, but in the meantime he publishes another volume of stories—*Winner Take Nothing*—which is almost up to its predecessor. In this collection he deals much more effectively than in *Death in the Afternoon* with that theme of contemporary decadence which is implied in his panegyric of the bullfighter. The first of these stories, *After the Storm*, is another of his variations—and one of the finest—on the theme of keeping up a code of decency among the hazards and pains of life. A fisherman goes out to plunder a wreck: he dives down to break in through a porthole, but inside he sees a woman with rings on her hands and her hair floating loose in the water, and he thinks about the passengers and crew being suddenly plunged to their deaths (he has almost been killed himself in a drunken fight the night before). He sees the cloud of sea birds screaming around, and he finds that he is unable to break the glass with his wrench and that he loses the anchor grapple with which he next tries to attack it. So he finally goes away and leaves the job to the Greeks, who blow the boat open and clean her out.

But in general the emotions of insecurity here obtrude themselves and dominate the book. Two of the stories deal with the hysteria of soldiers falling off the brink of their nerves under the strain of the experiences of the war, which here no longer presents an idyllic aspect; another deals with a group of patients in a hospital, at the same time crippled and hopeless; still another (a five-page masterpiece) with a waiter, who, both on his own and on his customers' account, is reluctant to go home at night, because he feels the importance of a 'clean well-lighted cafe' as a refuge from the 'nothing' that people fear. *God Rest You Merry, Gentlemen* repeats the theme of castration of *The Sun Also Rises;* and four of the stories are concerned more or less with male or female homosexuality. In the last story, *Fathers and Sons*, Hemingway reverts to the Michigan woods, as if to take the curse off the rest: young Nick had once enjoyed a nice Indian girl with plump legs and hard little breasts on the needles of the hemlock woods.

These stories and the interludes in *Death in the Afternoon* must have been written during the years that followed the stock-market crash. They are full of the apprehension of losing control of oneself which is aroused by the getting out of hand of a social-economic system, as well as of the fear of impotence which seems to accompany the loss of social mastery. And there is in such a story as *A Clean Well-Lighted Place* the feeling of having got to the end of everything, of having given up heroic attitudes and wanting only the illusion of peace.

IV

And now, in proportion as the characters in his stories run out of fortitude and bravado, he passes into a phase where he is occupied with building up his public personality. He has already now become a legend, as Mencken was in the twenties; he is the Hemingway of the handsome photographs with the sportsmen's tan and the outdoor grin, with the ominous resemblance to Clark Gable, who poses with giant marlin which he has just hauled in off Key West. And unluckily—but for an American inevitably—the opportunity soon presents itself to exploit this personality for profit: he turns up delivering Hemingway monologues in well-paying and trashy magazines; and the Hemingway of these loose disquisitions, arrogant, belligerent and boastful, is certainly the worst-invented character to be found in the author's work. If he is obnoxious, the effect is somewhat mitigated by the fact that he is intrinsically incredible.

There would be no point in mentioning this journalism at all, if it did not seem somewhat to have contributed to the writing of certain unsatisfactory books. *Green Hills of Africa* (1935) owes its failure to falling between the two *genres* of personal exhibitionism and fiction. 'The writer has attempted,' says Hemingway, 'to write an absolutely true book to see whether the shape of a country and the pattern of a month's action can, if truly presented, compete with a work of the imagination.' He does try to present his own rôle objectively, and there is a genuine Hemingway theme— the connection between success at big-game hunting and sexual self-respect—involved in his adventures as he presents them. But the sophisticated technique of the fiction writer comes to look artificial when it is applied to a series of real happenings; and the necessity of sticking to what really happened makes impossible the typical characters and incidents which give point to a work of fiction. The monologues by the false, the publicity, Hemingway with which the narrative is interspersed are almost as bad as the ones that he has been writing for the magazines. He inveighs with much scorn against the literary life and against the professional literary man of the cities; and then manages to give the impression that he himself is a professional literary man of the touchiest and most self-conscious kind. He delivers a self-confident lecture on the high possibilities of prose writing; and then produces such a sentence as the following: 'Going downhill steeply made these Spanish shooting boots too short in the toe and there was an old argument, about this length of boot and whether the bootmaker, whose part I had taken, unwittingly first, only as interpreter, and finally embraced his theory patriotically as a whole and, I believed, by logic, had overcome it by adding onto the heel.' As soon as Hemingway begins speaking in the first person, he seems to lose his bearings, not merely as a critic of life, but even as a craftsman.

In another and significant way, *Green Hills of Africa* is disappointing. *Death in the Afternoon* did provide a lot of data on bullfighting and build up for us the bullfighting world; but its successor tells us little about Africa. Hemingway keeps affirming—as if in accents of defiance against those who would engage his attention for social problems—his passionate enthusiasm for the African country and his perfect satisfaction with the hunter's life; but he has produced what must be one of the only books ever written which make Africa and its animals seem dull. Almost the only thing we learn about the animals is that Hemingway wants to kill them. And as for the natives, though there is one fine description of a tribe of marvelous trained runners, the principal impression we get of them is that they were simple and inferior people who enormously admired Hemingway.

It is not only that, as his critics of the Left had been complaining, he shows no interest in political issues, but that his interest in his fellow beings seems actually to be drying up. It is as if he were throwing himself on African hunting as something to live for and believe in, as something through which to realize himself; and as if, expecting of it too much, he had got out of it abnormally little, less than he is willing to admit. The disquiet of the Hemingway of the twenties had been, as I have said, undruggable—that is, in his books themselves, he had tried to express it, not drug it, had given it an appeasement in art; but now there sets in, in the Hemingway of the thirties, what seems to be a deliberate self-drugging. The situation is indicated objectively in *The Gambler, the Nun and the Radio,* one of the short stories of 1933, in which everything from daily bread to 'a belief in any new form of government' is characterized as 'the opium of the people' by an empty-hearted patient in a hospital.

But at last there did rush into this vacuum the blast of the social issue, which had been roaring in the wind like a forest fire.

Out of a series of short stories that Hemingway had written about a Florida waterside character he decided to make a little epic. The result was *To Have and Have Not,* which seems to me the poorest of all his stories. Certainly some deep agitation is working upon Hemingway the artist.

Craftsmanship and style, taste and sense, have all alike gone by the board. The negative attitude toward human beings has here become definitely malignant: the hero is like a wooden-headed Punch, always knocking people on the head (inferiors—Chinamen or Cubans); or, rather, he combines the characteristics of Punch with those of Popeye the Sailor in the animated cartoon in the movies. As the climax to a series of prodigies, this stupendous pirate-smuggler named Harry Morgan succeeds, alone, unarmed, and with only a hook for one hand—though at the cost of a mortal wound—in outwitting and destroying with their own weapons four men carrying revolvers and a machine gun, by whom he has been shanghaied in a launch. The only way in which Hemingway's outlaw suffers by comparison with Popeye is that his creator has not tried to make him plausible by explaining that he does it all on spinach.

The impotence of a decadent society has here been exploited deliberately, but less successfully than in the earlier short stories. Against a background of homosexuality, impotence and masturbation among the wealthy holiday-makers in Florida, Popeye-Morgan is shown gratifying his wife with the same indefatigable dexterity which he has displayed in his other feats; and there is a choral refrain of praise of his *cojones*, which wells up in the last pages of the book when the abandoned Mrs. Popeye regurgitates Molly Bloom's soliloquy.

To be a man in such a world of maggots is noble, but it is not enough. Besides the maggots, there are double-crossing rats, who will get you if they are given the slightest chance. What is most valid in *To Have and Have Not* is the idea—conveyed better, perhaps, in the first of the series of episodes than in the final scenes of massacre and agony—that in an atmosphere (here revolutionary Cuba) in which man has been set against man, in which it is always a question whether your companion is not preparing to cut your throat, the most sturdy and straightforward American will turn suspicious and cruel. Harry Morgan is made to realize as he dies that to fight this bad world alone is hopeless. Again Hemingway, with his barometric accuracy, has rendered a moral atmosphere that was prevalent at the moment he was writing—a moment when social relations were subjected to severe tensions, when they seemed sometimes already disintegrating. But the heroic Hemingway legend has at this point invaded his fiction and, inflaming and inflating his symbols, has produced an implausible hybrid, half Hemingway character, half nature myth.

Hemingway had not himself particularly labored this moral of individualism *versus* solidarity, but the critics of the Left labored it for him and received his least creditable piece of fiction as the delivery of a new revelation. The progress of the Communist faith among our writers since the beginning of the depression has followed a peculiar course. That the aims and beliefs of Marx and Lenin should have come through to the minds of intellectuals who had been educated in the bourgeois tradition as great awakeners of conscience, a great light, was quite natural and entirely desirable. But the conception of the dynamic Marxist will, the exaltation of the Marxist religion, seized the members of the professional classes like a capricious contagion or hurricane, which shakes one and leaves his neighbor standing, then returns to lay hold on the second after the first has become quiet again. In the moment of seizure, each one of them saw a scroll unrolled from the heavens, on which Marx and Lenin and Stalin, the Bolsheviks of 1917, the Soviets of the Five-Year Plan, and the GPU of the Moscow trials were all a part of the same great purpose. Later the convert, if he were capable of it, would get over his first phase of snow blindness and learn to see real people and conditions, would study the development of Marxism in terms of nations, periods, personalities, instead of logical deductions from abstract propositions or—as in the case of the more naïve or dishonest—of simple incantatory slogans. But for many there was at least a moment when the key to all the mysteries of human history seemed suddenly to have been placed in their hands, when an infallible guide to thought and behavior seemed to have been given them in a few easy formulas.

Hemingway was hit pretty late. He was still in *Death in the Afternoon* telling the 'world-savers,' sensibly enough, that they should 'get to see' the world 'clear and as a whole. Then any part you make will represent the whole, if it's made truly. The thing to do is work and learn to make it.' Later he jibed at the literary radicals, who talked but couldn't take it; and one finds even in *To Have and Have Not* a crack about a 'highly paid Hollywood director, whose brain is in the process of outlasting his liver so that he will end up calling himself a Communist, to save his soul.' Then the challenge of the fight itself—Hemingway never could resist a physical challenge—the natural impulse to dedicate oneself to something bigger than big-game hunting and bullfighting, and the fact that the class war had broken out in a country to which he was romantically attached, seem to have combined to make him align himself with the Communists as well as the Spanish Loyalists at a time when the Marxist philosophy had been pretty completely shelved by the Kremlin, now reactionary as well as corrupt, and when the Russians were lending the Loyalists only help enough to preserve, as they imagined would be possible, the balance of power against Fascism while they acted at the same time as a police force to beat down the real social revolution.

Hemingway raised money for the Loyalists, reported the battle fronts.

He even went so far as to make a speech at a congress of the League of American Writers, an organization rigged by the supporters of the Stalinist régime in Russia and full of precisely the type of literary revolutionists that he had been ridiculing a little while before. Soon the Stalinists had taken him in tow, and he was feverishly denouncing as Fascists other writers who criticized the Kremlin. It has been one of the expedients of the Stalin administration in maintaining its power and covering up its crimes to condemn on trumped-up charges of Fascist conspiracy, and even to kidnap and murder, its political opponents of the Left; and, along with the food and munitions, the Russians had brought to the war in Spain what the Austrian journalist Willi Schlamm called that diversion of doubtful value for the working class: 'Herr Vyshinsky's Grand Guignol.'

The result of this was a play, *The Fifth Column*, which, though it is good reading for the way the characters talk, is an exceedingly silly production. The hero, though an Anglo-American, is an agent of the Communist secret police, engaged in catching Fascist spies in Spain; and his principal exploit in the course of the play is clearing out, with the aid of a single Communist, an artillery post manned by seven Fascists. The scene is like a pushover and getaway from one of the cruder Hollywood Westerns. It is in the nature of a small boy's fantasy, and would probably be considered extravagant by most writers of books for boys.

The tendency on Hemingway's part to indulge himself in these boyish day-dreams seems to begin to get the better of his realism at the end of *A Farewell to Arms*, where the hero, after many adventures of fighting, escaping, love-making and drinking, rows his lady thirty-five kilometers on a cold and rainy night; and we have seen what it could do for Harry Morgan. Now, as if with the conviction that the cause and the efficiency of the GPU have added several cubits to his stature, he has let this tendency loose; and he has also found in the GPU's grim duty a pretext to give rein to the appetite for describing scenes of killing which has always been a feature of his work. He has progressed from grasshoppers and trout through bulls and lions and kudus to Chinamen and Cubans, and now to Fascists. Hitherto the act of destruction has given rise for him to complex emotions: he has identified himself not merely with the injurer but also with the injured; there has been a masochistic complement to the sadism. But now this paradox which splits our natures, and which has instigated some of Hemingway's best stories, need no longer present perplexities to his mind. The Fascists are dirty bastards, and to kill them is a righteous act. He who had made a separate peace, who had said farewell to arms, has found a reason for taking them up again in a spirit of rabietic fury unpleasantly reminiscent of the spy mania and the sacred anti-German rage which took possession of so many civilians and staff officers under the stimulus of the last war.

Not that the compensatory trauma of the typical Hemingway protagonist is totally absent even here. The main episode is the hero's brief love affair and voluntary breaking off with a beautiful and adoring girl whose acquaintance he has made in Spain. As a member of the Junior League and a graduate of Vassar, she represents for him—it seems a little hard on her—that leisure-class playworld from which he is trying to get away. But in view of the fact that from the very first scenes he treats her with more or less open contempt, the action is rather lacking in suspense as the sacrifice is rather feeble in moral value. One takes no stock at all in the intimation that Mr. Philip may later be sent to mortify himself in a camp for training Young Pioneers. And in the meantime he has fun killing Fascists.

In *The Fifth Column*, the drugging process has been carried further still: the hero, who has become finally indistinguishable from the false or publicity Hemingway, has here dosed himself not only with whiskey, but with a seductive and desirous woman, for whom he has the most admirable reasons for not taking any responsibility, with sacred rage, with the excitement of a bombardment, and with indulgence in that headiest of sports, for which he has now the same excellent reasons: the bagging of human beings.

V

You may fear, after reading *The Fifth Column*, that Hemingway will never sober up; but as you go on to his short stories of this period, you find that your apprehensions were unfounded. Three of these stories have a great deal more body—they are longer and more complex—than the comparatively meager anecdotes collected in *Winner Take Nothing*. And here are his real artistic successes with the material of his adventures in Africa, which make up for the miscarried *Green Hills: The Short Happy Life of Francis Macomber* and *The Snows of Kilimanjaro*, which disengage, by dramatizing them objectively, the themes he had attempted in the earlier book but that had never really got themselves presented. And here is at least a beginning of a real artistic utilization of Hemingway's experience in Spain: an incident of the war in two pages which outweighs the whole of *The Fifth Column* and all his Spanish dispatches, a glimpse of an old man, 'without politics,' who has so far occupied his life in taking care of eight pigeons, two goats and a cat, but who has now been dislodged and separated from his pets by the advance of the Fascist armies. It is a story which takes its place among the war prints of Callot and Goya, artists whose union of elegance with sharpness has already been recalled by Hemingway in his earlier battle pieces: a story which might have been written about almost any war.

And here—what is very remarkable—is a story, *The Capital of the World*, which finds an objective symbol for, precisely, what is wrong with *The Fifth Column*. A young boy who has come up from the country and waits on table in a pension in Madrid gets accidentally stabbed with a meat knife while playing at bullfighting with the dishwasher. This is the simple anecdote, but Hemingway has built in behind it all the life of the pension and the city: the priesthood, the working-class movement, the grown-up bullfighters who have broken down or missed out. 'The boy Paco,' Hemingway concludes, 'had never known about any of this nor about what all these people would be doing on the next day and on other days to come. He had no idea how they really lived nor how they ended. He did not realize they ended. He died, as the Spanish phrase has it, full of illusions. He had not had time in his life to lose any of them, or even, at the end, to complete an act of contrition.' So he registers in this very fine piece the discrepancy between the fantasies of boyhood and the realities of the grown-up world. Hemingway the artist, who feels things truly and cannot help recording what he feels, has actually said good-bye to these fantasies at a time when the war correspondent is making himself ridiculous by attempting to hang on to them still.

The emotion which principally comes through in *Francis Macomber* and *The Snows of Kilimanjaro*—as it figures also in *The Fifth Column*—is a growing antagonism to women. Looking back, one can see at this point that the tendency has been there all along. In *The Doctor and the Doctor's Wife*, the boy Nick goes out squirrel-hunting with his father instead of obeying the summons of his mother; in *Cross Country Snow*, he regretfully says farewell to male companionship on a skiing expedition in Switzerland, when he is obliged to go back to the States so that his wife can have her baby. The young man in *Hills Like White Elephants* compels his girl to have an abortion contrary to her wish; another story, *A Canary for One*, bites almost unbearably but exquisitely on the loneliness to be endured by a wife after she and her husband shall have separated; the peasant of *An Alpine Idyll* abuses the corpse of his wife (these last three appear under the general title *Men Without Women*). "Brett in *The Sun Also Rises* is an exclusively destructive force: she might be a better woman if she were mated with Jake, the American; but actually he is protected against her and is in a sense revenging his own sex through being unable to do anything for her sexually. Even the hero of *A Farewell to Arms* eventually destroys Catherine—after enjoying her abject devotion—by giving her a baby, itself born dead. The only women with whom Nick Adams' relations are perfectly satisfactory are the little

Indian girls of his boyhood who are in a position of hopeless social disadvantage and have no power over the behavior of the white male—so that he can get rid of them the moment he has done with them. Thus in *The Fifth Column* Mr. Philip brutally breaks off with Dorothy—he has been rescued from her demoralizing influence by his enlistment in the Communist crusade, just as the hero of *The Sun Also Rises* has been saved by his physical disability—to revert to a little Moorish whore. Even Harry Morgan, who is represented as satisfying his wife on the scale of a Paul Bunyan, deserts her in the end by dying and leaves her racked by the cruelest desire.[1]

And now this instinct to get the woman down presents itself frankly as a fear that the woman will get the man down. The men in both these African stories are married to American bitches of the most soul-destroying sort. The hero of *The Snows of Kilimanjaro* loses his soul and dies of futility on a hunting expedition in Africa, out of which he has failed to get what he had hoped. The story is not quite stripped clean of the trashy moral attitudes which have been coming to disfigure the author's work: the hero, a seriously intentioned and apparently promising writer, goes on a little sloppily over the dear early days in Paris when he was earnest, happy and poor, and blames a little hysterically the rich woman whom he has married and who has debased him. Yet it is one of Hemingway's remarkable stories. There is a wonderful piece of writing at the end when the reader is made to realize that what has seemed to be an escape by plane, with the sick man looking down on Africa, is only the dream of a dying man. The other story, *Francis Macomber*, perfectly realizes its purpose. Here the male saves his soul at the last minute, and then is actually shot down by his woman, who does not want him to have a soul. Here Hemingway has at last got what Thurber calls the war between men and women right out into the open and has written a terrific fable of the impossible civilized woman who despises the civilized man for his failure in initiative and nerve and then jealously tries to break him down as soon as he begins to exhibit any. (It ought to be noted, also, that whereas in *Green Hills of Africa* the descriptions tended to weigh down the narrative with their excessive circumstantiality, the landscapes and animals of *Francis Macomber* are alive and unfalteringly proportioned.)

Going back over Hemingway's books today, we can see clearly what an error of the politicos it was to accuse him of an indifference to society. His whole work is a criticism of society: he has responded to every pressure of the moral atmosphere of the time, as it is felt at the roots of human relations, with a sensitivity almost unrivaled. Even his preoccupation with licking the gang in the next block and being known as the best basketball player in high school has its meaning in the present epoch. After all, whatever is done in the world, political as well as athletic, depends on personal courage and strength. With Hemingway, courage and strength are always thought of in physical terms, so that he tends to give the impression that the bullfighter who can take it and dish it out is more of a man than any other kind of man, and that the sole duty of the revolutionary socialist is to get the counter-revolutionary gang before they get him.

But ideas, however correct, will never prevail by themselves: there must be people who are prepared to stand or fall with them, and the ability to act on principle is still subject to the same competitive laws which operate in sporting contests and sexual relations. Hemingway has expressed with genius the terrors of the modern man at the danger of losing control of his world, and he has also, within his scope, provided his own kind of antidote. This antidote, paradoxically, is almost entirely moral. Despite Hemingway's preoccupation with physical contests, his heroes are almost always defeated physically, nervously, practically: their victories are moral ones. He himself, when he trained himself stubbornly in his unconventional unmarketable art in a Paris which had other fashions, gave the prime example of such a victory; and if he has sometimes, under the menace of the general panic, seemed on the point of going to pieces as an artist, he has always pulled himself together the next moment. The principle of the Bourdon gauge, which is used to measure the pressure of liquids, is that a tube which has been curved into a coil will tend to straighten out in proportion as the liquid inside it is subjected to an increasing pressure.

The appearance of *For Whom the Bell Tolls* since this essay was written in 1939 carries the straightening process further. Here Hemingway has largely sloughed off his Stalinism and has reverted to seeing events in terms of individuals pitted against specific odds. His hero, an American teacher of Spanish who has enlisted on the side of the Loyalists, gives his life to what he regards as the cause of human liberation; but he is frustrated in the task that has been assigned him by the confusion of forces at cross-purposes that are throttling the Loyalist campaign. By the time that he comes to die, he has little to sustain him but the memory of his grandfather's record as a soldier in the American Civil War. The psychology of this young man is presented with a certain sobriety and detachment in comparison with Hemingway's other full-length heroes; and the author has here succeeded as in none of his earlier books in externalizing in plausible characters the elements of his own complex personality. With all this, there is an historical point of view which he has learned from his political adventures: he has aimed to reflect in this episode the whole course of the Spanish War and the tangle of tendencies involved in it.

The weaknesses of the book are its diffuseness—a shape that lacks the concision of his short stories, that sometimes sags and sometimes bulges; and a sort of exploitation of the material, an infusion of the operatic, that lends itself all too readily to the movies.

NOTE

1. There would probably be a chapter to write on the relation between Hemingway and Kipling, and certain assumptions about society which they share. They have much the same split attitude toward women. Kipling anticipates Hemingway in his beliefs that 'he travels the fastest that travels alone' and that 'the female of the species is more deadly than the male'; and Hemingway seems to reflect Kipling in the submissive infra-Anglo-Saxon women that make his heroes such perfect mistresses. The most striking example of this is the amoeba-like little Spanish girl, Maria, in *For Whom the Bell Tolls*. Like the docile native 'wives' of English officials in the early stories of Kipling, she lives only to serve her lord and to merge her identity with his; and this love affair with a woman in a sleeping-bag, lacking completely the kind of give and take that goes on between real men and women, has the all-too-perfect felicity of a youthful erotic dream. One suspects that *Without Benefit of Clergy* was read very early by Hemingway and that it made on him a lasting impression. The pathetic conclusion of this story of Kipling's seems unmistakably to be echoed at the end of *A Farewell to Arms*.

ROBERT PENN WARREN

Ernest Hemingway

In May, 1929, in *Scribner's Magazine*, the first installment of *A Farewell to Arms* appeared. The novel was completed in the issue of October, and was published in book form the same year. Ernest Hemingway was already regarded, by a limited literary public, as a writer of extraordinary freshness and power, as one of the makers, indeed, of a new American fiction. *A Farewell to Arms* more than justified the early enthusiasm of the connoisseurs for Hemingway, and extended his reputation from them to the public at large. Its great importance was at once acknowledged, and its reputation has survived through the changing fashions and interests of many years.

What was the immediate cause of its appeal? It told a truth about the first world war, and a truth about the generation who had fought it and whose lives, because of the war, had been wrenched from the expected pattern and the old values. Other writers had told or were to tell similar truths about this war. John Dos Passos in *Three Soldiers*, E.E. Cummings in *The Enormous Room*, William Faulkner in *Soldier's Pay*, Maxwell Anderson and Laurence Stallings in *What Price Glory?* All these writers had presented the pathos and endurance and gallantry of the individual caught and mangled in the great anonymous mechanism of a modern war fought for reasons that the individual could not understand, found insufficient to justify the event, or believed to be no reasons at all. And *A Farewell to Arms* was not the first

From *Robert Penn Warren: Selected Essays*. © 1958 by Robert Penn Warren. Originally published in the MSA edition of *A Farewell to Arms* © 1949 by Charles Scribner's Sons.

book to record the plight of the men and women who, because of the war, had been unable to come to terms with life in the old way. Hemingway himself in *The Sun Also Rises*, 1926, had given the picture of the dislocated life of young English and American expatriates in the bars of Paris, the "lost generation," as Gertrude Stein defined them. But before that, F. Scott Fitzgerald, who had been no nearer to the war than an officers' training camp, had written of the lost generation. For the young people about whom Fitzgerald wrote, even when they were not veterans and even when their love stories were enacted in parked cars, fraternity houses, and country clubs and not in the cafés and hotels of Paris, were like Hemingway's expatriates under the shadow of the war and were groping to find some satisfaction in a world from which the old values had been withdrawn. Hemingway's expatriates had turned their backs on the glitter of the Great Boom of the 1920's, and Fitzgerald's young men were usually drawn to the romance of wealth and indulgence, but this difference is superficial. If Hemingway's young men begin by repudiating the Great Boom, Fitzgerald's young men end with disappointment in what even success has to offer. "All the sad young men" of Fitzgerald—to take the title of one of his collections of stories—and the "lost generation" of Hemingway are seekers for landmarks and bearings in a terrain for which the maps have been mislaid.

A Farewell to Arms, which appeared ten years after the first world war and on the eve of the collapse of the Great Boom, seemed to sum up and bring to focus an inner meaning of the decade being finished. It worked thus, not because it disclosed the end results that the life of the decade was producing—the discontents and disasters that were beginning to be noticed even by unreflective people—but because it cut back to the beginning of the process, to the moment that had held within itself the explanation of the subsequent process.

Those who had grown up in the war, or in its shadow could look back nostalgically, as it were, to the lost moment of innocence of motive and purity of emotion. If those things had been tarnished or manhandled by the later business of living, they had, at least, existed, and on a grand scale. If they had been tarnished or manhandled, it was not through the fault of the individual who looked back to see the image of the old simple and heroic self in Frederick or Catherine, but through the impersonal grindings of the great machine of the universe. *A Farewell to Arms* served, in a way, as the great romantic alibi for a generation, and for those who aped and emulated that generation. It showed how cynicism or disillusionment, failure of spirit or the worship of material success, debauchery or despair, might have been grounded in heroism, simplicity, and fidelity that had met unmerited defeat.

The early tragedy could cast a kind of flattering and extenuating afterglow over what had come later. The battlefields of *A Farewell to Arms* explained the bars of *The Sun Also Rises*—and explained the young Krebs, of the story "Soldier's Home," who came back home to a Middle-Western town to accept his own slow disintegration.

This is not said in disparagement of *A Farewell to Arms*. It is, after all, a compliment to the hypnotic force of the book. For the hypnotic force of the book was felt from the first, and it is not unusual for such a book to be relished by its first readers for superficial reasons and not for the essential virtues that may engage those who come to it later.

In accounting for the immediate appeal of *A Farewell to Arms*, the history of the author himself is of some importance. In so far as the reader knew about Ernest Hemingway in 1929, he knew about a young man who seemed to typify in his own experience the central experience of his generation. Behind the story of *A Farewell to Arms* and his other books there was the shadow of his own story that could stamp his fiction with the authenticity of a document and, for the more impressionable, with the value of a revelation. He could give an ethic and a technique for living, even in the face of defeat or frustration, and yet his own story was the story that we have always loved: the American success story.

He was born in Oak Park, Illinois, in the Middle West—that region which it was fashionable to condemn (after Mencken and Sinclair Lewis) as romanceless, but which became endowed, paradoxically enough, with the romance of the American average. His father was a physician. There were two boys and four girls in the family. In the summers the family lived in northern Michigan, where there were Indians, and where lake, streams, and forests gave boyhood pursuits their appropriate setting. In the winters he went to school in Oak Park. He played football in high school, ran away from home, returned and, in 1917, graduated. After graduation he was for a short time a reporter on the *Kansas City Star*, but the war was on and he went to Italy as a volunteer ambulance driver. He was wounded and decorated, and after his recovery served in the Italian army as a soldier. For a time after the war he was a foreign correspondent for the *Toronto Star*, in the Near East.

In the years after the war Hemingway set about learning, quite consciously and with rigorous self-discipline, the craft and art of writing. During most of his apprenticeship he lived in Paris, one of the great number of expatriates who were drawn to the artistic capital of the world to learn to be writers, painters, sculptors, or dancers, or simply to enjoy on a low monetary exchange the freedom of life away from American or British conventions. "Young America," writes Ford Madox Ford, "from the limitless prairies leapt, released, on Paris. They stampeded with the madness of colts when you let down the slip-rails between dried pasture and green. The noise of their advancing drowned all sounds. Their innumerable forms hid the very trees on the boulevards. Their perpetual motion made you dizzy." And of Hemingway himself: "He was presented to me by Ezra [Pound] and Bill Bird and had rather the aspect of an Eton-Oxford, huskyish young captain of a midland regiment of His Britannic Majesty.... Into that animated din would drift Hemingway, balancing on the point of his toes, feinting at my head with hands as large as hams and relating sinister stories of Paris landlords. He told them with singularly choice words in a slow voice."[1]

The originality and force of Hemingway's early stories, published in little magazines and in limited editions in France, were recognized from the first by many who made their acquaintance. The seeds of his later work were in those stories of *In Our Time*, concerned chiefly with scenes of inland American life and a boy's growing awareness of that life in contrast to vivid flashes of the disorder and brutality of the war years and the immediate postwar years in Europe. There are both contrast and continuity between the two elements of *In Our Time*. There is the contrast between the lyric rendering of one aspect of the boyhood world and the realistic rendering of the world of war, but there is also a continuity, because in the boyhood world there are recurring intimations of the blackness into which experience can lead even in the peaceful setting of Michigan.

With the publication of *The Sun Also Rises*, in 1926, Hemingway's work reached a wider audience, and at the same time defined more clearly the line his genius was to follow and his role as one of the spokesmen for a generation. But *A Farewell to Arms* gave him his first substantial popular success and established his reputation. It was a brilliant and compelling novel; it provided the great alibi; it crowned the success story of the American boy from the Middle West, who had hunted and fished, played football in high school, been a newspaper reporter, gone to war and been wounded and decorated, wandered exotic lands as a foreign correspondent, lived the free life of the Latin Quarter of Paris, and, at the age of thirty, written a best seller—athlete, sportsman, correspondent, soldier, adventurer, and author.

It would be possible and even profitable to discuss *A Farewell to Arms* in isolation from Hemingway's other work. But Hemingway is a peculiarly personal writer, and for all the apparent objectivity and self-suppression in his method as a writer, his work, to an uncommon degree, forms a continuous whole. One part explains and interprets another part. It is true that there have been changes between early and late work, that there has been an increasing self-consciousness, that attitudes and methods that in the beginning were instinctive and simple have become calculated and elaborated. But the best way to understand one of his books is, nevertheless, to compare it with both earlier and later pieces and seek to discern motives and methods that underlie all of his work.

Perhaps the simplest way into the whole question is to consider what kind of world Hemingway writes about. A writer may write about his special world merely because he happens to know that world, but he may also write about that special world because it best dramatizes for him the issues and questions that are his fundamental concerns—because, in other words, that special world has a kind of symbolic significance for him. There is often—if we discount mere literary fashion and imitation—an inner and necessary reason for the writer's choice of his characters and situations. What situations and characters does Hemingway write about?

They are usually violent. There is the hard-drinking and sexually promiscuous world of *The Sun Also Rises*; the chaotic and brutal world of war, as in *A Farewell to Arms*, *For Whom the Bell Tolls*, many of the inserted sketches of *In Our Time*, the play *The Fifth Column*, and some of the stories; the world of sport, as in "Fifty Grand," "My Old Man," "The Undefeated," "The Snows of Kilimanjaro"; the world of crime, as in "The Killers," "The Gambler, the Nun, and the Radio," and *To Have and Have Not*. Even when the situation of a story does not fall into one of these categories, it usually involves a desperate risk, and behind it is the shadow of ruin, physical or spiritual. As for the typical characters, they are usually tough men, experienced in the hard worlds they inhabit, and not obviously given to emotional display or sensitive shrinking—men like Rinaldi or Frederick Henry of *A Farewell to Arms*, Robert Jordan of *For Whom the Bell Tolls*, Harry Morgan of *To Have and Have Not*, the big-game hunter of "The Snows of Kilimanjaro," the old bullfighter of "The Undefeated," or the pugilist of "Fifty Grand." Or if the typical character is not of this seasoned order, he is a very young man, or boy, first entering the violent world and learning his first adjustment to it.

We have said that the shadow of ruin is behind the typical Hemingway situation. The typical character faces defeat or death. But out of defeat or death the character usually manages to salvage something. And here we discover Hemingway's special interest in such situations and characters. His heroes are not squealers, welchers, compromisers, or cowards, and when they confront defeat they realize that the stance they take, the stoic endurance, the stiff upper lip mean a kind of victory. If they are to be defeated they are defeated upon their own terms; some of them have even courted their defeat; and certainly they have maintained, even in the practical defeat, an ideal of themselves—some definition of how a man should behave, formulated or unformulated—by which they have lived. They represent some notion of a code, some notion of honor, that makes a man a man, and that distinguishes him from people who merely follow their random impulses and who are, by consequence, "messy."

In case after case, we can illustrate this "principle of sportsmanship," as Edmund Wilson has called it, at the center of a story or novel. Robert Jordan, in *For Whom the Bell Tolls*, is somehow happy as he lies, wounded, behind the machine gun that is to cover the escape of his friends and his sweetheart from Franco's Fascists. The old bullfighter, in "The Undefeated," continues his incompetent fight even under the jeers and hoots of the crowd, until the bull is dead and he himself is mortally hurt. Francis Macomber, the rich young sportsman who goes lion-hunting in "The Short, Happy Life of Francis Macomber," and who has funked it and bolted before a wounded lion, at last learns the lesson that the code of the hunter demands that he go into the bush after an animal he has wounded. Brett, the heroine of *The Sun Also Rises*, gives up Romero, the young bullfighter with whom she is in love, because she knows she will ruin him, and her tight-lipped remark to Jake, the newspaper man who is the narrator of the novel, might almost serve as the motto of Hemingway's work: "You know it makes one feel rather good deciding not to be a bitch."

It is the discipline of the code that makes man human, a sense of style or good form. This applies not only in isolated, dramatic cases such as those listed above, but is a more pervasive thing that can give meaning, partially at least, to the confusions of living. The discipline of the soldier, the form of the athlete, the gameness of the sportsman, the technique of an artist can give some sense of the human order, and can achieve a moral significance. And here we see how Hemingway's concern with war and sport crosses his concern with literary style. If a writer can get the kind of style at which Hemingway, in *Green Hills of Africa*, professes to aim, then "nothing else matters. It is more important than anything else he can do." It is more important because, ultimately, it is a moral achievement. And no doubt for this reason, as well as for the reason of Henry James's concern with cruxes of a moral code, he is, as he says in *Green Hills of Africa*, an admirer of the work of Henry James, the devoted stylist.

But to return to the subject of Hemingway's world: the code and the discipline are important because they can give meaning to life that otherwise seems to have no meaning or justification. In other words, in a world without supernatural sanctions, in the God-abandoned world of modernity, man can realize an ideal meaning only in so far as he can define and maintain the code. The effort to do so, however limited and imperfect it may be, is the characteristically human effort and provides the tragic or pitiful human story. Hemingway's attitude on this point is much like that of Robert Louis Stevenson in "Pulvis et Umbra":

Poor soul, here for so little, cast among so many hardships, filled with desires so incommensurate and so inconsistent, savagely surrounded, savagely descended, irremediably condemned to prey upon his fellow lives: who should have blamed him had he been of a piece with his destiny and a being merely barbarous? And we look and behold him instead, filled with imperfect virtues ... an ideal of decency, to which he would rise if it were possible; a limit of shame, below which, if it be possible, he will not stoop.... Man is indeed marked for failure in his effort to do right. But where the best consistently miscarry how tenfold more remarkable that all should continue to strive; and surely we should find it both touching and inspiring, that in a field from which success is banished, our race should not cease to labor.... It matters not where we look, under what climate we observe him, in what stage of society, in what depth of ignorance, burthened with what erroneous morality; by campfires in Assiniboia, the snow powdering his shoulders, the wind plucking his blanket, as he sits, passing the ceremonial calumet and uttering his grave opinions like a Roman senator; on ships at sea, a man inured to hardship and vile pleasures, his brightest hope a fiddle in a tavern and a bedizened trull who sells herself to rob him, and he for all that, simple, innocent, cheerful, kindly like a child, constant to toil, brave to drown, for others; ... in the brothel, the discard of society, living mainly on strong drink, fed with affronts, a fool, a thief, the comrade of thieves, and even here keeping the point of honor and the touch of pity, often repaying the world's scorn with service, often standing firm upon a scruple, and at a certain cost, rejecting riches:—everywhere some virtue cherished or affected, everywhere some decency of thought or carriage, everywhere the ensign of man's ineffectual goodness! ... under every circumstance of failure, without hope, without help, without thanks, still obscurely fighting the lost fight of virtue, still clinging, in the brothel or on the scaffold, to some rag of honor, the poor jewel of their souls! They may seek to escape, and yet they cannot; it is not alone their privilege and glory, but their doom; they are condemned to some nobility....

Hemingway's code is more rigorous than Stevenson's and perhaps he finds fewer devoted to it, but, like Stevenson, he can find his characteristic

hero and characteristic story among the discards of society, and, like
Stevenson, is aware of the touching irony of that fact. But for the moment
the important thing in the parallel is that, for Stevenson, the world in which
this drama of pitiful aspiration and stoic endurance is played out, is
apparently a violent and meaningless world—"our rotary island loaded with
predatory life and more drenched with blood ... than ever mutinied ship,
scuds through space."

Neither Hemingway nor Stevenson invented this world. It had already
appeared in literature before their time, and that is a way of saying that this
cheerless vision had already begun to trouble men. It is the world we find
pictured (and denied) in Tennyson's "In Memoriam"—the world in which
human conduct is a product of "dying Nature's earth and lime." It is the
world pictured (and not denied) in Hardy and Housman, a world that seems
to be presided over by blind Doomsters (if by anybody), as Hardy put it in
his poem "Hap," or made by some brute and blackguard (if by anybody), as
Housman put it in his poem "The Chestnut Casts Its Flambeaux." It is the
world of Zola or Dreiser or Conrad or Faulkner. It is the world of, to use
Bertrand Russell's phrase, "secular hurryings through space." It is the God-
abandoned world, the world of Nature-as-all. We know where the literary
men got this picture. They got it from the scientists of the nineteenth
century. This is Hemingway's world, too, the world with nothing at center.

Over against this particular version of the naturalistic view of the world,
there was, of course, an argument for Divine Intelligence and a Divine
purpose, an argument that based itself on the beautiful system of nature, on
natural law. The closely knit order of the natural world, so the argument ran,
implies a Divine Intelligence. But if one calls Hemingway's attention to the
fact that the natural world is a world of order, his reply is on record in a story
called "A Natural History of the Dead." There he quotes from the traveler
Mungo Park, who, naked and starving in an African desert, observed a
beautiful little moss-flower and meditated thus:

> Can the Being who planted, watered, and brought to
> perfection, in this obscure part of the world, a thing which
> appears of so small importance, look with unconcern upon the
> situation and suffering of creatures formed after his own image?
> Surely not. Reflections like these would not allow me to despair:
> I started up and, disregarding both hunger and fatigue, travelled
> forward, assured that relief was at hand; and I was not
> disappointed.

And Hemingway continues:

> With a disposition to wonder and adore in like manner, as Bishop Stanley says [the author of *A Familiar History of Birds*], can any branch of Natural History be studied without increasing that faith, love and hope which we also, everyone of us, need in our journey through the wilderness of life? Let us therefore see what inspiration we may derive from the dead.

Then Hemingway presents the picture of a modern battlefield, where the bloated and decaying bodies give a perfect example of the natural order of chemistry—but scarcely an argument for faith, hope, and love. That picture is his answer to the argument that the order of nature implies meaning in the world.

In one of the stories, "A Clean, Well-Lighted Place," we find the best description of what underlies Hemingway's world of violent action. In the early stages of the story we see an old man sitting late in a Spanish café. Two waiters are speaking of him.

> "Last week he tried to commit suicide," one waiter said.
> "Why?"
> "He was in despair."
> "What about?"
> "Nothing."
> "How do you know it was nothing?"
> "He has plenty of money."

The despair beyond plenty of money—or beyond all the other gifts of the world: its nature becomes a little clearer at the end of the story when the older of the two waiters is left alone, reluctant too to leave the clean, well-lighted place:

> Turning off the electric light he continued the conversation with himself. It is the light of course but it is necessary that the place be clean and pleasant. You do not want music. Certainly you do not want music. Nor can you stand before a bar with dignity although that is all that is provided for these hours. What did he fear? It was not fear or dread. It was a nothing that he knew too well. It was all a nothing and a man was nothing too. It was only that and light was all it needed and a certain cleanness and order.

Some lived in it and never felt it but he knew it all was nada y pues nada y nada y pues nada. Our nada who art in nada, nada be thy name thy kingdom nada thy will be nada in nada as it is in nada. Give us this nada our daily nada and nada us our nada as we nada our nadas and nada us not into nada but deliver us from nada; pues nada. Hail nothing full of nothing, nothing is with thee. He smiled and stood before a bar with a shining steam pressure coffee machine.

"What's yours?" asked the barman.

"Nada."

At the end the old waiter is ready to go home:

Now, without thinking further, he would go home to his room. He would lie in bed and finally, with daylight, he would go to sleep. After all, he said to himself, it is probably only insomnia. Many must have it.

And the sleepless man—the man obsessed by death, by the meaninglessness of the world, by nothingness, by nada—is one of the recurring symbols in the work of Hemingway. In this phase Hemingway is a religious writer. The despair beyond plenty of money, the despair that makes a sleeplessness beyond insomnia, is the despair felt by a man who hungers for the sense of order and assurance that men seem to find in religious faith, but who cannot find grounds for his faith.

Another recurring symbol is the violent man. But the sleepless man and the violent man are not contradictory; they are complementary symbols. They represent phases of the same question, the same hungering for meaning in the world. The sleepless man is the man brooding upon nada, upon chaos, upon Nature-as-all. (For Nature-as-all equals moral chaos; even its bulls and lions and kudu are not admired by Hemingway as creatures of conscious self-discipline; their courage has a meaning only in so far as it symbolizes human courage.) The violent man is the man taking an action appropriate to the realization of the fact of nada. He is, in other words, engaged in the effort to discover human values in a naturalistic world.

Before we proceed with this line of discussion, it might be asked, "Why does Hemingway feel that the quest necessarily involves violence?" Now, at one level, the answer to this question would involve the whole matter of the bias toward violence in modern literature. But let us take it in its more immediate reference. The typical Hemingway hero is the man aware, or in the process of becoming aware, of nada. Death is the great nada. Therefore whatever code or creed the hero gets must, to be good, stick even in the face of death. It has to be good in the bull ring or on the battlefield and not merely in the study or lecture room. In fact, Hemingway is anti-intellectual, and has a great contempt for any type of solution arrived at without the testings of immediate experience.

So aside from the question of a dramatic sense that would favor violence, and aside from the mere matter of personal temperament (for Hemingway describes himself on more than one occasion as obsessed by death), the presentation of violence is appropriate in his work because death is the great nada. In taking violent risks man confronts in dramatic terms the issue of nada that is implicit in all of Hemingway's world.

But to return to our general line of discussion. There are two aspects to this violence that is involved in the quest of the Hemingway hero, two aspects that seem to represent an ambivalent attitude toward nature.

First, there is the conscious sinking into nature, as we may call it. On this line of reasoning we would find something like this: if there is at center only nada, then the only sure compensation in life, the only reality, is gratification of appetite, the relish of sensation.

Continually in the stories and novels one finds such sentences as this from *Green Hills of Africa:* ". . . drinking this, the first one of the day, the finest one there is, and looking at the thick bush we passed in the dark, feeling the cool wind of the night and smelling the good smell of Africa, I was altogether happy." What is constantly interesting in such sentences is the fact that happiness, a notion that we traditionally connect with a complicated state of being, with notions of virtue, of achievement, etc., is here equated with a set of merely agreeable sensations. For instance, in "Cross-Country Snow," one of the boys, George, says to the other, Nick, who in story after story is a sort of shadow of Hemingway himself, "Maybe we'll never go skiing again, Nick." And Nick replies, "We've got to. It isn't worth while if you can't." The sensations of skiing are the end of life. Or in another story, "Big Two-Hearted River: Part II," a story that is full of the sensation-as-happiness theme, we find this remark about Nick, who has been wading in a trout stream: "Nick climbed out onto the meadow and stood, water running down his trousers and out of his shoes, his shoes squelchy. He went over and sat on the logs. He did not want to rush his sensations any." The careful relish of sensation—that is what counts, always.

This intense awareness of the world of the senses is, of course, one of the things that made the early work of Hemingway seem, upon its first impact, so fresh and pure. Physical nature is nowhere rendered with greater vividness than in his work, and probably his only competitors in this department of literature are William Faulkner, among the modern, and Henry David Thoreau, among the older American writers. The meadows, forests, lakes, and trout streams of America, and the arid, sculpturesque mountains of Spain, appear with astonishing immediacy, an immediacy not dependent upon descriptive flourishes. But not only the appearance of landscape is important; a great deal of the freshness comes from the discrimination of sensation, the coldness of water in the "squelchy" shoes after wading, the tangy smell of dry sagebrush, the "cleanly" smell of grease and oil on a field piece.[2] Hemingway's appreciation of the aesthetic qualities of the physical world is important, but a peculiar poignancy is implicit in the rendering of those qualities; the beauty of the physical world is a background for the human predicament, and the very relishing of the beauty is merely a kind of desperate and momentary compensation possible in the midst of the predicament.

This careful relishing of the world of the senses comes to a climax in drinking and sex. Drink is the "giant-killer," the weapon against man's thought of nada. And so is sex, for that matter, though when sexual attraction achieves the status of love, the process is one that attempts to achieve a meaning rather than to forget meaninglessness in the world. In terms of drinking and sex, the typical Hemingway hero is a man of monel-metal stomach and Homeric prowess in the arts of love. And the typical situation is love, with some drinking, against the background of nada—of civilization gone to pot, of war, or of death—as we get it in all of the novels in one form or another, and in many of the stories.

It is important to remember, however, that the sinking into nature, even at the level of drinking and mere sexuality, is a self-conscious act. It is not the random gratification of appetite. We see this quite clearly in *The Sun Also Rises* in the contrast between Cohn, who is merely a random dabbler in the world of sensation, who is merely trying to amuse himself, and the initiates like Jake and Brett, who are aware of the nada at the center of things and whose dissipations, therefore, have a philosophical significance. The initiate in Hemingway's world raises the gratification of appetite to the level of a cult and a discipline.

The cult of sensation, as we have already indicated, passes over very readily into the cult of true love, for the typical love story is presented primarily in terms of the cult of sensation. (*A Farewell to Arms*, as we shall see when we come to a detailed study of that novel, is closely concerned with this transition.) Even in the cult of true love it is the moment that counts, and the individual. There is never any past or future to the love stories, and the lovers are always isolated, not moving within the framework of obligations of an ordinary human society. The notion of the cult—a secret cult composed of those who have been initiated into the secret of nada—is constantly played up.

In *A Farewell to Arms*, for instance, Catherine and Frederick are two against the world, a world that is, literally as well as figuratively, an alien world. The peculiar relationship between Frederick and the priest takes on a new significance if viewed in terms of the secret cult. We shall come to this topic later, but for the moment we can say that the priest is a priest of Divine Love, the subject about which he and Frederick converse in the hospital, and that Frederick himself is a kind of priest, one of the initiate in the end, of the cult of profane love. This same pattern of two against the world with an understanding confidant or interpreter, reappears in *For Whom the Bell Tolls*—with Pilar, the gipsy woman who understands "love," substituting for the priest of *A Farewell to Arms*.

The initiates of the cult of love are those who are aware of nada, but their effort, as members of the cult, is to find a meaning to put in place of the nada. That is, there is an attempt to make the relationship of love take on a religious significance in so far as it can give meaning to life. This general topic is not new with the work of Hemingway. It is one of the literary themes of the nineteenth century—and has, as a matter of fact, a longer history than that.

If the cult of love arises from and states itself in the language of the cult of sensation, it is an extension of the sinking-into-nature aspect of the typical Hemingway violence; but in so far as it involves a discipline and a search for a "faith," it leads us to the second aspect of the typical violence.

The violence, although in its first aspect it represents a sinking into nature, at the same time, in its second aspect, represents a conquest of nature, and of nada in man. It represents such a conquest, not because of the fact of violence, but because the violence appears in terms of a discipline, a style, and a code. It is, as we have already seen, in terms of a self-imposed discipline that the heroes make one gallant, though limited, effort to redeem the incoherence of the world: they attempt to impose some form upon the disorder of their lives, the technique of the bullfighter or sportsman, the discipline of the soldier, the fidelity of the lover, or even the code of the gangster, which, though brutal and apparently dehumanizing, has its own ethic. (Ole Anderson, in "The Killers," is willing to take his medicine without whining, and even recognizes some necessity and justice in his plight. Or the dying Mexican, in "The Gambler, the Nun, and the Radio," refuses to squeal despite the detective's argument: "One can, with honor, denounce one's assailant.")

If it is said that Frederick in *A Farewell to Arms* does not, when he deserts, exhibit the discipline of the soldier, the answer is simple: his obligation has been constantly presented as an obligation to the men in his immediate command, and he and the men in his command have never recognized an obligation to the total war—they recognize no meaning in the war and are bound together only by a squad sense and by their immediate respect for each other; when Frederick is separated from his men his obligation is gone. His true obligation then becomes the fidelity to Catherine.

The discipline, the form, is never quite capable of subduing the world, but fidelity to it is part of the gallantry of defeat. By fidelity to it the hero manages to keep one small place "clean" and "well-lighted," and manages to retain, or achieve for one last moment, his dignity. There should be, as the old Spanish waiter reflects, a "clean, well-lighted place" where one could keep one's dignity at the late hour.

We have said earlier that the typical Hemingway character is tough and, apparently, insensitive. But only apparently, for the fidelity to a code, to the discipline, may be the index to a sensitivity that allows the characters to see, at moments, their true plight. At times, and usually at times of stress, it is the tough man in the Hemingway world, the disciplined man, who is actually aware of pathos or tragedy. The individual toughness (which may be taken to be the private discipline demanded by the world) may find itself in conflict with the natural human reactions; but the Hemingway hero, though he may be aware of the claims of the natural reaction, the spontaneous human emotion, cannot surrender to it because he knows that the only way to hold on to the definition of himself, to "honor" or "dignity," is to maintain the discipline, the code. For example, when pity appears in the Hemingway world—as in "The Pursuit Race"—it does not appear in its maximum but in its minimum manifestation.

What this means in terms of style and method is the use of understatement. This understatement, stemming from the contrast between the sensitivity and the superimposed discipline, is a constant aspect of the work, an aspect that was caught in a cartoon in the *New Yorker*. The cartoon showed a brawny, muscle-knotted forearm and a hairy hand that clutched a rose. It was entitled "The Soul of Ernest Hemingway." Just as there is a margin of victory in the defeat of the Hemingway characters, so there is a little margin of sensitivity in their brutal and apparently insensitive world. Hence we have the ironical circumstance—a central circumstance in creating the pervasive irony of Hemingway's work—that the revelation of the values characteristic of his work arises from the most unpromising people and the most unpromising situations—the little streak of poetry or pathos in "The Pursuit Race," "The Killers," "My Old Man," "A Clean, Well-Lighted Place," or "The Undefeated." We have a perfect example of it in the last-named story. After the defeat of the old bullfighter, who is lying wounded on an operating table, Zurito, the picador, is about to cut off the old fellow's pigtail, the mark of his profession. But when the wounded man starts up, despite his pain, and says, "You couldn't do a thing like that," Zurito says, "I was joking." Zurito becomes aware that, after all, the old bullfighter is, in a way, undefeated, and deserves to die with his coleta on.

This locating of the poetic, the pathetic, or the tragic in the unpromising person or situation is not unique with Hemingway. It is something with which we are acquainted in a great deal of our literature since the Romantic Movement. In such literature, the sensibility is played down, and an antiromantic surface sheathes the work; the point is in the contrast. The impulse that led Hemingway to the simple character is akin to the one that drew Wordsworth to the same choice. Wordsworth felt that his unsophisticated peasants were more honest in their responses than the cultivated man, and were therefore more poetic. Instead of Wordsworth's peasant we have in Hemingway's work the bullfighter, the soldier, the revolutionist, the sportsman, and the gangster; instead of Wordsworth's children we have the young men like Nick, the person just on the verge of being initiated into the world. There are, of course, differences between the approach of Wordsworth and that of Hemingway, but there is little difference on the point of marginal sensibility. In one sense, both are anti-intellectual, and in such poems as "Resolution and Independence" or "Michael" one finds even closer ties.

I have just indicated a similarity between Wordsworth and Hemingway on the grounds of a romantic anti-intellectualism. But with Hemingway it is far more profound and radical than with Wordsworth. All we have to do to see the difference is to put Wordsworth's Preface to the *Lyrical Ballads* over against any number of passages from Hemingway. The intellectualism of the eighteenth century had merely put a veil of stereotyped language over the world and a veil of snobbism over a large area of human experience. That is Wordsworth's indictment. But Hemingway's indictment of the intellectualism of the past is that it wound up in the mire and blood of 1914 to 1918; that it was a pack of lies leading to death. We can put over against the Preface of Wordsworth, a passage from *A Farewell to Arms*:

> I was always embarrassed by the words sacred, glorious, and sacrifice and the expression in vain. We had heard them, sometimes standing in the rain almost out of earshot, so that only the shouted words came through, and had read them, on proclamations that were slapped up by billposters over other proclamations, now for a long time, and I had seen nothing sacred, and the things that were glorious had no glory and the sacrifices were like the stockyards at Chicago if nothing was done with the meat except to bury it. There were many words that you could not stand to hear and finally only the names of places had dignity.... Abstract words such as glory, honor, courage, or hallow were obscene beside the concrete names of villages, the numbers of roads, the names of rivers, the numbers of regiments and the dates.

I do not mean to say that the general revolution in style, and the revolt against the particular intellectualism of the nineteenth century, was a result of the first world war. As a matter of fact, that revolt was going on long before the war, but for Hemingway, and for many others, the war gave the situation a peculiar depth and urgency.

Perhaps we might scale the matter thus: Wordsworth was a revolutionist—he truly had a new view of the world—but his revolutionary view left great tracts of the world untouched; the Church of England, for instance. Arnold and Tennyson, a generation or so later, though not revolutionists themselves, are much more profoundly stirred by the revolutionary situation than ever Wordsworth was; that is, the area of the world involved in the debate was for them greater. Institutions are called into question in a more fundamental way. But they managed to hang on to their English God and their English institutions. With Hardy, the area of disturbance has grown greater, and what can be salvaged is much less. He, like the earlier Victorians, had a strong sense of community to sustain him in the face of the universe that was for him, as not finally for Arnold and Tennyson, unfriendly, or at least neutral and Godless. But his was a secret community, different from that of social institutions. It was a human communion that, as a matter of fact, was constantly being violated by institutions. Their violation of it is, in fact, a constant source of subject matter and a constant spring of irony. Nevertheless, Hardy could refer to himself as a meliorist. He could not keep company with Wordsworth or Tennyson or Arnold; and when Hardy, having been elected an Honorary Fellow of Magdalene College, Cambridge, was to be formally admitted, the

Master, Doctor Donaldson (as we know from A. C. Benson's *Diary*) was much afraid that Hardy might dislike the religious service. The occasion, however, went off very well, even though Hardy, after impressing the Master with his knowledge of ecclesiastical music, did remark, "Of course it's only a sentiment to me now." Hardy listened to a sermon by the Archdeacon of Zanzibar, who declared that God was "a God of *desire*—who both hated and loved—not a mild or impersonal force." But even though Hardy could not accept the God of the Bishop of Zanzibar, he still had faith in the constructive power of the secret community.

Now, in Hemingway we see something very like Hardy's secret community, but one much smaller, one whose definition has become much more specialized. Its members are those who know the code. They recognize each other, they know the password and the secret grip, but they are few in number, and each is set off against the world like a wounded lion ringed round by waiting hyenas (*Green Hills of Africa* gives us the hyena symbol— the animal whose death is comic because it is all hideously "appetite": wounded, it eats its own intestines). Furthermore, this secret community is not constructive; Hemingway is no meliorist. In fact, there are hints that somewhere in the back of his mind, and in behind his work, there is a kind of Spenglerian view of history: our civilization is running down. We get this most explicitly in *Green Hills of Africa*:

> A continent ages quickly once we come. The natives live in harmony with it. But the foreigner destroys, cuts down the trees, drains the water, so that the water supply is altered and in a short time the soil, once the sod is turned under, is cropped out and, next, it starts to blow away as it has blown away in every old country and as I had seen it start to blow in Canada. The earth gets tired of being exploited. A country wears out quickly unless man puts back in it all his residue and that of all his beasts. When he quits using beasts and uses machines, the earth defeats him quickly. The machine can't reproduce, nor does it fertilize the soil, and it eats what he cannot raise. A country was made to be as we found it. We are the intruders and after we are dead we may have ruined it but it will still be there and we don't know what the next changes are. I suppose they all end up like Mongolia.
>
> I would come back to Africa but not to make a living from it.... But I would come back to where it pleased me to live; to really live. Not just let my life pass. Our people went to America because that was the place for them to go then. It had been a good country

and we had made a bloody mess of it and I would go, now, somewhere else as we had always had the right to go somewhere else and as we had always gone. You could always come back. Let the others come to America who did not know that they had come too late. Our people had seen it at its best and fought for it when it was well worth fighting for. Now I would go somewhere else.

This is the most explicit statement, but the view is implicit in case after case. The general human community, the general human project, has gone to pot. There is only the little secret community of, paradoxically enough, individualists who have resigned from the general community, and who are strong enough to live without any of the illusions, lies, and big words of the herd. At least, this is the case up to the novel *To Have and Have Not*, which appeared in 1937. In that novel and in *For Whom the Bell Tolls*, Hemingway attempts to bring his individualistic hero back to society, to give him a common stake with the fate of other men.

But to return to the matter of Wordsworth and Hemingway. What in Wordsworth is merely simple or innocent is in Hemingway violent: the gangster or bullfighter replaces the leech-gatherer or the child. Hemingway's world is a more disordered world, and the sensibility of his characters is more ironically in contrast with their world. The most immediate consideration here is the playing down of the sensibility as such, the sheathing of it in the code of toughness. Gertrude Stein's tribute is here relevant: "Hemingway is the shyest and proudest and sweetest-smelling storyteller of my reading." But this shyness manifests itself in the irony. In this, of course, Hemingway's irony corresponds to the Byronic irony. But the relation to Byron is even more fundamental. The pity is valid only when it is wrung from the man who has been seasoned by experience. Therefore a premium is placed on the fact of violent experience. The "dumb ox" character, commented on by Wyndham Lewis, represents the Wordsworthian peasant; the character with the code of the tough guy, the initiate, the man cultivating honor, gallantry, and recklessness, represents the Byronic aristocrat.

The failures of Hemingway, like his successes, are rooted in this situation. The successes occur in those instances where Hemingway accepts the essential limitations of his premises—that is, when there is an equilibrium between the dramatization and the characteristic Hemingway "point," when the system of ironies and understatements is coherent. On the other hand, the failures occur when we feel that Hemingway has not respected the limitations of his premises—that is, when the dramatization seems to be "rigged" and the violence, therefore, merely theatrical. The characteristic irony, or understatement, in such cases, seems to be too self-conscious. For example, let us glance at Hemingway's most spectacular failure, *To Have and Have Not*. The point of the novel is based on the contrast between the smuggler and the rich owners of the yachts along the quay. But the irony is essentially an irony without any center of reference. It is superficial, for, as Philip Rahv indicates, the only difference between the smuggler and the rich is that the rich were successful in their buccaneering. The revelation that comes to the smuggler dying in his launch—"a man alone ain't got no ... chance"—is a meaningless revelation, for it has no reference to the actual dramatization. It is, finally, a failure in intellectual analysis of the situation.

There is, I believe, a good chance that *For Whom the Bell Tolls* will not turn out to be Hemingway's best novel (an honor I should reserve for *A Farewell to Arms*) primarily because in this most ambitious of the novels Hemingway does not accept the limitations of his premises. I do not mean to imply that it is on a level with *To Have and Have Not*. There is a subtler irony in the later novel. I have pointed out that the irony in *To Have and Have Not* is that of the contrast between the smuggler and the rich in the yachts along the pier; that is, it is a simple irony, in direct line with the ostensible surface direction of the story. But the irony in *For Whom the Bell Tolls* runs counter to the ostensible surface direction of the story. As surface, we have a conflict between the forces of light and the forces of darkness, freedom versus fascism, etc. Hero and heroine are clearly and completely and romantically aligned on the side of light. We are prepared to see the Fascist atrocities and the general human kindness of the Loyalists. It happens to work out the other way. The scene of horror is the massacre by the Loyalists, not by the Fascists. Again, in the attack on El Sordo's hill by the Fascists, we are introduced to a young Fascist lieutenant, whose bosom friend is killed in the attack. We are suddenly given this little human glimpse—against the grain of the surface. But this incident, we discover later, is preparation for the very end of the novel. We leave the hero lying wounded, preparing to cover the retreat of his friends. The man who is over the sights of the machine gun as the book ends is the Fascist lieutenant, whom we have been made to know as a man, not as a monster. This general ironical conditioning of the overt story line is reflected also in the attitude of Anselmo, who kills but cannot believe in killing. In other words, the irony here is much more functional, and more complicated, than that of *To Have and Have Not*; the irony affirms that the human values may transcend the party lines.

Much has been said to the effect that *To Have and Have Not* and *For Whom the Bell Tolls* represent a basic change of point of view, an enlargement of what I have called the secret community. Now no doubt that is the intention behind both books, but the temper of both books, the good one and the bad one, is the old temper, the cast of characters is the old cast, and the assumptions lying far below the explicit intention are the old assumptions.

The monotony and self-imitation, into which Hemingway's work sometimes falls, are again an effect of a failure in dramatization. Hemingway, apparently, can dramatize his "point" in only one basic situation and with only one set of characters. He has, as we have seen, only two key characters, with certain variations from them by way of contrast or counterpoint. His best women characters, by the way, are those who most nearly approximate the men; that is, they embody the masculine virtues and point of view characteristic of Hemingway's work.

But the monotony is not merely a monotony deriving from the characters as types; it derives, rather, from the limitations of the author's sensibility, which seems to come alive in only one issue. A more flexible sensibility, one capable of making nicer discriminations, might discover great variety in such key characters and situations. But Hemingway's successes are due, in part at least, to the close co-ordination that he sometimes achieves between the character and the situation, and the sensibility as it reflects itself in the style.

The style characteristically is simple, even to the point of monotony. The characteristic sentence is simple, or compound; and if compound, there is no implied subtlety in the co-ordination of the clauses. The paragraph structure is, characteristically, based on simple sequence. There is an obvious relation between this style and the characters and situations with which the author is concerned—a relation of dramatic decorum. (There are, on the other hand, examples, especially in the novels, of other, more fluent, lyrical effects, but even here this fluency is founded on the conjunction *and*; it is a rhythmical and not a logical fluency. And the lyrical quality is simply a manifestation of that marginal sensibility, as can be demonstrated by an analysis of the occasions on which it appears.)

But there is a more fundamental aspect of the question, an aspect that involves not the sensibility of the characters but the sensibility of the author. The short, simple rhythms, the succession of coordinate clauses, the general lack of subordination—all suggest a dislocated and ununified world. The figures who live in this world live a sort of hand-to-mouth existence perceptually, and conceptually they hardly live at all. Subordination implies some exercise of discrimination—the sifting of reality through the intellect. But in Hemingway we see a romantic anti-intellectualism.

In Wordsworth, too, we see this strain of anti-intellectualism. He, too, wishes to clear away the distorting sophistications of the intellect, and to keep his eye on the object. The formulations of the intellect create the "veil of familiarity" that he would clear away. His mode, too, was to take unpromising material and reveal in it the lyric potentiality. He, too, was interested in the margin of sensibility. He, too, wished to respect the facts, and could have understood Hemingway's rejection of the big abstract words in favor of "the concrete names of villages, the numbers of roads, the names of rivers, the numbers of regiments and the dates."

The passage from *A Farewell to Arms* from which the above quotation comes is, of course, the passage most commonly used to explain the attitude behind Hemingway's style. But we can put with it other passages of a similar import, and best of all a sentence from the story "Soldier's Home." Krebs, the boy who has been through the war and who comes back home to find himself cut off from life, had "acquired the nausea in regard to experience that is the result of untruth or exaggeration." He is a casualty, not of bullet or bayonet, but of the big, abstract words. Hemingway's style is, in a way, an attempt to provide an antidote for that "nausea."

A Farewell to Arms is a love story. It is a compelling story at the merely personal level, but it is much more compelling and significant when we see the figures of the lovers silhouetted against the flame-streaked blackness of war, of a collapsing world, of nada. For there is a story behind the love story. That story is the quest for meaning and certitude in a world that seems to offer nothing of the sort. It is, in a sense, a religious book; if it does not offer a religious solution it is nevertheless conditioned by the religious problem.

The very first scene of the book, though seemingly casual, is important if we are to understand the deeper motivations of the story. It is the scene at the officers' mess where the captain baits the priest. "Priest every night five against one," the captain explains to Frederick. But Frederick, we see in this and later scenes, takes no part in the baiting. There is a bond between him and the priest, a bond that they both recognize. This becomes clear when, after the officers have advised Frederick where he should go on his leave to find the best girls, the priest turns to him and says that he would like to have him to go to Abruzzi, his own province:

> "There is good hunting. You would like the people and though it is cold it is clear and dry. You could stay with my family. My father is a famous hunter."
>
> "Come on," said the captain. "We go whorehouse before it shuts."

"Goodnight," I said to the priest.
"Goodnight," he said.

In this preliminary contrast between the officers, who invite the hero to go the brothel, and the priest, who invites him to go to the cold, clear, dry country, we have in its simplest form the issue of the novel.

Frederick does go with the officers that night, and on his leave he does go to the cities, "to the smoke of cafés and nights when the room whirled and you needed to look at the wall to make it stop, nights in bed, drunk, when you knew that that was all there was, and the strange excitement of waking and not knowing who it was with you, and the world all unreal in the dark and so exciting that you must resume again unknowing and not caring in the night, sure that this was all and all and all and not caring." Frederick, at the opening of the novel, lives in the world of random and meaningless appetite, knowing that it is all and all and all, or thinking that he knows that. But behind that there is a dissatisfaction and disgust. Upon his return from his leave, sitting in the officers' mess, he tries to tell the priest how he is sorry that he had not gone to the clear, cold, dry country—the priest's home, which takes on the shadowy symbolic significance of another kind of life, another view of the world. The priest had always known that other country.

> He had always known what I did not know and what, when I learned it, I was always able to forget. But I did not know that then, although I learned it later.

What Frederick learns later is the story behind the love story of the book.

But this theme is not merely stated at the opening of the novel and then absorbed into the action. It appears later, at crucial points, to define the line of meaning in the action. When, for example, Frederick is wounded, the priest visits him in the hospital. Their conversation makes even plainer the religious background of the novel. The priest has said that he would like to go back after the war to the Abruzzi. He continues:

> "It does not matter. But there in my country it is understood that a man may love God. It is not a dirty joke."
> "I understand."
> He looked at me and smiled.
> "You understand but you do not love God."
> "No."

"You do not love Him at all?" he asked.

"I am afraid of him in the night sometimes."

"You should love Him."

"I don't love much."

"Yes," he said. "You do. What you tell me about in the nights. That is not love. That is only passion and lust. When you love you wish to do things for. You wish to sacrifice for. You wish to serve."

"I don't love."

"You will. I know you will. Then you will be happy."

We have here two important items. First, there is the definition of Frederick as the sleepless man, the man haunted by nada. Second, at this stage in the novel, the end of Book I, the true meaning of the love story with Catherine has not yet been defined. It is still at the level of appetite. The priest's role is to indicate the next stage of the story, the discovery of the true nature of love, the "wish to do things for." And he accomplishes this by indicating a parallel between secular love and Divine Love, a parallel which implies Frederick's quest for meaning and certitude. And to emphasize further this idea, Frederick, after the priest leaves, muses on the high, clean country of the Abruzzi, the priest's home that has already been endowed with the symbolic significance of the religious view of the world.

In the middle of Book II (chapter xviii), in which the love story begins to take on the significance that the priest had predicted, the point is indicated by a bit of dialogue between the lovers.

"Couldn't we be married privately some way? Then if anything happened to me or if you had a child."

"There's no way to be married except by church or state. We are married privately. You see, darling, it would mean everything to me if I had any religion. But I haven't any religion."

"You gave me the Saint Anthony."

"That was for luck. Some one gave it to me."

"Then nothing worries you?"

"Only being sent away from you. You're my religion. You're all I've got."

Again, toward the end of Book IV (chapter xxxv), just before Frederick and Catherine make their escape into Switzerland, Frederick is talking with a friend, the old Count Greffi, who has just said that he thought H.G. Wells's novel *Mr. Britling Sees It Through* a very good study of the English middle-class soul. But Frederick twists the word *soul* into another meaning.

> "I don't know about the soul."
> "Poor boy. We none of us know about the soul. Are you *Croyant?*"
> "At night."

Later in the same conversation the Count returns to the topic:

> "And if you ever become devout pray for me if I am dead. I am asking several of my friends to do that. I had expected to become devout myself but it has not come." I thought he smiled sadly but I could not tell. He was so old and his face was very wrinkled, so that a smile used so many lines that all gradations were lost.
>   "I might become very devout," I said. "Anyway, I will pray for you."
>   "I had always expected to become devout. All my family died very devout. But somehow it does not come."
>   "It's too early."
>   "Maybe it is too late. Perhaps I have outlived my religious feeling."
>   "My own comes only at night."
>   "Then too you are in love. Do not forget that is a religious feeling."

So here we find, again, Frederick defined as the sleepless man, and the relation established between secular love and Divine Love.

In the end, with the death of Catherine, Frederick discovers that the attempt to find a substitute for universal meaning in the limited meaning of the personal relationship is doomed to failure. It is doomed because it is liable to all the accidents of a world in which human beings are like the ants running back and forth on a log burning in a campfire and in which death is, as Catherine says just before her own death, "just a dirty trick." But this is not to deny the value of the effort, or to deny the value of the discipline, the code, the stoic endurance, the things that make it true—or half true—that "nothing ever happens to the brave."

This question of the characteristic discipline takes us back to the beginning of the book, and to the context from which Frederick's effort arises. We have already mentioned the contrast between the officers of the mess and the priest. It is a contrast between the man who is aware of the issue of meaning in life and those who are unaware of it, who give themselves over to the mere flow of accident, the contrast between the disciplined and the undisciplined. But the contrast is not merely between the priest and the officers. Frederick's friend, the surgeon Rinaldi, is another who is on the same "side" of the contrast as the priest. He may go to the brothel with his brother officers, he may even bait the priest a little, but his personal relationship with Frederick indicates his affiliations; he is one of the initiate. Furthermore, he has the discipline of his profession, and, as we have seen, in the Hemingway world, the discipline that seems to be merely technical, the style of the artist or the form of the athlete or bullfighter, may be an index to a moral value. "Already," Rinaldi says, "I am only happy when I am working." (Already the seeking of pleasure in sensation is inadequate for Rinaldi.) This point appears more sharply in the remarks about the doctor who first attends to Frederick's wounded leg. He is incompetent and does not wish to take the responsibility for a decision.

> Before he came back three doctors came into the room. I have noticed that doctors who fail in the practice of medicine have a tendency to seek one another's company and aid in consultation. A doctor who cannot take out your appendix properly will recommend to you a doctor who will be unable to remove your tonsils with success. These were three such doctors.

In contrast with them there is Doctor Valentini, who is competent, who is willing to take responsibility, and who, as a kind of mark of his role, speaks the same lingo, with the same bantering, ironical tone, as Rinaldi—the tone that is the mark of the initiate.

So we have the world of the novel divided into two groups, the initiate and the uninitiate, the aware and the unaware, the disciplined and the undisciplined. In the first group are Frederick, Catherine, Rinaldi, Valentini, Count Greffi, the old man who cut the paper silhouettes "for pleasure," and Passini, Manera, and the other ambulance men in Frederick's command. In the second group are the officers of the mess, the incompetent doctors, the "legitimate hero" Ettore, and the "patriots"—all the people who do not know what is really at stake, who are deluded by the big words, who do not have the discipline. They are the messy people, the people who surrender to the flow and illusion of things. It is this second group who provide the context of the novel, and more especially the context from which Frederick moves toward his final complete awareness.

The final awareness means, as we have said, that the individual is thrown back upon his private discipline and his private capacity to endure. The hero cuts himself off from the herd, the confused world, which symbolically appears as the routed army at Caporetto. And, as Malcolm Cowley has pointed out,[3] the plunge into the flooded Tagliamento, when Frederick escapes from the battle police, has the significance of a rite. By this "baptism" Frederick is reborn into another world; he comes out into the world of the man alone, no longer supported by and involved in society.

> Anger was washed away in the river along with my obligation. Although that ceased when the carabiniere put his hands on my collar. I would like to have had the uniform off although I did not care much about the outward forms. I had taken off the stars, but that was for convenience. It was no point of honor. I was not against them. I was through. I wished them all the luck. There were the good ones, and the brave ones, and the calm ones and the sensible ones, and they deserved it. But it was not my show any more and I wished this bloody train would get to Maestre and I would eat and stop thinking.

So Frederick, by a decision, does what the boy[4] Nick does as the result of the accident of a wound. He makes a "separate peace." And from the waters of the flooded Tagliamento arises the Hemingway hero in his purest form, with human history and obligation washed away, ready to enact the last phase of his appropriate drama, and learn from his inevitable defeat the lesson of lonely fortitude.

This is not the time to attempt to give a final appraisal of Hemingway's work as a whole or even of this particular novel—if there is ever a time for a "final" appraisal. But we may touch on some of the objections which have been brought against his work.

First, there is the objection that his work is immoral or dirty or disgusting. This objection appeared in various quarters against *A Farewell to Arms* at the time of its first publication. For instance, Robert Herrick wrote that if suppression were to be justified at all it would be justified in this case. He said that the book had no significance, was merely a "lustful indulgence," and smelled of the "boudoir," and summarized his view by calling it "garbage."[5] That objection has, for the most part, died out, but its echoes can still be occasionally heard, and now and then at rare intervals some bigot or high-minded but uninstructed moralist will object to the inclusion of *A Farewell to Arms* in a college course.

The answer to this moralistic objection is fundamentally an answer to the charge that the book has no meaning. The answer would seek to establish the fact that the book does deal seriously with a moral and philosophical issue, which, for better or worse, does exist in the modern world in substantially the terms presented by Hemingway. This means that the book, even if it does not end with a solution that is generally acceptable, still embodies a moral effort and is another document of the human effort to achieve ideal values. As for the bad effect it may have on some readers, the best answer is perhaps to be found in a quotation from Thomas Hardy, who is now sanctified but whose most famous novels, *Tess of the D'Urbervilles* and *Jude the Obscure*, once suffered the attacks of the dogmatic moralists, and one of whose books was burned by a bishop:

> Of the effects of such sincere presentation on weak minds, when the courses of the characters are not exemplary and the rewards and punishments ill adjusted to deserts, it is not our duty to consider too closely. A novel which does moral injury to a dozen imbeciles, and has bracing results upon intellects of normal vigor, can justify its existence; and probably a novel was never written by the purest-minded author for which there could not be found some moral invalid or other whom it was capable of harming.[6]

Second, there is the objection that Hemingway's work, especially of the period before *To Have and Have Not*, has no social relevance, that it is off the main stream of modern life, and that it has no concern with the economic structure of society. Critics who hold this general view regard Hemingway, like Joseph Conrad and perhaps like Henry James, as an exotic. There are several possible lines of retort to this objection. One line is well stated in the following passage by David Daiches if we substitute the name of Hemingway for Conrad:

> Thus it is no reproach to Conrad that he does not concern himself at all with the economic and social background underlying human relationships in modern civilization, for he never sets out to study those relationships. The Marxists cannot accuse him of cowardice or falsification, because in this case the charge is not relevant [though it might be relevant to *To Have and Have Not* or to *For Whom the Bell Tolls*]. That, from the point of view of the man with a theory, there are accidents in history, no one can deny. And if a writer chooses to discuss those accidents

rather than the events which follow the main stream of historical causation, the economic, or other, determinist can only shrug his shoulder and maintain that these events are less instructive to the students than are the major events which he chooses to study; but he cannot accuse the writer of falsehood or distortion.[7]

That much is granted by one of the ablest critics of the group who would find Hemingway an exotic. But a second line of retort would fix on the word *instructive* in the foregoing passage, and would ask what kind of instruction, if any, is to be expected of fiction, as fiction. Is the kind of instruction expected of fiction in direct competition, at the same level, with the kind of instruction offered in Political Science I or Economics II? If that is the case, then out with Shakespeare and Keats and in with Upton Sinclair.

Perhaps *instruction* is not a relevant word, after all, for this case. This is a very thorny and debatable question, but it can be ventured that what good fiction gives us is the stimulation of a powerful image of human nature trying to fulfill itself, and not instruction in an abstract sense. The economic man and political man are important aspects of human nature and may well constitute part of the *materials* of fiction. Neither the economic nor the political man is the complete man; other concerns may still be important enough to engage the attention of a writer—such concerns as love, death, courage, the point of honor, and the moral scruple. A man has to live with other men in terms not only of economic and political arrangements but also of moral arrangements; and he has to live with himself, he has to define himself. It can truly be said that these concerns are all interrelated in fact, but it might be dangerously dogmatic to insist that a writer should not bring one aspect into sharp, dramatic focus.

And it might be dangerously dogmatic to insist that Hemingway's ideas are not relevant to modern life. The mere fact that they exist and have stirred a great many people is a testimony to their relevance. Or to introduce a variation on that theme, it might be dogmatic to object to his work on the ground that he has few basic ideas. The history of literature seems to show that good artists may have very few *basic* ideas. They may have many ideas, but the ideas do not lead a life of democratic give-and-take, of genial camaraderie. No, there are usually one or two basic, obsessive ones. Like Savonarola, the artist may well say: "*Le mie cose erano poche e grandi.*" And the ideas of the artist are grand simply because they are intensely felt, intensely realized—not because they are, by objective standards, by public, statistical standards, "important." No, that kind of public, statistical importance may be a condition of their being grand but is not of the special essence of their grandeur. (Perhaps not even the condition—perhaps the grandeur inheres in the fact that the artistic work shows us a parable of meaning—how idea is felt and how passion becomes idea through order.)

An artist may need few basic ideas, but in assessing his work we must introduce another criterion in addition to that of intensity. We must introduce the criterion of area. An artist's basic ideas do not operate in splendid isolation; to a greater or lesser degree, they prove themselves by their conquest of other ideas. Or again differently, the focus is a focus of experience, and the area of experience involved gives us another criterion of condition, the criterion of area. Perhaps an example would be helpful here. We have said that Hemingway is concerned with the scruple of honor, that this is a basic idea in his work. But we find that he applies this idea to a relatively small area of experience. In fact, we never see a story in which the issue involves the problem of definition of the scruple, nor do we ever see a story in which honor calls for a slow, grinding, day-to-day conquest of nagging difficulties. In other words, the idea is submitted to the test of a relatively small area of experience, to experience of a hand-picked sort, and to characters of a limited range.

But within that range, within the area in which he finds congenial material and in which competing ideas do not intrude themselves too strongly, Hemingway's expressive capacity is very powerful and the degree of intensity is very great. He is concerned not to report variety of human nature or human situation, or to analyze the forces operating in society, but to communicate a certain feeling about, a certain attitude toward, a special issue. That is, he is essentially a lyric rather than a dramatic writer, and for the lyric writer virtue depends upon the intensity with which the personal vision is rendered rather than upon the creation of a variety of characters whose visions are in conflict among themselves. And though Hemingway has not given—and never intended to give—a documented diagnosis of our age, he has given us one of the most compelling symbols of a personal response to our age.

NOTES

1. Introduction to the Modern Library edition of *A Farewell to Arms*.

2. Commented on by Ford Madox Ford in his introduction to the Modern Library edition of *A Farewell to Arms*.

3. Introduction to the *Portable Hemingway*, The Viking Press. In this general connection one may consider the strategic advantage that Hemingway has in that it is the Italian army from which his hero deserts. If his hero had, for instance, deserted from the American army, the American reader's resistance to accepting the act would have been

much greater—the reader's own immediate loyalties, etc., would have been betrayed by Frederick's act. And by the same token the resistance to the symbolic meaning of the act—the resigning from society—would have been much greater. The reader is led to accept the act because the desertion is from a "foreign" army. The point is indicated in a passage of dialogue between Frederick and Catherine. Frederick complains that he doesn't want them to have to live in secret and on the run like criminals.

"I feel like a criminal. I've deserted from the army."

"Darling, *please* be sensible. It's not deserting from the army. It's only the Italian army."

It may be objected that since Hemingway himself saw service on the Italian front it is only natural that his story should be laid there and that by consequence the fact has no symbolic significance and no significance as fictional strategy. But the fact that circumstances of personal history dictated the setting of the story does not prevent the author from seizing on and using the advantages inherent in the situation.

4. *In Our Time*, chapter vi.

5. "What Is Dirt?" *Bookman*, November, 1929.

6. "The Profitable Reading of Fiction," in *Life and Art, Essays, Notes and Letters*.

7. For a contrary view of the work of Conrad, see my essay on p. 31.

CARLOS BAKER

The Way It Was

"The job of the last twenty-five years was for the writer or artist to get what there was to be got (artistically) out of the world extant."

—Ezra Pound[1]

I. PLACE, FACT, SCENE

"A writer's job is to tell the truth," said Hemingway in 1942.[2] He had believed it for twenty years and he would continue to believe it as long as he lived. No other writer of our time had so fiercely asserted, so pugnaciously defended, or so consistently exemplified the writer's obligation to speak truly. His standard of truth-telling remained, moreover, so high and so rigorous that he was ordinarily unwilling to admit secondary evidence, whether literary evidence or evidence picked up from other sources than his own experience. "I only know what I have seen," was a statement which came often to his lips and pen. What he had personally done, or what he knew unforgettably by having gone through one version of it, was what he was interested in telling about. This is not to say that he refused to invent freely. But he always made it a sacrosanct point to invent in terms of what he actually knew from having been there.

The primary intent of his writing, from first to last, was to seize and project for the reader what he often called "the way it was." This is a

From *Hemingway: The Writer as Artist*. © 1972 by Carlos Baker. Published by Princeton University Press.

characteristically simple phrase for a concept of extraordinary complexity, and Hemingway's conception of its meaning subtly changed several times in the course of his career—always in the direction of greater complexity. At the core of the concept, however, one can invariably discern the operation of three esthetic instruments: the sense of place, the sense of fact, and the sense of scene.

The first of these, obviously a strong passion with Hemingway, is the sense of place. "Unless you have geography, background," he once told George Antheil, "you have nothing."[3] You have, that is to say, a dramatic vacuum. Few writers have been more place-conscious. Few have so carefully charted out the geographical groundwork of their novels while managing to keep background so conspicuously unobtrusive. Few, accordingly, have been able to record more economically and graphically the way it is when you walk through the streets of Paris in search of breakfast at a corner café. Or when your footfalls echo among surrounding walls on the ancient cobblestones of early morning Venice, heading for the market-place beside the Adriatic. Or when, at around six o'clock of a Spanish dawn, you watch the bulls running from the corrals at the Puerta Rochapea through the streets of Pamplona towards the bullring.

"When I woke it was the sound of the rocket exploding that announced the release of the bulls from the corrals at the edge of town.... Down below the narrow street was empty. All the balconies were crowded with people. Suddenly a crowd came down the street. They were all running, packed close together. They passed along and up the street toward the bullring and behind them came more men running faster, and then some stragglers who were really running. Behind them was a little bare space, and then the bulls, galloping, tossing their heads up and down. It all went out of sight around the corner. One man fell, rolled to the gutter, and lay quiet. But the bulls went right on and did not notice him. They were all running together."[4]

This scene is as morning-fresh as a design in India ink on clean white paper. First is the bare white street, seen from above, quiet and empty. Then one sees the first packed clot of runners. Behind these are the thinner ranks of those who move faster because closer to the bulls. Then the almost comic stragglers, who are "really running." Brilliantly behind these shines the "little bare space," a desperate margin for error. Then the clot of running bulls— closing the design, except of course for the man in the gutter making himself, like the designer's initials, as inconspicuous as possible.

The continuing freshness of such occasions as this might be associated with Hemingway's lifelong habit of early waking. More likely, the freshness arises because Hemingway loves continental cities, makes it almost a fetish to know them with an artist's eye, and has trained himself rigorously to see and retain those aspects of a place that make it *that place*, even though, with an odd skill, he manages at the same time to render these aspects generically.

As with the cities—and Hemingway's preference is for the Latin cities—so with the marshes, rivers, lakes, troutstreams, gulf-streams, groves, forests, hills, and gullies, from Wyoming to Tanganyika, from the Tagliamento to the Irati, and from Key West to the Golden Horn. "None can care for literature itself," said Stevenson, somewhere, "who do not take a special pleasure in the sound of names." Hemingway's love of names is obvious. It belongs to his sense of place. But like the rest of his language, it is under strict control. One never finds, as so often happens in the novels of Thomas Wolfe or the poetry of Carl Sandburg, the mere riot and revel of place-names, played upon like guitar-strings for the music they contain. Hemingway likes the words *country* and *land*. It is astonishing how often they recur in his work without being obtrusive. He likes to move from place to place, and to be firmly grounded, for the time being, in whatever place he has chosen. It may be the banks of the Big Two-Hearted River of Northern Michigan or its Spanish equivalent above Burguete. It may be the Guadarrama hilltop where El Sordo died, or the Veneto marshes where Colonel Cantwell shot his last mallards from a duckblind. Wherever it is, it is solid and permanent, both in itself and in the books.

The earliest of his published work, descriptively speaking, shows an almost neoclassical restraint. Take a sample passage from *The Sun Also Rises*, not his earliest but fairly representative. This one concerns the Irati Valley fishing-trip of Jake Barnes and Bill Gorton.

"It was a beech wood and the trees were very old. Their roots bulked above the ground and the branches were twisted. We walked on the road between the thick trunks of the old beeches and the sunlight came through the leaves in light patches on the grass. The trees were big, and the foliage was thick but it was not gloomy. There was no undergrowth, only the smooth grass, very green and fresh, and the big gray trees were well spaced as though it were a park. 'This is country,' Bill said."[5]

It is such country as an impressionist might paint almost exactly in the terms, and the subdued colors, which Hemingway employs. More than this, however, is the fact that in such a paragraph Dr. Samuel Johnson's Imlac could find little to criticize. Even the arrangement of the beech trees themselves, like the choice of the words, is clean and classical. The foliage is thick, but there is no gloom. Here is neither teeming undergrowth nor its verbal equivalent. The sage of Johnson's *Rasselas* advises all aspirant poets against numbering the streaks of the tulip or describing in detail the different shades of the verdure of the forest. Young Hemingway, still an aspirant poet, follows the advice. When he has finished, it is possible to say (and we supply our own inflection for Bill Gorton's words): "This is country."

For all the restraint, the avoidance of color-flaunting adjectives, and the plainsong sentences (five compound to one complex), the paragraph is loaded with precisely observed fact: beech wood, old trees, exposed roots, twisted branches, thick trunks, sunpatches, smooth green grass, foliage which casts a shade without excluding light. One cannot say that he has been given a generalized landscape—there are too many exact factual observations. On the other hand, the uniquenesses of the place receive no special emphasis. One recognizes easily the generic type of the clean and orderly grove. where weeds and brush do not flourish because of the shade, and the grass gets only enough light to rise to carpet-level. Undoubtedly, as in the neoclassical esthetic, the intent is to provide a generic frame within which the reader is at liberty to insert his own uniquenesses—as many or as few as his imagination may supply.

Along with the sense of place, and as a part of it, is the sense of fact. Facts march through all his pages in a stream as continuous as the refugee wagons in Thrace or the military camions on the road from the Isonzo. Speculation, whether by the author or by the characters, is ordinarily kept to a minimum. But facts, visible or audible or tangible facts, facts baldly stated, facts without verbal paraphernalia to inhibit their striking power, are the stuff of Hemingway's prose.

Sometimes, especially in the early work, the facts seem too many for the effect apparently intended, though even here the reader should be on guard against misconstruing the intention of a given passage. It is hard to discover, nevertheless, what purpose beyond the establishment of the sense of place is served by Barnes's complete itinerary of his walk with Bill Gorton through the streets of Paris.[6] The direction is from Madame Lecomte's restaurant on the Île St. Louis across to the left bank of the Seine, and eventually up the Boulevard du Port Royal to the Café Select. The walk fills only two pages. Yet it seems much longer and does not further the action appreciably except to provide Jake and Bill with healthy after-dinner exercise. At Madame Lecomte's (the facts again), they have eaten "a roast chicken, new green beans, mashed potatoes, a salad, and some apple pie and cheese." To the native Parisian, or a foreigner who knows the city, the pleasure in the after-dinner itinerary would consist in the happy shock of recognition. For others, the inclusion of so many of the facts of municipal or gastronomic geography—so many more than are justified by their dramatic purpose—may seem excessive.

Still, this is the way it was that time in Paris. Here lay the bridges and the streets, the squares and the cafés. If you followed them in the prescribed order, you came to the café where Lady Brett Ashley sat on a high stool at the bar, her crossed legs stockingless, her eyes crinkling at the corners.

If an imaginative fusion of the sense of place and the sense of fact is to occur, and if, out of the fusing process, dramatic life is to arise, a third element is required. This may be called the sense of scene. Places are less than geography, facts lie inert and uncoordinated, unless the imagination runs through them like a vitalizing current and the total picture moves and quickens. How was it, for example, that second day of the San Fermin fiesta in the Pamplona bullring after Romero had killed the first bull?

"They had hitched the mules to the dead bull and then the whips cracked, the men ran, and the mules, straining forward, their legs pushing, broke into a gallop, and the bull, one horn up, his head on its side, swept a swath smoothly across the sand and out the red gate."[7]

Here are a dead bull, men, mules, whips, sand, and a red gate like a closing curtain—the place and the facts. But here also, in this remarkably graphic sentence, are the seven verbs, the two adverbs, and the five adverbial phrases which fuse and coordinate the diverse facts of place and thing and set them in rapid motion. If one feels that the sentence is very satisfying as a scene, and wishes to know why, the answer might well lie where it so often lies in a successful lyric poem—that is, in our sense of difficulty overcome. Between the inertness of the dead bull when he is merely *hitched* (a placid verb) and the smooth speed with which the body finally *sweeps* across the sand and out of sight, come the verbs of sweating effort: *crack*, *run*, *strain*, and *break*. It is precisely at the verb *broke* that the sentence stops straining and moves into the smooth glide of its close. The massing, in that section of the sentence, of a half-dozen *s*'s, compounded with the *th* sounds of *swath* and *smoothly*, can hardly have been inadvertent. They ease (or grease) the path of the bull's departure.

The pattern in the quoted passage is that of a task undertaken, striven through, and smoothly completed: order and success. For another graphic sentence, so arranged as to show the precise opposites—total disorder and total failure—one might take the following example from *Death in the Afternoon*. The protagonist is a "phenomenon," a bullfighter who has lost his nerve.

"In your mind you see the phenomenon, sweating, white-faced, and sick with fear, unable to look at the horn or go near it, a couple of swords on the ground, capes all around him, running in at an angle on the bull hoping the sword will strike a vital spot, cushions sailing down into the ring and the steers ready to come in."[8]

In this passage, place has become predicament. The facts, thrown in almost helter-skelter, imply the desperate inward fear which is responsible for the creation of the outward disorder. Verbs are held to a minimum, and their natural naked power is limited with qualifications. The phenomenon is *unable to look*, and *hoping to strike*, not *looking* and *striking*. He runs, but it is at a bad angle. The disorder of the swords on the ground and the capes all around is increased by the scaling-in of seat-cushions from the benches, the audience's insult to gross cowardice. The author-spectator's crowning insult is the allusion to the steers, who by comparison with the enraged bull are bovine, old-womanly creatures. On being admitted to the ring, they will quiet and lead away the bull the phenomenon could not kill.

The sense of place and the sense of fact are indispensable to Hemingway's art. But the true craft, by which diversities are unified and compelled into graphic collaboration, comes about through the operation of the sense of scene. Often, moving through the Latin language countries, watching the crowd from a café table or a barrera bench, Hemingway seems like a lineal descendant of Browning's observer in *How It Strikes a Contemporary.*

> You saw go up and down Valladolid
> A man of mark, to know next time you saw ...
> Scenting the world, looking it full in face.

II. WHAT HAPPENED

Although they are clearly fundamental to any consideration of Hemingway's esthetic aims, place, fact, and scene are together no more than one phase of a more complex observational interest. The skillful writer can make them work in harmony, with place and fact like teamed horses under the dominance of the sense of scene. The result is often as striking and satisfactory to watch as a good chariot race. But the event is, after all, mainly an extrinsic matter. These are not Plato's horses of the soul.

The complementary phase is inward: a state of mind causally related to the extrinsic events and accurately presented in direct relation to those events. When Samuel Putnam asked Hemingway in the late twenties for a definition of his aims, the answer was: "Put down what I see and what I feel in the best and simplest way I can tell it."[9] Taken as absolute standards, of course, bestness and simplicity will often be at variance, a fact of which Hemingway at that date was apparently becoming more and more conscious. But his aim from the beginning had been to show, if he could, the precise relationship between what he saw and what he felt.

It is characteristic of Hemingway, with his genuine scorn for overintellectualized criticism, that he has himself refused to employ critical jargon in the presentation of his esthetic ideas. It is also evident, however, that early in his career, probably about 1922, he had evolved an esthetic principle which might be called "the discipline of double perception." The term is not quite exact, since the aim of double perception is ultimately a singleness of vision. This is the kind of vision everyone experiences when his two eyes, though each sees the same set of objects from slightly disparate angles, work together to produce a unified picture with a sense of depth to it. According to Hemingway, he was trying very hard for this double perception about the time of his return from the Near East in the fall of 1922. Aside from knowing "truly" what he "really" felt in the presence of any given piece of action, he found that his greatest difficulty lay in putting down on paper "what really happened in action; what the actual things were which produced the emotion" felt by the observer. No wonder that he was finding it hard to get "the real thing, the sequence of motion and fact which made the emotion." Whatever that real thing was, if you stated it "purely" enough and were likewise lucky, there was a chance that your statement of it would be valid, esthetically and emotionally valid, forever.[10]

Fundamental to the task is the deletion of one's own preconceptions. Such and such was the way it *ought* to be, the way you *assumed* it was. But "oughts" and "assumptions" are dangerous ground for a man to stand on who wishes to take the word of no one else, and to achieve in esthetics what René Descartes thought he had achieved in philosophy, namely, a start at the start. The hope was that the genuinely serious and determined writer-observer might be able in time to penetrate behind the illusions which all our preconceptions play upon the act of clear seeing.

It would then become his task to perfect himself in the discipline of double perception. To make something so humanly true that it will outlast the vagaries of time and change, yet will still speak directly to one's own changing time, he must somehow reach a state of objective awareness between two poles, one inward-outward and the other outward-inward. The first need (though not always first in order of time) is the ability to look within and to describe that complex of mixed emotions which a given set of circumstances has produced in the observer's mind. The other necessity is to locate and to state factually and exactly that outer complex of motion and fact which produced the emotional reaction.

This second class of things and circumstances, considered in their relations to the emotional complexes of the first class, would be precisely what T.S. Eliot called "objective correlatives."[11] His statement calls them variously "a set of objects, a situation, a chain of events which shall be the formula of that particular emotion; such that when the external facts, which must terminate in sensory experience, are given, the emotion is immediately evoked." He states further that the idea of artistic "inevitability" consists in the "complete adequacy of the external to the emotion." Mr. Eliot's generic description fits Hemingway's customary performance. Yet it may be noticed that Eliot's most frequent practice, as distinguished from his theoretical formulation, is to fashion his objective correlatives into a series of complex *literary* symbols. These are designed to elicit a more or less controlled emotional response from the reader (like the Wagnerian passage in *The Waste Land*), depending to some degree on the extent of his cultural holdings. With Hemingway, on the other hand, the objective correlatives are not so much inserted and adapted as observed and encompassed. They are to be traced back, not to anterior literature and art objects, but to things actually seen and known by direct experience of the world.

Hemingway's method has this special advantage over Eliot's—that one's ability to grasp the emotional suggestions embodied in an objective correlative depends almost solely on two factors: the reader's sensitivity to emotional suggestion, and the degree of his imaginative and sympathetic involvement in the story which is being told. With Eliot these two factors are likewise emphatically present, but a third is added. This third, which in a measure controls and delimits the first two, is the factor of "literary" experience. One's emotional response to the Wagnerian passage cannot be really full unless he knows its origin, can see it in both its original and its new and secondary context, and can make certain quick comparisons between the two. Some, though not all, of Eliot's correlatives accordingly show a "twice-removed" quality which in a measure pales and rarefies them. They cannot always achieve the full-bloodedness and immediacy of correlatives taken directly from the actual set of empirical circumstances which produced in the author the emotion which he is seeking to convey to the reader.

The objective correlatives in Hemingway appear to be of two main types, arbitrarily separable though always working together in a variety of ways. The first may be called *things-in-context*: that particular arrangement of facts in their relations to one another which constitutes a static field of perception. The second type may be called *things-in-motion*, since the arrangement of facts in their relations one to another is almost never wholly static. One might call any combination of the two types by the generic term of *what happened*, where the idea of happening implies a sequence of events in a certain order in time, though any event in the sequence can be arrested to form a static field of observation. If you have *what happened* in this special sense, you will have a chance of reproducing, in a perspective with depth, "the way it was."

To write for permanence, therefore, is to find and set down those things-in-context and things-in-motion which evoked a reaction in the writer as observer. Yet even the presence of both of these correlatives will not suffice to produce the total effect unless one also knows and says what he "really felt" in their presence. The important corollary idea of selection, meaning the elimination of the irrelevant and the unimportant at both poles, is clearly implied in Hemingway's phrase, "stated purely enough." During the five years of his early apprenticeship and the next five in which he developed his skills with such remarkable rapidity, the discipline of double perception was for Hemingway the leading esthetic principle. It is hard to imagine a better—or more difficult—task for the young writer to attempt. Although other principles later arose to supplement this first one, it still continued to occupy one whole side of his attention.

III. TRUTH AND FALLACY

The basis of Hemingway's continuing power, and the real backbone of his eminence, is in practical esthetics. "Pure" or theoretical esthetics, of that special bloodless order which can argue to all hours without a glance at concretions, holds little interest for an artist of so pragmatic and empirical a cast of mind. One might even doubt that theoretical esthetics is of real interest to any genuine artist, unless in his alter ego he happens also to be a philosophical critic. If that is true, his artistic life is always in some danger, as Hemingway's is not. In esthetics as in his personal philosophy, he strove very hard to stay free of the wrong kind of illusion, and out from under the control of any cut-and-dried system, always trying instead to keep his eye trained on the thing in itself and the effect of the thing in himself. The actual, he wrote in 1949, is "made of knowledge, experience, wine, bread, oil, salt, vinegar, bed, early mornings, nights, days, the sea, men, women, dogs, beloved motor cars, bicycles, hills and valleys, the appearance and disappearance of trains on straight and curved tracks ... cock grouse drumming on a basswood log, the smell of sweetgrass and fresh-smoked leather and Sicily."[12] Given the knowledge and experience of these and their unnamed equivalents, the artist can be at home in the world. If he is a practical esthetician whose aim is to "invent truly," he is on firm ground. By experience he knows what will do. By observation he knows what will go— like the eminently practical Aristotle of the *Poetics*.

It was once remarked, though not by Aristotle, that the province of esthetics is the true and the beautiful, the province of morality the good. Of Hemingway as a moral writer there will be much to say. It is clear that the strongest conviction in Hemingway the esthetician—the principle underlying his sense of place and fact and scene, the principle supporting his "discipline of double perception"—is the importance of telling truth.

To get at the truth of anything is hard enough. For the young artist the task is complicated by the fact that he must steer his way with the utmost care among a set of fallacies, placed like sand-bunkers around a green, or concealed traps around desirable bait. Three of these fallacies stand out: the pathetic, the apathetic, and what may be called the kinetographic.

Ruskin named the first.[13] It is *pathetic* because it comes about through excess of emotion. It is fallacious because, when we are really dominated by an emotion, it is extremely difficult to see things as they are. The curious may read Hemingway's own half-serious opinions on the subject in a disquisition on "erectile writing," which was written to satirize Waldo Frank's *Virgin Spain* in *Death in the Afternoon*.[14] Fundamentally, as that essay makes plain, the pathetic fallacy is an error in perception. But secondarily and by a logical sequence, it is an error of expression, since what has been wrongly seen cannot be rightly described. The intensity of the emotion felt by the writer, if let go on its own, will determine his choice of words. In Charles Kingsley's *Alton Locke*, Ruskin finds an example in which the writing has been made irrational by the author's failure to control the intensity of his emotion. A girl has died in the surf and the seamen bring her body in.

> They rowed her in across the rolling foam—
> The cruel, crawling foam.

"The foam is not cruel," says Ruskin, "neither does it crawl. The state of mind which attributes to it these characters of a living creature is one in which the reason is unhinged by grief. All violent feelings have the same effect. They produce in us a falseness in all our impressions of external things, which I would generally characterize as the pathetic fallacy."

Ruskin goes on to say that the greatest artists do not often admit this kind of falseness of impression and expression. It is only the second or third rankers who much delight in it. It is a form of self-deception, one of the orders of sentimentality. The good writers are not the creatures of their emotions; theirs is a sanity which helps them to see the world clearly and to see it whole.

Beginning with a standard of performance which rigorously excluded the pathetic fallacy, Hemingway adhered to it with a faith just short of fanatical, all his life. Emotion was of course both permissible and, under proper control, necessary. Excess of emotion, however, was never to be allowed. It would falsify both impression and expression. So many of our habits of seeing and saying take their origin from recollected emotion gone stale. If one could cut loose from these habits, three immediate results might be expected. First, you could see what you really saw rather than what you thought you saw. Second, you could know what you felt rather than "what you were supposed to feel." Third, you could say outright what you really saw and felt instead of setting down a false (and, in the bad sense, a literary) version of it.

Hemingway's earliest plan, therefore, was to start cleanly and all afresh to see what effects could be achieved by straight observation of action, set forth in unadorned prose. The immediate upshot of the effort was the kind of writing presented in the Paris edition of *in our time*. This, for example, on part of Act One at a bullfight:

"They whack-whacked the white horse on the legs and he kneed himself up. The picador twisted the stirrups straight and pulled and hauled up into the saddle. The horse's entrails hung down in a blue bunch and swung backward and forward as he began to canter, the monos whacking him on the back of his legs with the rods. He cantered jerkily along the barrera. He stopped stiff and one of the monos held his bridle and walked him forward. The picador kicked in his spurs, leaned forward and shook his lance at the bull. Blood pumped regularly from between the horse's front legs. He was nervously unsteady. The bull could not make up his mind to charge."[15]

This 120-word miniature is a writer's apprentice-exercise, a minute of a Spanish committee meeting. Without ignoring the beginning (a horse has been gored by a bull) or the end (the horse will be gored again and will die), the young writer is concentrating on the middle of an action. He puts down what he sees, exactly as he sees it. He eliminates from his view the panorama, the weather, the crowd, the waiting matadors, the price of the seats, the hardness of the bench on which he sits, the odor of his neighbor, the color of the sky, the degree of the temperature. Instead he watches the horse, and what takes place immediately around the horse, with a tremendous intensity of concentration. He is not guessing, even when he speaks of the horse's nervous unsteadiness or the bull's indecision. These are immediately visible qualities, shown by the animals through their actions. The prose is as clean as the observation. Nothing is ornamental. None but essential modifiers are called, and only a few are chosen. No similes, no metaphors, no literary allusions, no pathetic illusions, no balanced clauses. There is only one trick, and that is a good one: the three-time use of the word *forward*, which adds to the intensity of the account because "forward" is where the bull stands with one wet horn. Otherwise there is nothing in the least fancy. There is only an ancient horse, in very bad shape, waiting for the *coup de grâce.*

Though he never chose similar subjects himself, Ruskin might well have admired Hemingway's "story." He could have placed it alongside Thackeray's account of Amelia in *Vanity Fair:* that time in Chapter 32 in Brussels when she prays quietly for the well-being of her husband George, in ignorance of the fact that he lies dead at Waterloo. Ruskin's term for the literature of straight statement, without moralizing elaboration or rococo interior decorating, is the "Make-What-You-Will-Of-It" school of fiction— a school diametrically opposed to the school of the pathetic fallacy. Scholars at the Spartan school of "What-You-Will" are content to let well enough alone. Like Hemingway at the Spanish committee-meeting, they say the thing the way it was and let the minutes stand as written.

The passage on the horse also steers clear of the apathetic fallacy, where the reason is so cold and tight that the matter of emotion is squeezed out entirely. At first glance, it is true, one might suppose that Hemingway had ignored both his own and the reader's emotions. The account includes no overt allusion to how the observer felt in the presence of Rosinante Agonistes. There is no evident plucking of the heart-strings, no visible pump inserted into the springs of human sympathy.

Yet the close reader can entertain no real doubt. The passage is neither cold, austere, nor cruel. Pity for the horse (if you are a member of that sector of mankind which pities wounded horses) is revealed by the artist's selection of details: the horse's awkward struggle to a standing position, the swinging of the exposed entrails, the jerkiness of the canter, the bite of the spurs, and the awful regularity of the pumping of the blood. A kind of implicit enmity towards the picador and the ring-servants comes out in verbs like *whack-whacked, pulled and hauled,* the second *whacking,* and the *kicking-in* of the spurs. The pity and the enmity are so firmly in check that at first—to use Aristotle's ethical terms—we suppose a *defect* of sympathy. By the same token, the *extreme* of excessive pathos is carefully avoided. What remains is the *mean,* the province of the writer who seeks to avoid both the apathetic and the pathetic fallacies.

Such an esthetic theory of the "emotive mean" leaves the practitioner open to certain criticisms. What about scope, it is asked, and what about depth? Where is the rest of the act? Who were the parents of the horse that we may establish some sort of sympathetic rapport with him? "Hemingway's art," wrote Wyndham Lewis in 1934, "is an art of the surface—and, as I look at it, none the worse for that."[16] Lewis failed, like many of his contemporaries, to look at this particular art long enough. Had he done so, he might have seen what Hemingway was doing with images and with suggestion far below the surfaces of his better stories—though not too far to be overlooked by the close and sympathetic reader. He also ignored Henry James' observation, which applies to all of Hemingway's miniatures: "an exemplary anecdote" may be also "a little rounded drama."[17] Many of our best critics have consistently underrated Hemingway's esthetic intelligence.

If his chosen approach led to pejorative judgments, or even to the suggested kind of limitation on depth and scope, Hemingway as an apprentice craftsman was temporarily prepared to accept them. He began, as he knew he must, by centering attention on action, and on what he felt to be the simpler modes of action. "I was trying to learn to write, commencing with the simplest things," he said in 1932, speaking of his program in 1922.[18] As in the laboratory study of biology, one works up only very gradually to more complex organisms. If he were to begin on the human instead of the frog, the young biologist's ignorance might betray him into the most unscientific (which is to say, untrue) conceptions, and he would have the further hazard of getting lost among the ganglia. Hemingway's writing after 1922 was most certainly none the worse for his rigorous self-imposed apprentice training. He advanced well beyond the early state without losing sight of its importance. He continued to employ what he had learned there at the same time that he continued to learn other things.

The most dangerous pitfall for the young Hemingway was what may be called the kinetographic fallacy. This consists in the supposition that we can get the best art by an absolutely true description of what takes place in observed action. It will be kinetic because it must move by definition. It will be graphic because it is a picture. We write down what we see men doing, what they say, what they look like to us. We hold a mirror and a microphone up to life, and report, with absolute though selective precision, the reflections and the noises.

The dangers of such a program, if it is rigorously followed, are clear. The absolutist desire to see and say the truth and nothing but the truth may keep the best-intentioned writer from doing both. No artist who reports the action of men and animals, merely as such, will record things as they are, or really grasp and project "the way it was." He will record actions from the outside, only as they *look* to be. Facts will be distorted in the very attempt to avoid distortion.

The account of the wounded horse cannot be called distortion. But it does nevertheless consist in a concentration so intense that the miniature itself can be appreciated without remembering the larger context of the bullfight, the arena, the town, and the nation in which the described events took place. The spreading context can, of course, be supplied by the reader's imagination. But one could probably argue that the artist is not justified in overworking his reader's imagination to quite this extent.

Between the "defect" of too little detail and the "excess" of the sand-pile technique (where everything is put in, whether it is relevant or not, until we have a bulk on the horizon too considerable to ignore), there is a mean. By the time Hemingway wrote *The Sun Also Rises*, he was rounding out his writing by allowing the possible to enter his picture of the actual. He was beginning to admit guesses, fictions, motivations, imaginations in far greater profusion than he had done in 1922. He felt justified in doing so because he had so firmly avoided guessing throughout his apprenticeship. Now he had had sufficient experience of the kinetographic reporting of the actual so that he could trust himself to invent, though never to invent except in terms of carefully observed experience. Hemingway, therefore, did not so much avoid as transcend the kinetographic fallacy. His own summary of the "mean position" continued, of course, to stress the importance of truth-telling: "A writer's job is to tell the truth." Then he went on. "His standard of fidelity to the truth must be so high that his invention" which comes always and invariably "out of his experience, should produce a truer account than anything factual can be."[19] This remark, set down in 1942, is the essence of twenty years of experience. It runs very close to a pronouncement by Coleridge, who also based his views on common sense and long experience: "A poet ought not to pick nature's pocket: let him borrow, and so borrow as to repay by the very act of borrowing. Examine nature accurately, but write from recollection; and trust more to your imagination than your memory."[20]

Hemingway's nearly absolute devotion to what is true, coming in an age when absolute devotions are so rare, is not only the dominant drive in his whole esthetic life, but also the firmest guarantee that his works will survive. He continuously entertained a healthy and essentially humble conviction that the truth is difficult to come by, though sometimes it may drop by chance into a writer's lap. The good parts of a book, as he told Fitzgerald in 1929, may be only something a writer is lucky enough to overhear, or they may be the wreck of his "whole damned life."[21] But if both partake of the nature of truth, one is as good as the other, though their scope will naturally differ. Any form of truth, however, if it is put into an art form, will help the writing to survive the erosions of time. For the truth is a sturdy core, impervious to the winds of faddist doctrine and the temporary weather of an age.

IV. THE BEAUTIFUL

From truth it is only a step to beauty and *aisthetes*—"one who perceives"—is ordinarily associated with the perception of the beautiful. Although Hemingway the esthetician has spoken much of truth, he has had little to say about what constitutes for him the nature of the beautiful. In the fiction itself there is scarcely any overt emphasis on beauty for its own sake. Remembering Ruskin, one might call Hemingway's the "make-what-you-will-of-it" approach to the perception of the beautiful. It is as if Hemingway tacitly agreed with the dictum of Herbert Read: "To live according to natural law, this is also the release of the imagination. In discovering truth, we create beauty."[22]

With respect to the beautiful it appears to be a basic assumption in Hemingway's esthetic that what is true, in the sense of being natural and untinkered-with, is also beautiful. Ugliness in Hemingway is almost invariably associated with the abnormal and the unnatural: the unwomanly woman, for example, or the unmanly man. The unclean, the furtive, the cowardly, the enslaved all show an aspect of the sinister. Beauty in Hemingway is the beauty of land, of men and women, of the nobler animals, of the clean, the honest, the well-lighted, the nonconcealing, the brave.

One version of the alliance between the natural and the beautiful was very well summarized by the Emperor Marcus Aurelius.

"The hanging-down of grapes, the brow of the lion, the froth of a foaming wild boar, though by themselves considered they are far from beauty, yet because they happen naturally, they are both comely and beautiful."[23]

The comely is the becoming, the fitting, that which is felt to be naturally right. Whenever in the reading of Hemingway one finds himself arrested by the beauty of a passage, he may discover also that its essential naturalness, in the moral dimension of stoic esthetics, helps to explain its essential beauty.

Following the lead of the Emperor, one might turn to the examples of the rhinoceros and the kudu bull in the *Green Hills of Africa*, one of Hemingway's least appreciated books.[24] About the rhino:

"There he was, long-hulked, heavy-sided, prehistoric-looking, the hide like vulcanized rubber and faintly transparent looking, scarred with a badly healed horn wound that the birds had pecked at, his tail thick, round, and pointed, flat many-legged ticks crawling on him, his ears fringed with hair, tiny pig eyes, moss growing on the base of his horn that grew forward from his nose. M'Cola looked at him and shook his head. I agreed with him. This was the hell of an animal."

Confronted by this passage, the naturalist might well argue that this is the way a dead rhinoceros looks. This is the nature of the beast, and if we follow Marcus Aurelius it would be necessary to conclude that the rhinoceros, since he happens naturally, is a thing of beauty and a joy forever. Yet to argue thus he would have to ignore the very careful accumulation of points in Hemingway's description which suggest the unnatural and the abnormal. The prehistoric look, for example, is not of this present world; the vulcanized-rubber appearance of the skin, though very distinctly of this world, is somehow artificial and ugly on an animal. The horn wound, badly healed and pecked at by the tick birds, has the force of an abnormality. So does the allusion to the verminous ticks, comparable to the horror of flies around a horse's cruppet mentioned elsewhere in the same book. The eyes are out of proportion, and the moss at the base of the horn seems an unnatural growth, like festoons of mildew on a neglected book. This is an offensive animal, disproportioned in its long hulk, abnormal in its appurtenances, a kind of mistaken hybrid, not what you would expect an animal to look like—esthetically wrong, in short, and generally objectionable.

Against such disproportion, abnormality, and unnatural naturalness, one might place the unposed portrait of the kudu bull, killed at long last after many days of unsuccessful hunting.

"It was a huge, beautiful kudu bull, stone-dead, on his side, his horns in great dark spirals, widespread and unbelievable as he lay dead five yards from where we stood.... I looked at him, big, long-legged, a smooth gray with the white stripes and the great curling, sweeping horns, brown as walnut meats, and ivory-pointed, at the big ears and the great, lovely, heavy-maned neck, the white chevron between his eyes and the white of his muzzle and I stooped over and touched him to try to believe it. He was lying on the side where the bullet had gone in and there was not a mark on him and he smelled sweet and lovely like the breath of cattle and the odor of thyme after rain."

This is the true hunter's esthetic appreciation. Even the non-hunter, whose conscientious or temperamental objection to killing would not permit him to write in just this way, can share the hunter's admiration for the graceful, strong, handsomely proportioned animal. The size, the clean natural colors, the wholeness ("there was not a mark on him"), and the sweet natural smell which distinguishes the grazing animals from the meat-eaters, are all factors in the kudu's esthetic attractiveness. "Beautiful ... lovely ... lovely." Words like these, in the context of the weary hunt now successfully crowned with antlers, are used without apology. Here is the hunter's and the esthetician's dream of an animal, as the rhinoceros was a kind of tickridden nightmare.

The quality of beauty in Hemingway's work seems to come as naturally as the leaves to a tree. Yet the carefully ordered accounts of natural scenery in his pages reveal, on close examination, a deliberate and intelligent artifice. The description is nearly always directly functional within an action. The beauty—or ugliness—of the land is made to belong to the ugliness—or beauty—of the human events which occur in its midst. Sometimes, as in Frank Norris, natural beauty stands in quiet contrast to whatever it is that men and women are doing in its presence. Hemingway uses this old trick of the naturalistic writers charily and rarely; it is never emphasized in the black-jack manner of, say, Norris in *The Octopus*, or Steinbeck in *The Wayward Bus*. What we tend to get in Hemingway is a subtle interweaving of the natural conditions in the background and the human conditions in the foreground or the middle-distance.

While examining portraits by divers Italian masters, Hemingway always carefully studied the backgrounds, as if to find corroboration in another art for his ideas about the importance of natural settings in prose fiction. As he well knew total effect depends upon placing figures in a context—verbal, schematic and scenic—and in this respect he is as good a "contextualist" as T.S. Eliot, who adopted if he did not invent this special application of the term. Although Hemingway had rigorously trained himself in the accurate observation of natural objects, his precision of rendering did not prevent these objects from being put to symbolic use. The discipline of double perception requires an ability to penetrate both to the essential qualities of a natural scene and to the essential qualities of a subjective reaction to the scene. These, working together in a dozen ways, produce the total effect.

Hemingway's sense of beauty is stirred, his heart is moved, as much by human beings as by landscapes or the more handsome animals. Here again the normative judgment comes into operation. He scorns perversions of any kind. Whatever is abnormal or unnatural according to his measurement is ugly according to his conclusion. People about their normal business, or people who are able under abnormal circumstances to behave like normal human beings, ordinarily strike him with the impact of the beautiful though he may not use the word in that connection.

The point may be illustrated by choosing an example of a set of human beings of no extrinsic beauty at all, but modern, unlovely, dirty, urban, and tough. This is a group portrait of the matadors' representatives, the trusted banderilleros who have gathered to appraise the bulls the morning before a *corrida*.

"The representatives, usually short men in caps, not yet shaven for the day, with a great variety of accents, but all with the same hard eyes, argue and discuss."[25]

Goya would have fancied these people; Browning's poet-observer could have met them in Valladolid. Though by themselves considered they are far from beauty, yet because they happen naturally, in the morning chiaroscuro of the plaza corrals, they are both comely and beautiful to the eye of a true esthetician.

Anyone so minded could object to the foregoing position on the grounds that the natural is not by any means always to be equated with the moral. The neohumanists habitually opposed the moral to the natural; they argued that only through the operation of the inner check could the natural be housebroken into conformity with acceptable social standards. Dozens of examples could be assembled to show how anti-social and either amoral or immoral the natural man can be when he really lets himself go.

If such objections were not merely captious, they would be simply irrelevant. The neohumanists, great though their gifts were, could most of them lay no just claim to an understanding of practical esthetics.[26] For the first requirement of esthetics, at least in the area where Hemingway works, is that it shall be based on a moral view of the world. With Anton Chekhov's moral statement that "the aim of fiction is absolute and honest truth," he would agree entirely. He would also agree with Marcus Aurelius that the natural is comely and beautiful, though Hemingway offers evidence throughout his work that the natural must be defined within certain normative and essentially moral limits. Working with the concepts of truth and beauty, it thus becomes possible to see "the way it was" as an idea of empirical truth, taking due account of ugliness and deformity, but warmed and illuminated from within by the strong love of natural beauty.

V. THE SABIDURÍAN

To complete the portrait of Hemingway as esthetician, it is necessary to look at what may be called the underside of the painting. The upper side is of course that whole face of his effort as artist which has as its purpose the seeing and saying of truth and "natural" beauty. Truth-telling (whether the "objective" portrayal of things and events in the phenomenal world, or the "subjective" representation of mental-emotional responses to these things and events) is one great criterion by which the worth of writing may be judged. For the upper side of Hemingway's esthetic there is perhaps no better general statement than that of Conrad in his celebrated preface to *The Nigger of the Narcissus*.

"The artist ... like the thinker or the scientist, seeks the truth.... And art itself may be defined as a single-minded attempt to render the highest kind of justice to the visible universe.... It is an attempt to find in its forms, in its colours, in its light, in its shadows, in the aspects of matter and in the facts of life what of each is fundamental, what is enduring and essential...."

Although Hemingway's admiration for Conrad later became less intense than formerly, his evident agreement with such statements as the one just quoted gave him, in the years 1923–1924, good reason to defend Conrad against his fashionable detractors, and to refuse to share in the disparagement which was at its height about the time of Conrad's death. When Ford issued the Conrad memorial supplement in the *transatlantic* for September, 1924, Hemingway made his own position clear.[27]

"The second book of Conrad's that I read was *Lord Jim* [said Hemingway]. I was unable to finish it. It is therefore all I have left of him. For I cannot reread them. That may be what my friends mean by saying he is a bad writer. But from nothing else that I have ever read have I gotten what every book of Conrad has given me."

Knowing that he could not reread them, he had saved up four of the novels to be used as a combination anodyne and stimulant whenever his disgust "with writing, writers, and everything written of and to write would be too much." In Toronto the preceding autumn he had used up three, one after the other, borrowing them from a friend who owned a uniform set. When his newspaper sent him to cover the attempt to locate anthracite coal in the Sudbury Basin mining district north of Georgian Bay in Ontario, he bought three back numbers of the *Pictorial Review* and read *The Rover*, "sitting up in bed in the Nickle Range Hotel."

"When morning came [he continued] I had used up all my Conrad like a drunkard. I had hoped it would last me the trip, and felt like a young man who has blown his patrimony. But, I thought, he will write more stories. He has lots of time."

The later reviews had all superciliously agreed that *The Rover* was a bad book. But now Conrad was dead, and "I wish to God," said Hemingway, "they would have taken some great acknowledged technician of a literary figure and left [Conrad] to write his bad stories."

The fashionable derogation of Conrad was often accompanied by the praise of T.S. Eliot as a "good writer." As for Hemingway:

"If I knew that by grinding Mr. Eliot into a fine dry powder and sprinkling that powder over Mr. Conrad's grave, Mr. Conrad would shortly reappear, looking very annoyed at the forced return, and commence writing, I would leave for London early tomorrow morning with a sausage-grinder."

Hemingway neither ground in London nor sprinkled in Canterbury. Had he done so, the topic of conversation between exhumed and exhumer might well have been Conrad's preface. In that very eloquent defence of fiction, Conrad makes three other memorable points besides insisting that the artist must seek truth.

The first is on the language of prose. The phrases "like pebbles fresh from a brook" which Ford Madox Ford admired in the early work of Hemingway were not achieved without the most careful attention to the act of verbal selection. Hemingway told Samuel Putnam in 1926 that "easy writing makes hard reading," and that he wished, if he could, to "strip language clean, to lay it bare down to the bone."[28] In practice this meant the studied deletion of all words and phrases which were in any way false. One of the difficulties with language, as many good writers have felt and as Hemingway said, is that "all our words from loose using have lost their edge."[29] Recognizing this fact, Hemingway always wrote slowly and revised carefully, cutting, eliding, substituting, experimenting with syntax to see what a sentence could most economically carry, and then throwing out all words that could be spared.

Such an artist would be obliged to agree with Conrad: "It is only through an unremitting never-discouraged care for the shape and ring of sentences ... that the light of magic suggestiveness may be brought to play for an evanescent instant over the commonplace surface of words: of the old, old words, worn thin, defaced by ages of careless usage." Magic suggestiveness is a phrase not to be found anywhere in the published writings of Hemingway; yet everywhere in his language the magic of suggestion is at work among the old, old words. If their surfaces are commonplace, their interiors bear the imaginative supercharging which only the true artist can bring to them. And this positive charge, which on being released plays not over but beneath the verbal surfaces, is one phase of the underside of Hemingway's distinguished achievement in prose.

The second phase is what Conrad calls "communication through temperament." The Spanish word *sabiduría* comes very close to the context of this idea. It may be defined as a kind of natural knowledge, nothing like the "wisdom" of professional philosophers, but a knowledge available under the surface of their lives to all responsive human beings. According to Conrad, "the artist appeals to that part of our being which is not dependent on wisdom: to that in us which is a gift and not an acquisition—and therefore more permanently enduring.... Fiction, if it at all aspires to be art, appeals to temperament. And in truth it must be ... the appeal of one temperament to all the other innumerable temperaments whose subtle and resistless power endows passing events with their true meaning, and creates the moral, the emotional atmosphere of the place and time." One may remark in passing that the closing phrase, "the emotional atmosphere of the place and time," is a very concise description for a part of what Hemingway means by "the way it was." Conrad goes on to say that the artist's appeal must be realized through the senses—provided of course that it is the artist's high desire to reach the secret spring of responsive emotions.

This is also the theory and practice of Hemingway. As one watches the establishment and development of the sabidurian images in his novels or the more ambitious short stories, one comes to see, as Mr. Theodore Bardacke has recently noticed, "this underlying use of associations and emotional suggestion," visible and even audible through the "objectively reported details." It is precisely this power which enabled Mr. Malcolm Cowley to say that "Hemingway's prose at its best gives a sense of depth and of moving forward on different levels that is lacking in even the best of his imitators." Hemingway's own term for it is "the kind of writing that can be done ... if anyone is serious enough and has luck. There is a fourth and fifth dimension that can be gotten."[30]

In a number of his works, seriously charging and recharging the old, old words and the natural, non-literary temperamental images, Hemingway the sabidurían precisely did such a job. We respond to it as naturally as savages to thunder, or as Dr. Jung's patients to the recurrent opposed symbols of the "Wise Old Man" and "the Shadow." Whether we accept Jung's hypothesis of inherited patterns in the cells of the brain, or try to explain our responses by modern versions of Bentham's psychological hedonism, need not concern us here. However we explain the fact, it operates all through Hemingway's prose.

The total entity we respond to in a work of art is what Conrad's preface calls "the presented vision." It may be a vision of "regret or pity, of terror or mirth." The point is that in its presence no reasonably sensitive human being is an island; he is a part of the mainland. For the presented vision arouses "in the hearts of the beholders that feeling of unavoidable solidarity; of the solidarity in mysterious origin, in toil, in joy, in hope, in uncertain fate, which binds men to each other and all mankind to the visible world."

Hemingway is very clear on this matter of the presented vision. "All good books," he wrote in 1933, "are alike in that they are truer than if they had really happened and after you are finished reading one you will feel that all that happened to you and afterwards it all belongs to you; the good and the bad, the ecstasy, the remorse and sorrow, the people and the places and how the weather was. If you can get so that you can give that to people, then you are a writer."

No two individualist authors will perfectly agree in generals or in particulars. In every author, esthetically and culturally speaking, one finds a muted echo of Blake's "I must create my own system or be enslaved by another man's." Hemingway would never write the matter of Conrad's preface in the manner of Conrad. Yet he would wholly agree with Conrad in saying to all who demand other things of the artist: "My task which I am trying to achieve is, by the power of the written word to make you hear, to make you feel—it is, before all, to make you *see*. That—and no more, and it is everything." It is everything because it encompasses both the upper- and the underside of all we know as human beings. If the artist achieves his task, it will mean that by all the means at his disposal he has transferred to his reader the true essence of "the way it was."

NOTES

1. Ezra Pound, quoted in Samuel Putnam, *Paris Was Our Mistress*, New York, 1947, p. 154

2. *Men at War*, New York, 1942, introduction, p. xv.

3. George Antheil, *Bad Boy of Music*, p. 278.

4. *SAR*, pp. 165–166.

5. *AR*, p. 120.

6. S*AR*, pp. 79–80.

7. *SAR*, p. 175.

8. *DIA*, p. 226.

9. Samuel Putnam, *op.cit.*, pp. 128–129.

10. *DIA*, p. 2.

11. T.S. Eliot, *The Sacred Wood*, London, 1920, pp. 92–93.

12. Introd. to Elio Vittorini's novel, *In Sicily*, New York, 1949.

13. John Ruskin, *Modern Painters*, New York, 1865, Vol. 3, pp. 156–172.

14. *DIA*, p. 53.

15. *First 49*, p. 262.

16. *Men Without Art*, London, 1934, p. 19.

17. *Works*, New York edition, vol. 13, preface, p. v.

18. *DIA*, p. 2.

19. *Men at War*, introd., p. xv.

20. *Table Talk* in *Works*, ed. Shedd, New York, 1853, Vol. 6, pp. 345–346.

21. EH to FSF, from Madrid, 9/4/29.

22. Quoted by Kenneth Rexroth in review of Read's *Collected Poems*, *New York Times Book Review*, June 17, 1951, p. 5.

23. *Meditations*, Book III, section ii.

24. *GHOA*, pp. 79 and 231.

25. *DIA*, p. 27.

26. For Hemingway's humorous comment on this group, see *DIA*, p. 139.

27. *transatlantic review* 2 (October 1924), pp. 341–342. Information in part from W.L. McGeary.

28. Samuel Putnam, *op.cit.*, p. 128.

29. *DIA*, p. 71.

30. "Theodore Bardacke, "Hemingway's Women," in J.K.M. McCaffery, ed., *Ernest Hemingway: The Man and His Work*, New York, 1950, p. 341; see also Malcolm Cowley, *The Portable Hemingway*, introd., p. xviii. Cf. Hemingway, *GHOA*, pp. 26–27.

JOHN HOLLANDER

Hemingway's Extraordinary Actuality

Of all the Hemingway material to be posthumously unveiled, short stories dating from before World War II would surely be the most welcome. This awkward volume *The Fifth Column and the First Forty-Nine Stories* brings together four previously uncollected stories mostly set in Madrid during the siege, with *The Fifth Column*, Hemingway's play set in the same scene. This last is already familiar to us through inclusion in the canonical old Modern Library Giant edition of forty-nine short stories (until Scribner's removed it, for undisclosed reasons when they took over the collected stories reprint again in the Fifties). These four stories are all a bit long-winded: they are not of the genre of the World War I sketches. They propound a world of desperation, military blunders, a senseless slaying of a civilian in a café, the necessary dirtiness of turning in a spy, and the crippling aspect of the International presence on the Loyalist side. Within that world, familiar Hemingwayan acts of grace occur, in a kind of lowkeyed way, and the genuine people are mostly being hurt. The Spaniards all speak the patented Hemingway dialect, no contractions and *muy formal*. But the stories are authentic enough, and are quite better than the worst of those in the collected volume. It only seems a pity that these were not included in it, instead of appearing in this somewhat artificial format: "The Denunciation," "The Butterfly and the Tank," "Night Before Battle," and "Under the Ridge"

From *Ernest Hemingway* (Modern Critical Views), edited by Harold Bloom. © 1985 by John Hollander.

together take up 62 pages. In any event, once the publishers were committed to such a presentation, they might at least have included a note on the publishing history of its contents. But such a selection does cause us to reflect on the nature of his best stories. They belong to what may turn out to have been, save for *The Sun Also Rises*, his major genre. Hemingway's marvelous delicacy, his wielding of the powerful right cross, as it were, of nuance after so many jabs of apparent bald presentation of fact, his deployment of the resonances of a conversational phrase that remains unmatched—except in Joyce's *Dubliners*—by all of his followers, including the frequently formidable John O'Hara, are all more clearly manifest in his sketches than in his *grandes machines*. His best stories reveal a narrator who is a much greater figure and more clearly touched by a bit of nobility than any of his fictional heroes, whether earlier anti-heroes or later naively sentimental ones to whom we cannot help but condescend. It is not only the celebrated tone of voice of the narration (troped, as always, by a palpable style—but what else is new?) enabling it to personify itself so well, which accounts for these stories' peculiarly lyrical power. (And even Nick Adams is characterized by the sensibility which is internal monologue in, say, the "Big Two-Hearted River" stories, and so which he shares with the putatively more distanced narration). It is the very fabric of what some Frenchified critics would call the narratology, the very telling of the tale of telling, which itself pitches these accounts of episodes and moments at, and not above, the tension of the lyre.

Wallace Stevens wrote of Hemingway in 1942 as a poet; "the most significant of living poets, so far as the subject of extraordinary actuality is concerned." In one of his *Adagia* Stevens observed that "In the poem of extraordinary actuality, consciousness takes the place of imagination," and he might as well have been characterizing not only the stories themselves, but the pregnant parataxis which forever refuses to allow of trivial connections, and which marks several levels of Hemingway's writing. The cursive sentence structure manifests a refusal to subordinate clauses, not out of fake naïveté, nor out of a weak misconstruction of Gertrude Stein, but rather, in a language supremely conscious of persons in places, in order to avoid the reductiveness that exposition and description, in their zeal to account for the way things seem to be, often effect. A certain kind of trivial literary history would link Hemingway's manner to another sort of reduction, the stripping of the rhetorical varnish demanded by the aesthetic programs of Continental modernism. But any serious reader knows such rhetoric to be of the nature of the wood itself, and that varnish, stain, paint, raw creosoted surfaces, or whatever, merely represent differing rhetorical projections.

Yet beyond the styling of the prose, Hemingway's parataxis stands between larger elements, full of possibility and silence like the white spaces between printed stanzas of verse. The impossibility of allegorizing the italicized interchapters (those beautifully crafted lyrical vignettes—or are they more like dramatic monologues?) placed between the reminiscent stories in *In Our Time* in order to make them fit the stories they precede or follow, marks the effect of another level of poetical parataxis. Insofar as they act like macaronic refrains in some other language, placed between stanzas of a ballad, they seem to connect in one way while (or, perhaps, *by*) palpably disconnecting even further. Insofar as they present an unmeditative present in narrowed vignette, and a more fully realized past, they mediate between the opening of Wordsworth's "Tintern Abbey," say, and the standard vulgar cinematic dissolve into flashback.

Nowhere is Hemingway's poetry of "extraordinary actuality" more fully realized, perhaps, than in a story which he once declared to be a favorite, the one from *Men Without Women* called "Hills Like White Elephants." In this sketch, which Dorothy Parker rightly perceived as "delicate and tragic," an American couple waiting for a train at a small station in Spain are overheard, in about six pages of dialogue, while a bout of what must be a continuing disagreement about an abortion (the young man keeps maintaining that "It's perfectly simple;" the young woman knows that it, and much else, is not) gradually decays. The dialogue is framed by bits of description—rather like stage directions in their length and frequency of occurrence, but also unlike them, for the most part, in that they keep cutting away from the dialogue to describe a passage of scenery, or to recall such a passage previously invoked. The story opens with an observation of a bit of the landscape: "The hills across the Ebro were long and white," and the ellipsis of the more epistemologically plausible example—"Seen from the small railroad station in Castile on a hot afternoon, the extensive ridge of hills across the valley of the Ebro looked white"—moves the sentence from the rhetoric of novelistic point of view into that of lyrical trope. After some preliminary dialogue about ordering drinks, the narration observes that the girl "was looking off at the line of hills. They were white in the sun and the country was brown and dry."

> "They look like white elephants," she said.
> "I've never seen one," the man drank his beer.
> "No, you wouldn't have."

Even were it not for the synecdochal title, the apparent-white-elephantness of the hills has become a counter in their conversation, and leads to the first indication of the trouble between them, the passage from disillusion to dissolution which the vignette of talk and scene embraces:

> "Well, let's try and have a fine time."
>
> "All right. I was trying. I said the mountains looked like white elephants. Wasn't that bright?"
>
> "That was bright."
>
> "I wanted to try this new drink. That's all we do, isn't it—look at things and try new drinks?"
>
> "I guess so."
>
> The girl looked across at the hills.
>
> "They're lovely hills," she said. "They don't really look like white elephants. I just meant the coloring of their skin through the trees."

The girl's *looking* at the hills describes a totally different act from the disaffected sightseeing of the "look at things and try new drinks," of course, and the hills have been privileged by the narration to begin with. Even when she retracts her formulation about the white elephants, in the interests of maintaining the surface of the "fine time," she cannot abandon her observation entirely. What for the reader of novels constitutes her slip about the "skin" of the hills, operates in the poem of the sketch to reaffirm the truth and rightness and brightness of the original and originating trope: The ridge of hills, low peaked and undulant, lined up in circus fashion, trunk to tail, parade across the middle-high horizon, calm, beneficent, reaffirming the health of distant vision. The narration, and the girl, both know this. But this image of possibility and delight is tragically and inevitably linked, by the ways of the world, to a darker, narrower emblem, and as soon as the conversation moves to the matter of the abortion, the girl's pregnancy itself becomes part of the matter. Proverbially, the "white elephant" of unwanted possession, the objectified burden (which comes, as *Brewer's Dictionary of Phrase and Fable* elegantly puts it, from the story of a Siamese king who "used to make a present of a white elephant to courtiers he wished to ruin"), the ugly and useless bric-a-brac, gets allusively stuck to that pregnancy, even as the girl's momentarily repressed sense of her body (what will she look like to herself in her ninth month?) may perhaps be reflected as well.

And it is this touch of a more narrowed emblem which darkens the long, white *symbole* of the hills. After a later turn of unsatisfactory false resolution (she agrees to the operation, he returns with "I don't want you to do it if you feel that way") the narration again cuts away (and again, one can hardly avoid the cinematic verb) to what is there:

> The girl stood up and walked to the end of the station. Across, on the other side, were fields of grain and trees along the banks of the Ebro. Far away, beyond the river, were mountains. The shadow of a cloud moved across the field of grain and she saw the river through the trees.
>
> "And we could have all this," she said. "And we could have everything and every day we make it more impossible."

This is a more pictorial landscape now, and less of a visionary one. And yet, its mode of accessibility to the reading eye, the nearby growth of grain and tree, the promise of plenitude and the promise of continuity in the glimpse of the river—all of these lost before to the beyondness of the elephantine hills—now comprise a full figure of what the girl calls "all this." The parataxis of what should in more expository narrative be the adduced moral, and which is here replaced by the girl's statement, seems far more delicate than another famous moment of cutting from dialogue to glimpse of scene in American literature. The cloud about to pass in front of the moon in Robert Frost's "The Death of the Hired Man" fills in a few minutes of the wife's waiting for her husband to report on the condition of the old man who, it will turn out, has died. The wife says:

> "I'll sit and see if that small sailing cloud
> Will hit or miss the moon."
> It hit the moon.
> Then there were three there, making a dim row,
> The moon, the little silver cloud, and she.

The *ad hoc omen* ("It hit the moon") decays into a schematic trope in the last line, explicitly connecting the phenomenon and the interpeting observer. But Hemingway's glimpse is more elusively parabolic than this, and certainly more Wordsworthian in one mode even as it is less so in another.

In general, the riddling power of a figure like that of the hills lies in the way Hemingway's narrative controls the mode of figuration. The hills are, at the outset, simply *there*, as given as given can be; then they are grasped by the girl, become more and more rhetorically problematic as the brief dialogue unrolls, and finally vanish behind a later, sadder kind of landscape. And yet their beauty is nobler than their narrowed emblematic meaning, and that beauty calls up a wider and stronger evocation (like that of, say, the shadow of the distant poplar tree falling across the face of Tennyson's sleeping Mariana). I have twice used the term "cut" to describe the movement away from dialogue to glimpse of scene in this story. I should not have thought that early readers of it would have felt anything cinematic about it—indeed, what became momentarily celebrated about the story was the girl's string of seven *pleases* in her request, at the end of all their discourse, that the young man stop talking. (Virginia Woolf, in a singularly obtuse review of *Men Without Women* in 1927, expresses nothing but impatience with the dialogue, and sneers; "At last we are inclined to cry out with the little girl 'Would you please ...'" How she can call the quite grown-up young woman, fully equipped with a dose of *Weltschmerz*, a "little girl" is most curious and suggests that she thinks the operation in question to be a tonsillectomy.) It would not be until the days of 1960's Italian cinema that the amazing resemblance of this story to an Antonioni shooting script—in the relation of dialogue and shots of landscape cut away to as a move in the dialogue itself, rather than as mere punctuation, and ultimately in the way in which dialogue and uninterpreted glimpse of scene interpret each other—would become apparent. But the poetics of that kind of film, and the poetics of extraordinary actuality in Hemingway, are connected by more than analogy, for the literary-historical line from Hemingway to the novels of Pavese and on to the films of Antonioni is quite clear.

In stories like this one, like "God Rest You Merry, Gentlemen," like "The Light of the World" and, inevitably, like "A Clean, Well-Lighted Place," the unfolding of the central tropes has the kind of power of lyrical movement and tells a tale of the genesis of complex meaning which the more familiar chronicling of the longer stories may not be able to achieve. They may make even the Kilimanjaro and Macomber stories seem, some day, like anecdotes.

EARL ROVIT AND GERRY BRENNER

Of Tyros and Tutors

Hemingway's vision, based on his need to relate his isolate self to all that was not-self, was, as we have seen, an intensely lyrical vision; yet he is not a poet but a writer of fiction.[1] When he says in *Green Hills of Africa* that he is striving to create a prose "much more difficult than poetry," he is not indulging in casual hyperbole. He is actually stating quite accurately the dilemma that his aesthetic demands and his storytelling talents forced upon him. Given his insatiable drive to make his identity metaphysically secure through attaching it to the things of the universe by, as it were, emotional adhesion, we might have expected him to write a prose equivalent to "Song of Myself" or *The Waste Land*. In these poems—as in the last chapter of *Death in the Afternoon*, in Harry's remembrances of things past in "The Snows of Kilimanjaro," or in the preface to Vittorini's *In Sicily*—the principles of aesthetic and metaphysical structure fuse in the device of the evocative catalog. The metaphysical selves of the artists (their identities, in the full sense) are created and realized in their recollected moments of sincere emotional response; these, in turn, are re-created artistically as the fragments they have shored against their ruins.[2]

But Hemingway differed from both Whitman and Eliot in very significant ways. Unlike Whitman, he prized the adamant separateness of his isolate self, as we can see in his choice to be an administrator of death rather

---

From *Ernest Hemingway*. ©1986 by G.K. Hall & Co.

than a wooer of it. He fiercely resisted any potential loss of self, even a loss that might have given him the incalculable gain of transcendent mergence. There is in Hemingway a curious deficiency in the capacity to love which becomes manifest when we compare him to Whitman; the latter could write love poems to "sweet soothing death" and become whole in the spirit of total communion; Hemingway's book on bullfighting is a kind of love song to killing that insures him the role of eternal opposition. "The kelson of the creation is love," sang Whitman. But for Hemingway the kelson had cracked right down the middle, and the creation had become a form of combat in which "the conditions are that the winner shall take nothing."

And, unlike Eliot—whose revulsion at the world was matched by his revulsion at his own sensory responses—Hemingway could not deny the fundamental joie de vivre of experiencing physical action, of delighting in the increased awareness of life and self that the operation of his five senses so abundantly offered him. Eliot could try to enter the realms of all-acceptant love by a firm denial of the self that he found so distasteful; once there, his "vision of the street" could become softened into a prayerful meditation where "the fire and the rose are one." But Hemingway's deficiencies in his powers to love are matched by his incapacity to really hate. He can be contemptuous; he can be shocked and outraged; he can be arrogantly superior. But lacking a sense of real security in the universe, he lacked also the necessary bases of self-righteousness and self-unity, the sources of hatred. And thus again, for precisely the reverse reasons as with Whitman, Hemingway was forced into the role of eternal opposition in total conflict with everything that was Other.

This introductory discussion is pertinent if it helps us to realize why Hemingway had no choice except to dramatize his lyric vision. The uncompromising split that he felt between himself and the universe could be made to yield an objective correlative of his emotions only through the tensions of the dialectic form. Action and reaction, force and shock, challenge and response these are the relentless antagonists that will engage in dubious battle throughout Hemingway's fiction; the battlefield, the locus of contact and the point of arrest, is the willed awareness of the human spirit, Hemingway's spirit, recording with precision the attacks and counterattacks, the retreats, the acts of bravery and cowardice, the casualties and the irreparable damages. To examine the dramatic tension that provides the action of his fictions, we will have to examine in some detail the famous Hemingway "Hero" and Hemingway's "Code" within the general frame of reference that we have been developing.[3]

There are, as criticism has come slowly to recognize, not one but two Hemingway heroes; or, to use Philip Young's designations, the "Nick-Adams-hero" and the "code-hero." The generic Nick Adams character, who lives through the course of Hemingway's fiction, appears first as the shocked invisible "voice" of the miniatures of *in our time;* he grows up through Hemingway's three volumes of short stories and at least four of his novels, sometimes changing his name to Jake Barnes, Frederic Henry, Mr. Frazer, Macomber, Harry, Robert Jordan, Richard Cantwell; and he makes his final appearances (appropriately unnamed as when he first entered the fictional stage) in Hemingway's last two published stories in 1957. The code-hero also figures in Hemingway's earliest fiction. He dies of a *cogida* as Maera in *in our time,* and he is resurrected in a considerable variety of shapes, forms, and accents (usually non-American) through the bulk of Hemingway's creative output. His manifestations would include Belmonte in *The Sun Also Rises;* Manuel in "The Undefeated"; the Major in "In Another Country"; Harry Morgan; Wilson in "The Short Happy Life of Francis Macomber"; Cayetano Ruiz in "The Gambler, the Nun, and the Radio"; El Sordo; and Santiago.

For convenience sake we will refer to the Nick Adams hero as the tyro and to the "code-hero" as the tutor; for it is basically an educational relationship, albeit one-sided, that binds them together. The tyro, faced with the overwhelming confusion and hurt (*nada*) inherent in an attempt to live an active sensual life, admires the deliberate self-containment of the tutor (a much "simpler man") who is seemingly not beset with inner uncertainties. Accordingly, the tyro tries to model his behavior on the pattern he discerns. However, the tyro is not a simple man; being in fact a near projection of Hemingway himself, he never attains the state of serene unself-consciousness—what James once called nastily "the deep intellectual repose"—that seems to come naturally to the tutor. What he can learn, however, is the appearance of that self-containment. He can laboriously train himself in the conventions of the appearance of "the code"; and he can so severely practice those external restraints as to be provided with a pragmatic defense against the horrors that never cease to assault him.

It may be salutary to digress slightly to what we can call "The Education of Nick Adams" because there is some inevitable confusion surrounding it. In one sense the education is thoroughly abortive; Nick at the end of his multicheckered career is as terrified and lost as he was, for example, in his encounter with the stark, machined horror of the Chicago gangsters in "The Killers." In the following quotation is the tyro, aged somewhere in his mid-fifties, trying to cope with the loss of his eyesight

("Get a Seeing-Eyed Dog"): "Because I am not doing too well at this. That I can promise you. But what else can you do? Nothing, he thought. There's nothing you can do. But maybe, as you go along, you will get good at it." The tyro, with his unfair inheritance from Hemingway of a particularly fecund and hyperactive imagination of disaster, has lost nothing of his capacities to be afraid—in spite of his long indoctrination in the craft of courage. In fact, he has rather increased his capacities, for his accumulated experience of horror has taught him many more things of which to be afraid. Measured pragmatically, however—and the defense never pretends to be more than a pragmatic one—Nick does survive for an astonishingly long time. He does, as Hemingway puts it, get pretty good at it as he goes along.

If we sketch briefly Nick's biography, we will be able to judge somewhat better the values of his education and to note also the varying ways that Hemingway employed him as shock absorber and seismographer of emotional stress. Nick is born, roughly at the turn of the twentieth century, somewhere in the Midwest. His father, a physician, is fond of hunting and shooting, and is concerned to teach Nick the proper ways of handling a rod and a gun. Dr. Adams has incredibly sharp eyesight and is a better wing-shot than Nick will ever be. He is also intimidated by his wife—a suspiciously indistinct character who is a blur of polite nagging and vague religious sentiments—and, on one occasion, Nick is shocked to see his father back down from a fight. The pattern of cowardice and intimidation, never actually explained, comes to a disgusting (to Nick) finale when his father commits suicide in the 1920s with Nick's grandfather's gun. The grandfather becomes elected as Nick's spiritual father—a tutorial hero because of his reputed bravery during the Civil War.

As a boy, Nick's adventures distill the excitements, perplexities, and terrors that are classically supposed to accompany adolescence. He witnesses a lynching in Ohio, a Caesarean delivery by jack-knife, and a razor suicide in an Indian camp; he has a very satisfactory initiation into sex with an Ojibway Indian girl whom he later discovers to be promiscuous. He also undergoes a puppy-love affair with a "nice" girl, which he is tremulously strong enough to break off. Unexplainedly "on the road," he comes into contact with sentimental whores, sinister homosexuals, and a vaudeville team of professional assassins. His characteristic response to these situations is open-eyed shock; he registers the events as though he were a slowmotion camera, but rarely if ever does he actively participate in them. He never gets into a fight; he does not argue; he does not retreat to protect his sensibilities. Like the camera, he has a curious masochistic quality of total acceptance and receptivity. At about this point we begin to suspect that the adventures of

Nick Adams are approximately as realistic as "The Adventures of Tom Swift," although any individual episode in the serial is gratifyingly convincing. We begin to suspect that Hemingway's tyro figure is a projection into the nightmare possibilities of confusion, pain, and immolation; that his adventures are mythic fantasies, guided by the rhythms of intense fear and alienation. That, in short, Nick Adams is a sacrificial victim, bound time and time again to the slaughtering-table to be almost slaughtered in order that his creator and readers may be free of fear.

The pattern continues and proliferates when Nick joins the Italian Army fighting the Austrians in northeastern Italy. He is blown up at Fossalta di Piave, where he feels his soul go out of his body, go off, and then return. For a long time after this he has to leave the light burning at night to keep his soul in place. His convalescence at the hospital in Milan is aided and abetted by a love affair with a British nurse, but he is finally returned to the Austrian front as a morale advertisement—in spite of the fact that he is in a severe state of combat trauma. He returns briefly to the United States to go fishing, and then reembarks for Europe where he remains except for sporadic visits to hunt in Wyoming and to recuperate from an accident in a Montana hospital. Somewhere along the line he has become by profession a writer—more often a newspaperman—and he has also married. There is surprisingly little information about his domestic life, other than that he is afraid his approaching fatherhood will restrain his athletic diversions. Much later we discover that he has been married and divorced three times; but, in general, the nightmare terrors of banal marital existence are avoided in the episodes of his adventures.

We catch glimpses of his life in the 1920s—skiing in Switzerland, riding his bicycle through Paris streets, developing an air of expertise on the running of the bulls in Spain and the empty carousing of the American bohemians throughout Europe. Details of isolated horror in World War I crop up in his memories from time to time, and the action of the Greeks in breaking the legs of their baggage animals and dumping them in the harbor at Smyrna (Izmir) becomes a kind of climactic leitmotiv in the aria of his remembered terrors. But meanwhile there has been a gradual hardening of his powers to resist the shocks that he seems desperately impelled to pursue. He slowly edges away from the margins of nervous collapse as a war convalescent who has seen too many helmets full of brains. Painfully during the 1920s, he masters his physical responses and rather proudly subjects himself to situations of violence and disgust as though (like the red-headed veteran in *To Have and Have Not*) these occasions give him an opportunity to prove that he can not only absorb punishment but also take a perverted pleasure in it.

The 1930s extend his experience to the fishing waters between Cuba and Key West, safaris to Africa, and the Loyalist front in the Spanish War. Nick, who has become increasingly resistant to shock, reacts now more as a clinical observer than as an outraged participant. In fact, there is evidence that he even manipulates events consciously to increase a stress situation, as when—through "the always dirty desire to see how people act under an emotional conflict, that makes writers such attractive friends"[4]—he triggers off a rather unpleasant series of consequences that leads to the execution of one man and the guilty shame of another. His exposures to the cynicism of political chicanery in the command levels of the Spanish War are followed by disgust with the military stupidities and vanities of the higher echelons that control the operations of World War II. The threat of old age and physical debility appears in his collection of terrors in the late 1930s, becomes a more dense specter in the 1940s, and assumes haunting proportions in the 1950s in his recurrent fear of blindness. The question of suicide, introduced in the early 1930s, remains a foreboding undercurrent in his ethical reflections through the 1940s and 1950s; and it is probably significant that his first aggressive denunciation of the act becomes reluctantly mollified. And, finally, a marginal interest in Catholic attitudes toward life and death, which appears in the 1920s, maintains its steady flow throughout his career, without seeming to engage his deeper levels of concern.

Such is Nick Adams, surely not, as one critic explains, a man whose life's story "differs in no essential way from that of almost any middleclass American male who started life at the beginning of the present century or even with the generation of 1920."[5] There is little that is realistically representative in the career of Nicholas Adams, nor is there meant to be. In a sense—which his name suggests—he is a released devil of our innocence, an enfleshment of our conscious and unconscious fears dispatched to do battle with the frightening possibilities that an always uncertain future holds over our heads. He is the whipping-boy of our fearful awareness, the pragmatic probability extrapolated into a possible tomorrow to serve as a propitiary buffer against the evils that tomorrow may or may not bring. He suffers our accidents and defeats before they happen to us. Like Tiresias, he is doomed to foresuffer them all—to witness the infidelities and deaths of our loved ones; to enact our cowardices and indecisions; to struggle against the internal and external diseases that inexorably pursue us; in short, to die the innumerable times we project our deaths in our imaginations. But for all this he is a far from impotent counter in the game in which the winner takes nothing. Hemingway plays him, the sacrificial card in his hand, to finesse the ruthless king; he is the defeated victim, but in experiencing his defeat,

Hemingway (and we) can ring ourselves in invisible armor so that we will be undefeated if and when the catastrophes of our imagination do actually occur. On this level, then, the Nick Adams projection is a vital defensive weapon in Hemingway's combat with the universe.

The tutor, on the other hand, is a much less complicated figure than the tyro; but he is certainly no more realistic. If the tyro is in general a projection of the possibilities of an inadequate response to "the terrible ambiguities of an immediate experience" (Jung's phrase), the tutor is the embodied wish-fulfillment of a successful response. He is "a tough boy," which Colonel Cantwell defines as "a man who will make his play and then back it up. Or just a man who backs his play" (*A*, 48–49). The seemingly innocuous amendment to the definition underlines one distinction between the tutor and the tyro. The fully developed tyro is "the man who will make his play and then back it up." The tutor is "just a man who backs his play." The difference, so deceptively small, encompasses the whole range of man's conscious awareness of himself while engaged in action; it includes his capacities not only to reflect and to imagine but also to be aware of reflecting and imagining. This human burden the tyro must always carry, but from it the tutor is free; this, indeed, is what makes the tutor "a simpler man." He is so simple, in fact, that he is closer to brute animality than to "humanness."[6] For example, we cite Manuel of "The Undefeated" as he is facing the bull that will not charge:

> He thought in bull-fight terms. Sometimes he had a thought and the particular piece of slang would not come into his mind and he could not realize the thought. His instincts and his knowledge worked automatically, and his brain worked slowly and in words. He knew all about bulls. He did not have to think about them. He just did the right thing. His eyes noted things and his body performed the necessary measures without thought. If he thought about it, he would be gone. (*SS*, 260)

Thought and action (or reaction) are simultaneous for Manuel; he is "just a man who backs his play," and hence his responses will be inevitably adequate to the challenge he is trained to accept. The tyro, as we see often in Hemingway's works, must try to stop himself from thinking. There is an inevitable hiatus between challenge and response, action and reaction; it is here, in Hemingway's diagnosis, that man's greatest danger takes place. The broken circuit, the incomplete synapse, the failure of the nerve: all these phrases designate that emotional paralysis, or shock, which Hemingway had every reason to fear, and which on a collective basis may very well be the major disease of twentieth-century man. Thus the trained tyro is "the man who will make his play and then back it up"; unable to become a fully responsive mechanism of instincts, he can try to condition himself to force the right responses under stress.

The tutor takes a surprisingly large variety of forms in Hemingway's fiction, but, in each of his manifestations, he is always "the professional." With two significant exceptions, his activities are confined to areas where he can perform within the predictabilities of his training—fighting bulls, bootlegging whiskey and Chinamen, facing lion charges, and landing large fish. The exceptional stories recount, in part, the adventures of tutors who encounter challenges beyond the jurisdiction of their professional preparations; these are in "Fifty Grand" and "In Another Country."

"Fifty Grand," one of Hemingway's most humorous stories, recalls Ring Lardner's "Champion" in tone and situation. The tutor is Jack Brennan— loutish, parsimonious, overaged welter-weight champion of the world. Believing honestly that he will lose his title to the challenger, Walcott, he bets fifty thousand dollars against himself. He does not know, however, that a gambling syndicate has arranged for Walcott to throw the fight. In the eleventh round, when it is obvious that Brennan (who has been making an honest fight thus far) will eventually lose on points, Walcott deliberately fouls him and seriously hurts him in the process. The situation is supremely comical: if Brennan abides by the rules of boxing, as well as by the imperatives of his creature instincts (he is in much pain) and his professional conditioning, he will retain his championship and lose fifty thousand dollars. Instead, he waves off the referee and brutally fouls Walcott twice, losing the fight on a foul and winning his bet. And he remarks toward the end of the story, "It's funny how fast you can think when it means that much money" (SS, 326).

One critic has dubbed this to be a story of the "honor-and-courage-among-thieves" variety, finding Brennan a satisfactory code hero in the peculiar milieu of his operations.[7] This interpretation, however, misses the humor and the point of the story. What we have is an exposure in veniality to the noncommitted first-person narrator (the tyro), and an indication that professionals (tutors) can be trusted only within their special areas of mastery. Brennan breaks the code in betting against himself, and when he is challenged by the foul, he is thrown like the rest of us into a decision-making problem where his training is useless. His exercise of "fast" thinking under stress transforms him from a fully responsive mechanism of instincts into an instinctive machine of avarice.

"In Another Country," surely one of Hemingway's masterpieces in the short story form, also takes a professional into a challenge situation for which he has not been prepared, but with very different results from the satiric "Fifty Grand." The Major of the story is Hemingway's most attractive tutor figure, and he is also the most intelligent and sensitive. A professional soldier, and before the war a champion fencer, he is undergoing mechanical therapy for a wound which has left his fencing hand shrunken to baby size. Disabling wounds and death are foreseeable eventualities for professional soldiers, and the Major accepts his lot with equanimity. Out of a sense of duty he reports to the hospital every afternoon to be treated by the therapeutic machines (designed to rehabilitate industrial accidents), even though he does not believe in their efficacy. When he engages the tyro (the first-person narrator) in conversation, he insists with characteristic professionalism that the boy speak Italian grammatically. As Hemingway presents him, the Major is a figure of considerable dignity and somewhat stuffy rectitude who "did not believe in bravery," presumably because, like Santiago, he chooses precision and exactness over the uncontrollable results of impulse action.

But one afternoon he comes to the hospital in an irritable mood and provokes the tyro into a rude argument over marriage, declaiming angrily that a man must not marry. "If he is to lose everything, he should not place himself in a position to lose that. He should not place himself in a position to lose. He should find things he cannot lose" (*SS*, 271). He makes a telephone call and returns to the room where the tyro is sitting.

> He was wearing his cape and had his cap on, and he came directly toward my machine and put his arm on my shoulder.
>
> "I am so sorry," he said, and patted me on the shoulder with his good hand. "I would not be rude. My wife has just died. You must forgive me."
>
> "Oh—" I said, feeling sick for him. "I am *so* sorry."
>
> He stood there biting his lower lip. "It is very difficult," he said. "I cannot resign myself."
>
> He looked straight past me and out through the window. Then he began to cry. "I am utterly unable to resign myself," he said and choked. And then crying, his head up looking at nothing, carrying himself straight and soldierly, with tears on both his cheeks and biting his lips, he walked past the machines and out the door. (*SS*, 272)

One final paragraph concludes the story, in which we are told that the Major returns for his regular treatments three days later with mourning crepe on his uniform sleeve. The doctors had placed photographs of wounds before and after treatment in front of his machine. "The photographs did not make much difference to the major because he only looked out of the window" (*SS*, 272).

This is the one certain case in Hemingway's work where the tutor rises far beyond the artificial boundaries that restrict his need to make decisions. As we have seen, the code of professionalism with its severe conditioning in special pragmatic skills and attitudes is designed to minimize the multiplicity of possibilities existing in any challenge situation. Or, to express it more simply, the professional attitude creates an arbitrary chart of the future—like a contour map of preselected terrain—in which only a few items are considered significant and the rest are ignored. The rationale for the adoption of such a code is suggested in the Major's passionate cry: "[Man] should not place himself in a position to lose. He should find things he cannot lose." He will eventually lose everything when he loses himself, but along the way he will be able to control his losses and also the sequence of "holding attacks" through which he wages his battles.

If such a life code were adhered to strictly, a man would have to be either "the dumb ox" (the "simpler man") of so much Hemingway criticism or an unbelievable monster of machined egotism living, as it were, in an almost impregnable pillbox with no exits or entrances. The Major of this story is neither; his adoption of a code of life does not preclude his exposure to the risks of the incalculable in spite of his angry cry of outrage. Because he is human, he has loved; and, to continue the military metaphor, he has wittingly exposed his flanks to undefendable attack. His commitment to love and his shock at his wife's death have placed him "in another country" than the one he has prepared to defend. That other country is nothing less than the human condition itself, for the human will is always vulnerable to ruthless destruction. And Hemingway's ultimate test of human performance is the degree of stripped courage and dignity that man can discover in himself in his moments of absolute despair. It would have been quite simple for the Major to have died well; his challenge is far greater than his own death (a challenge that Hemingway has typically considered a relatively easy one to face). The Major, in losing his wife, suffers a death of himself accompanied by the absurdity of his own continued life. It is meaninglessness—*nada*—that confronts the Major in full assault.

And like Jesus in "Today is Friday," the Major is "good in there." He is badly broken, but not destroyed. He refuses to resign himself to the chaos of unmeaning, but he refuses also to deny the actuality of his fearsome defeat. He holds tight to the superficial conventions of his training—the empty forms of innate courtesy and soldierly duty—and sits within them to begin the laborious process of making the broken places within himself strong again. His response can be characterized as neither acceptance nor denial; he is neither victim nor rebel. The least and the best that can be said of him is that he survives with dignity, and it is possible that he may be considered Hemingway's most eloquent portrait of ideal heroism—unquixotic, unathletic, profoundly humanistic.

The characteristic of dignity, so important to Hemingway as to have furnished him with one of the major themes in his fiction, is relevant to our discussion at this point. The peculiar problems of twentieth-century life have made the depictions of human dignity almost anomalous in modern literature. Our characteristic heroes have been antiheroes or nonheroes, aggressive doomed men in revolt or essentially pathetic dupes at the mercy of nonmalicious and implacable victimization. Dignity in either situation is difficult to ascribe to such heroes who tend by choice to divest themselves of the traditional values of rational intelligence and moral integrity on which dignity has always rested. The great majority of modern heroes in literature are purposely grotesque—picaresque saints, rebels, victims, and underground men of all shapes and colors. Their individual value as artistic achievements and embodiments of viable life attitudes is undeniable, but dignity is a quality largely beyond their grasp.[8] Hemingway's attempt to retain the ideal of dignity without falsifying the ignobility of the modern human condition (that impulse in his work that leads many commentators to associate his beliefs with those of classical Stoicism) is one of his signal triumphs as a modern writer. And it is generally through his characterizations of the tutor figure that this quality of dignity is manifested.

Besides the Major we can find dignity in Manuel ("The Undefeated"), in Anselmo of *For Whom the Bell Tolls*, in the old men of "A Clean Well-Lighted Place" and of "Old Man at the Bridge," and finally in Santiago. It is probably significant that all of these examples are older men. Dignity certainly does not come automatically with age in Hemingway's fiction, but it is usually denied to youth with its passions and penchant for illusions.[9] A minimal degree of native intelligence is a basic requirement: basic also are the qualities of real humility and self-abnegation. Thus characters like Harry Morgan, Cayetano Ruiz, Wilson, or El Sordo—all in some fashion tutor figures and models of a kind of excellence—are on the lower levels of Hemingway's portraits of heroism. This point should be remembered since too many evaluations of Hemingway's life code mistakenly assume that Hemingway's code heroes can be lumped togther in an indiscriminate stereotype of brute primitivism and animal virtues.

One other point should be made concerning the tutor figure. We have noted that the great majority of them are non-American (Spanish bullfighters, Mexican gamblers, British white hunters, etc.), and that the ones of greatest excellence, of dignity, are all non-Americans and men of mature or advanced age. We also noted earlier that Hemingway's nubile heroines are likewise non-Americans and that, if they do not grow progressively younger as Hemingway writes over a period of some thirty years, they do not noticeably age either. His heroines would seem to be so many variations on his archetype, the Ojibway Trudy. These two examples of repetitive characterization offer some evidence for legitimate speculation. Just as we have seen that the Nick Adams projection can be understood as a compulsive fantasy figure closely related to one aspect of Hemingway's self-image, so these two other consistent figurations are comparable fantasy projections. It takes no great Freudian sophistication to recognize in the tutor figure a father image. Purified of the weaknesses that shame Nick in his real hunting-and-fishing father, the substitute retains the capacity to "doctor" or heal by emulation. All the tutor fathers are childless (Harry Morgan has a brood of daughters); and, in suffering the sea change of denationalization and conversion to Catholicism, they are moved by Hemingway into another country where they can be loved and respected by their tyro sons without reservation. The heroines, similarly, seem purified mother figures; at once completely satisfying and undemanding, they are handy oceanic reservoirs of temporary regression and security. The incest motif that obtrudes from *Across the River and into the Trees* can thus be seen as a rather consistent modulation on the erotic concerns in Hemingway's fiction.

The relationship between Colonel Cantwell and Renata affords an opportunity of investigating the Hemingway heroines somewhat more closely.[10] Renata is "almost nineteen," the age at which Nick Adams and Cantwell suffered the great wound at Fossalta di Piave. Cantwell refers to Renata and to her symbolic portrait as "boy" and "daughter," suggesting that Hemingway is employing the device of "symbolic doubling" (Carlos Baker's term) to make Renata not only the mother image (the daughter inversion is a standard Freudian trick) of Cantwell, but also his alter ego or anima—that is, himself some thirty years earlier. The temporary gift of the two emeralds which Renata presents to Cantwell is clearly symbolic of Cantwell's youthful virility; and Renata's name ("the reborn") would seem to make this reading decisive.

Extending this interpretation to Hemingway's other typical heroines, Catherine Barkley and Maria, we find that the double function of each is likewise present but less obvious. Each becomes absolutely identified with her lover: "There isn't any me. I'm you." And in the physical act of union—symbolically appropriate in a womblike sleeping bag or under a blanket in a Venetian gondola—the tyro figure makes a complete regression to a prenatal state of oneness with himself and the mother. Finally we may note that in *The Old Man and the Sea*, Hemingway's last published major work, the impulse to regression is complete. The tyro has split into the young boy, Manolo, and the hero, Santiago, while the Hemingway heroine (the mother and anima) has assumed its primordial symbolic shape as *la mar*, the eternal, feminine sea.

We are neither interested nor qualified to conduct a fully developed psychoanalytic study of Hemingway's fiction, several of which have been attempted;[11] but an elementary analytic reading can illuminate some of the conditions of Hemingway's art. The point worth grasping here, as we have been insisting, is that Hemingway's aesthetic concerns are not with the depiction of objective reality, but with the fantasy projections of his inner consciousness. The mirror of his art is held up to his own nature, not Nature; and, if he succeeded in casting a definition of the human condition that has been useful to twentieth-century readers, it is because his own human condition, painfully and honestly transmuted into evocative prose in a lifetime of disciplined writing, was in some way deeply representative of the condition of humanity. We can never know how aware he was of the direction his art took. We do know it was compulsively intent on recording those emotional shocks that gave him a feeling of immortality. We know also that he wrote in order that he could live, and when he could no longer "get rid of it" (the disintegrating shocks) through writing them out, he ceased to live. The pattern of his work is consistently rooted in a dramatization of the traumatic births of his tortured psyche, relentlessly struggling to rid itself of its horrors. An examination of one of the problems recurrent in Hemingway criticism may be persuasive in showing that the real pain in Hemingway's fiction is residual in his personality, and that he may very well be talking about his own theory of writing when he asks through Professor MacWalsey in *To Have and Have Not*, "why must all the operations in life be performed without an anaesthetic?"[12]

The inconsistency of Hemingway's sociopolitical beliefs has been, since the middle 1930s, a stumbling block or source of embarrassment to Hemingway's critics, both the friendly and the hostile. A writer, like everyone else, has every right to change his mind on cardinal principles of belief; but a writer, especially a great writer, is under obligation to leave a trail of evidence behind him in his shifts of opinion, so that his devious course can be followed. In the miniatures of *in our time* (1924), Hemingway proclaimed the "separate peace"; and he officially ratified it in the famous baptismal plunge into the Tagliamento River in *A Farewell to Arms* (1929):

> You had lost your cars and your men as a floorwalker loses the stock of his department in a fire. There was, however, no insurance. You were out of it now. You had no more obligation....
>
> Anger was washed away in the river along with any obligation.
> ... I had taken off the stars, but that was for convenience. It was no point of honor. I was not against them. I was through. I wished them all the luck.... But it was not my show anymore. (232)

Frederic Henry's political "lone-wolfism" and his disseverance from any body of authority is strictly held to through *Death in the Afternoon* (1932) and *Green Hills of Africa* (1935); if anything, his determination to be uninvolved is more pronounced. And yet, in an amazingly sudden turnabout, Hemingway renounces the separate peace with Harry Morgan's dramatically unmotivated dying speech in *To Have and Have Not* (1937): "No matter how a man alone ain't got no bloody ... chance" (225). And the shift is spelled out as clearly as possible with Robert Jordan's voluntary enlistment against fascism in *For Whom the Bell Tolls* (1940).

The nub of the literary critical confusion in Hemingway's political shifts is that Robert Jordan submits to Communist discipline for reasons precisely antithetical to those that impel Frederic Henry's desertion. Henry stands for the concrete immediacy of experience and is "embarrassed by the words sacred, glorious, and sacrifice and the expression in vain." He concludes that only place names have dignity, and that abstract words "such as glory, honor, courage, or hallow" are obscene. Eleven years later, Robert Jordan, referring to his participation in the Loyalist Cause as a "crusade," attempts to define how he feels:

> You felt, in spite of all bureaucracy and inefficiency and party strife something that was like the feeling you expected to have and did not have when you made your first communion. It was a feeling of consecration to a duty toward all of the oppressed of the world which would be as difficult and embarrassing to speak about as religious experience.... It gave you a part in something that you could believe in wholly and completely and in which you felt an absolute botherhood with the others who were engaged in it. It was something that you had never known before but that

you had experienced now and you gave such importance to it and
the reasons for it that your own death seemed of complete
unimportance.... (*FW*, 235)

The disparity between Jordan's and Henry's positions can never be
adequately explained by Hemingway's reactions to world events, for it is
doubtful that political or social ideas seriously engaged his creative
consciousness. As a man and as a newspaper correspondent, Hemingway was
in a better position to assess European social and political developments than
probably any other writer of the period. His dispatches and articles in the
1920s and 1930s are evidence that he possessed a keen political eye for what
was important in the news; yet he rarely uses this material except in a
superficial way, and none of his fictions are truly political. The significant
line of development between the filing for a separate peace in 1929 and the
return to brotherhood in 1940 can, however, be suggested on a
psychoanalytic level of interpretation.

   The interior struggle symbolized in *A Farewell to Arms* is fairly easy to
follow. The tyro, Henry, undergoes a series of unjust brutalities at the hands
of mysterious forces beyond his understanding. He is blown up and
seriously wounded (symbolically castrated), only to be nursed back to
wholeness and security by Catherine (the anima-mother). This idyllic union
in the hospital is only a temporary stay, however (prefigured, in part, by the
fact of Catherine's pregnancy), and the tyro returns to the war. His
opportunity for rebellion arrives during the chaos of the Caporetto retreat.
His ambulance unit picks up two wandering sergeants from an engineering
detachment, and, when they run off, he shoots one of them, aiming at the
one "who had talked the most." Neither of the sergeants is described or
characterized in any detail. Henry's actual desertion takes place at the bridge
when the forces of tyranny are imaged in the merciless battle police with
their "beautiful detachment and devotion to stern justice" (*F*, 224). In the
face of certain execution he leaps into the water and escapes to his anima-
mother at Stresa. There he meets Catherine and learns that the authorities
have tracked him down. During the night he and Catherine escape over the
lake to Switzerland where the idyll is resumed outside of Montreux. Finally
Catherine dies giving birth to a still-born baby boy, and the tyro is left alone
in the rain.

   On a psychoanalytic level Henry's separate peace is attained at the
expense of becoming an orphan and a half-man. Parricide, matricide, incest,
and narcissistic suicide are clumsily ponderous terms to apply to anything as
delicate as *A Farewell to Arms*, but they describe what happens in the

symbolic construct of the novel. Henry's wholeness is attainable only through the anima-mother who is from the earliest time of their meeting inexorably doomed. The father-images are split between the engineering sergeants (one of whom Henry inexplicably kills), the ruthless battle police, and the anonymous authorities. The tyro revolts against the tutor (symbolically killing one of his manifestations, but not all of them) and indirectly destroys his mother and anima. At the end of the novel he has, it is true, a separate peace with the universe, but he is bereft of any affectional contact with it.[13]

While Hemingway was writing the second draft of *A Farewell to Arms*, he learned of his own father's suicide.[14] We have every right to expect that this fact would influence the interior drama of Hemingway's fiction. The first point we notice is that, after the publication of *A Farewell to Arms*, Hemingway's fictional output noticeably slows down. *Winner Take Nothing* (1933) contains fourteen stories, and among them are some of the bitterest in the Hemingway canon: "A Natural History of the Dead," "The Mother of a Queen," "God Rest You Merry, Gentlemen." The famous *nada* prayer of "A Clean Well-Lighted Place" and "the opium of the people" speech of "The Gambler, the Nun, and the Radio" are in this collection. The volume is also notable for its savage concern with homosexuality and castration, and it is surely remarkable that not one of the stories has a love interest. The anima-mother is nonexistent, and only in "The Gambler, the Nun, and the Radio" is there a tyro-tutor relationship. In that story, however, Cayetano Ruiz is an exceptionally inadequate father image and Mr. Frazer, the tyro, concludes the action by reaching for a bottle of "giant killer" while reflecting that anything that serves as an opiate against the pain of life is a good.

The other two volumes between *A Farewell to Arms* and *To Have and Have Not* are nonfictional treatises on the pleasures of killing. In *Death in the Afternoon* (1932) not only are there long detailed descriptions of men killing bulls and bulls killing men and horses, but a rather elaborate justification for an interest in such murders:

> Killing cleanly and in a way which gives you aesthetic pleasure and pride has always been one of the greatest enjoyments of a part of the human race. One of its greatest pleasures, aside from the purely aesthetic ones ... is the feeling of rebellion against death which comes from its administering. Once you accept the rule of death thou shalt not kill is an easily and a naturally obeyed commandment. But when a man is still in rebellion against death he has pleasure in taking to himself one of the Godlike attributes;

that of giving it. This is one of the most profound feelings in those men who enjoy killing. (232–33)

Green Hills of Africa (1935), which continues the interest in killing, moves from the spectator's viewpoint behind the *barrera* to the participant, Hemingway, behind the sights of a .220 Springfield. Hemingway recounts his slaughter of a wide variety of animal life, but if there is a climax to the book, it occurs in the description of a giant sable bull that got away from him, although he had gut-shot it. Both volumes with their emphasis on compulsive killing suggest that the separate peace is still in effect. In terms of our analysis it seems likely that the tyro, desperately fragmented, can only strike out again and again in repetitive acts of destruction. That the targets of his destruction are male animals of rather noble stature is not surprising; the father image has treacherously escaped the tyro by removing himself from gun-range (although he has been "gut-shot"), and the symbolic animals must fall until the Oedipal fury is exhausted.

To Have and Have Not (1937)[15] marks, as we have seen, the clear recantation of the separate peace. And since social and political analysis must stumble over the abrupt switch in position, we are justified in searching the inward mechanisms of the novel for an indication of what has happened. Harry Morgan, whose prototype seems to have been invented in "After the Storm" (1932), is one of Hemingway's most brutalized characters. As tutor or father image, he is, on the one hand, degraded in speech patterns, utterly lacking in dignity, and morally unscrupulous; on the other hand, his elemental power is indicated by his physical strength and endurance (his delighted lust in killing, and his admirable sexual prowess with his wife). The symbolic thrust of the novel is directed to wound-castrate him (his arm must be amputated) and finally to destroy him in a carnage of gore and pain so that the fragmented tyro may become whole. However, this has been done already in Hemingway's previous two works of nonfiction at nearly the same level of intensity, and with no obvious therapeutic value. The differences may be explained as follows. The classic formula, "A man must kill his father in order to become a man," requires not only the death of the father but the death of the son-killer and his emergence as man; in his rebirth he becomes his own father. And this is the pattern in *To Have and Have Not* which is lacking in the preceding work.

In the crucial third section of this novel, Hemingway introduces the tyro figure, Emilio, the good Cuban revolutionary. Harry Morgan, a character not overly given to sentiment or affection, thinks of him as "a kind of nice kid." Emilio voices the rebellion theme, as he explains to Harry what his movement stands for: "We want to do away with all the old politicians, with all the American imperialism that strangles us, with the tyranny of the army. We want to start clean and give every man a chance" (*TH*, 166). Harry listens to him tolerantly and unmoved, reflecting that "He was a nice-looking boy all right. Pleasant talking too" (169). And then with the dispassionate efficiency of a ritual executioner, he blasts his head off. In the ensuing barrage, the three other Cubans are killed, and Harry is shot in the stomach. Like the sable bull, he is "gut-shot," but unlike the sable bull, his death has been fully propitiary. The son has become reborn in the father, and Harry's last words rejecting the philosophy of "a man alone" are the words of the son-become-father. In the chaotic, disorganized, melodramatic structure of *To Have and Have Not*, which could stand almost as an objective correlative of the disintegration of the Caporetto retreat, the tyro ceases to be a separate "piece" of the whole, and is ready for the experience of integration chronicled in *For Whom the Bell Tolls*.

But there are still several serious gaps in the symbolic drama. There is, as it were, a missing act between *Green Hills of Africa* and *To Have and Have Not*. And fortunately, we have three short stories, originally published in the summer and fall of 1936, that do provide the missing elements in the process of reintegration. These stories, two of which are among Hemingway's best, are "The Capital of the World" (first entitled "The Horns of the Bull"), "The Snows of Kilimanjaro," and "The Short Happy Life of Francis Macomber." We have already looked in some detail at one of them, and "The Capital of the World" is easily disposed of in terms of this discussion. The tyro hero of that story, Paco, is killed in a fight with a symbolic bull (butcher knives strapped to a kitchen chair) which in turn must be a symbolic father. He sacrifices himself with the same kind of naive idealism that Emilio, the Cuban revolutionary, entertained; and, like Emilio, he dies "as the Spanish phrase has it, full of illusions" (*SS*, 51). In Hemingway's writings that precede "The Capital of the World," the tyro does the killing exclusively; here sacrifice rather than destruction is emphasized, which indicates that the movement away from the separate peace has commenced.

Both "The Snows of Kilimanjaro" and "The Short Happy Life of Francis Macomber" introduce new elements into the drama. In both, the tyro is dead at the end of the story, he dies "full of illusions"; and he symbolically shucks off his past self to emerge a new man. The new radical factor introduced in these stories is the "bitch-heroine" or the "wicked-mother" figure, a character only vaguely prefigured in Hemingway's earlier fiction (specifically in several of the stories of *In Our Time*), and nowhere else evident after 1936 except in concealed form in the character of Pilar in *For*

Whom the Bell Tolls. "The Short Happy Life of Francis Macomber" is a clear portrait of the dramatic changes in Hemingway's world of fantasy projection, signaling the establishment of a new perspective on which the later mergence and emergence of the tyro can be based.

The Macomber marriage, Hemingway tells us, has "a sound basis of union. Margot was too beautiful for Macomber to divorce her and Macomber had too much money for Margot ever to leave him" (*SS*, 22).[16] The action of the story will effect a decisive break in this unhealthy union, as it will also unmask to the tyro the identity of his real antagonist, the mother-image, and pave the way for a reconciliation with the father. The locale of the story—a safari in the African jungle—is unprecedented in Hemingway's landscapes as a fictional setting, and is highly appropriate for the tropical depths of awareness from which the story rises. The action opens with Macomber repeating Hemingway's unsuccessful attempts with the giant sable bull in *Green Hills of Africa*; Francis gut-shoots a lion and runs in cowardice from its retaliatory charge. He suffers the contempt of tutor-father Wilson and of wicked-mother Margot, as well as his own overwhelming self-disgust. Note, though, that this action is an exact parallel of the declaration of a separate peace in *A Farewell to Arms*, viewed with an entirely different system of emotional valuation. In 1929 the failure to deal masterfully with authority and the flight from it were transformed into acts of heroic nobility. Frederic Henry's final isolation at the end of the novel was treated lingeringly as a particularly poignant result of blindly malicious injustice. Now blame has been transferred from the impersonal "world" to the self-conscious tyro, signaling the first stage in a return to health and creativity.

The immediate consequences of Francis's failure with the lion are Margot's rejection and betrayal of him with father-image Wilson and the completion of Francis's self-disgust and thorough alienation. He is now in the situation of the Hemingway of *Death in the Afternoon* and *Green Hills of Africa*, but without the temporary recourse to random killing. He hates Wilson, but he cannot act on that hatred because of his own sense of fear and unworthiness. In the chase after the bull buffaloes, he dramatically loses his fear in his hatred and performs meritoriously with the buffalo—becoming a reborn man. The denouement to the drama is inevitable. In his second facing of the wounded buffalo's charge, when it is clear that he will react like a man, Margot blasts his brains out with a 6.5 Mannlicher. But here, as in "The Snows of Kilimanjaro," the true villain, the mother, has been exposed; and the separation between tyro and mother is healthily effected.

Macomber's relationship to Wilson has also been clarified. The father has been taught to respect the son, and the son can afford to feel brotherly affection for the father. Interestingly, there is no specific father image in "The Snows of Kilimanjaro." The mountain top, hitherto unapproachable because of Harry's gangrenous unworthiness, seems to fulfill Wilson's function on a more exalted plane. And the hyena, hermaphroditic and vicious, which we observed to be an extension of Helen, becomes even more closely identified with the wicked-mother figure. In sum, the self-realization of the tyro can come only when he has become man enough to tear himself free from dependence on the mother. Then, and only then, can he face his father on equal terms, symbolically becoming one with him. "The Snows of Kilimanjaro" and "The Short Happy Life of Francis Macomber" crystallize this orientation in Hemingway's fantasy life and, on a psychological level, make Harry Morgan's recantation of the separate peace understandable. It remains only to carry this discussion through Hemingway's later fiction to complete the arc of its inner struggle.

For Whom the Bell Tolls is something of an anomaly in Hemingway's fiction. Far and away his longest sustained prose narrative, it is thickly populated for a Hemingway novel, creatively agile in its handling of space and shifting of backgrounds. In terms of our argument it seems significant that the writing pace was extremely fast and regular (the book took almost exactly eighteen months to write and revise);[17] it seems fair to assume that the "inner-breakthrough" of 1936–37 had released in Hemingway prolific creative powers after a dry period of almost ten years. Further, the style of *For Whom the Bell Tolls* is much more freely flowing than the brittle staccato periods that had been characteristic of Hemingway's prose. And, most significantly, it is, with the possible exception of *The Old Man and the Sea*, Hemingway's most serene work. There are scenes of violence and horror, to be sure, but these are narrated at a distance. Pilar's description of the slaughter of the Fascists and Maria's account of her parents' murders and of her own violation are violent memories recollected in something that approaches tranquillity. Even El Sordo's stand on the mountain top is placed at a narrative distance from the reader, since it is viewed by the impersonal narrator and describes the fate of a guerrilla band only peripherally connected with the main characters of interest. It would be too much to call this novel a pastoral idyll. But the emotional center of the fiction—in sometimes jarring contrast to the action described—almost from the very beginning resonates with a harmony in perfect accord with Jordan's previously quoted speech on "communion," as well as with the Donnean echoes of the title. Indeed, it is even worth wondering whether the complete quotation from which the title derives—"No man is an *Island*, intire of it

selfe; every man is a peece of the *Continent* ... I am involved in *Mankinde.*"—
is, as it is usually considered, a justification for taking part in a foreign war.
More likely is Hemingway's announcement of his achieved "at-one-ment" in
himself.

At any rate, such is the way the novel reads on its lower levels; it is a
happy fairy tale where all the seeming evils only appear to be evil, and all the
goods gain in radiance as the novel progresses. The disasters at the end are
merely the inevitabilities of death, and since life has been telescoped into a
seventy-hour period, death can be accepted with an almost-Whitmanesque
readiness: "There is no such thing as a shortness of time, though. You should
have sense enough to know that too. I have been all my life in these hills since
I have been here. Anselmo is my oldest friend.... Agustin, with his vile mouth,
is my brother, and I never had a brother. Maria is my true love and my wife.
I never had a true love. I never had a wife. She is also my sister, and I never
had a sister, and my daughter, and I never will have a daughter. I hate to leave
a thing that is so good" (*FW,* 381). And these statements by the tyro figure
are, in terms of the symbolic inner drama, perfectly true. The good father,
Anselmo, has become his oldest friend; the bad father, Pablo, has repented of
his treachery and become a helper. The gypsy witch mother, Pilar, has
refrained from capturing him in the domineering nets of bad incest, and has
metamorphosed into the fairy godmother, bestower of all blessings. In that
role she gives him an anima-mother, Maria. The inner drama achieves such
a harmony of relationships that "drama," a word to denote a system of
tensions, is probably inaccurate; it would be better to characterize the
psychoanalytic area of action as the inner tableau.

The last two fictions can be treated much more cursorily. Ten years
elapsed between the publication of *For Whom the Bell Tolls* and *Across the River
and into the Trees.* It is worth remarking that in that period Hemingway began
to refer to himself as "Papa." We have already noticed the effects of "the
symbolic doubling" in the 1950 novel. The tyro, Richard Cantwell, becomes
his own father-image, projecting his anima into the noble mother, Renata.
Characteristically, this results in Cantwell's being forced to attack himself in
lieu of an external antagonist, and this he does through the device of the
cardiac condition. This novel, the most static of Hemingway's fiction, is
largely composed of the tyro father's self-beratements and self-defenses. It
does not make for good fiction, but is extremely interesting as a relatively
naked exposure of the drama beneath the drama.

And finally, as we suggested earlier, *The Old Man and the Sea* (1952)
completes the cycle of the arc. Santiago is father tyro, the sea is anima-
mother, and the boy is a displaced remembrance of the hero as a young man.

The antagonist, the male marlin, is Santiago's brother, and the parable of maturity or age is cast in fresh poetic terms. The ultimate regression of the psyche to immersion in the primordial is given an authoritative and substantive treatment. There are the scavenger sharks and the Portuguese men of war to disrupt the surfaces of unity and peace; but these are merely the last thrashings of life which, in time, will subside and submerge themselves into the great boundless all.

Two concluding items need reemphasis. As a tool for measuring the worth of a work of art, psychoanalytic criticism is of arguable value. Some critics may allow that it can be fruitful with inferior works—like *To Have and Have Not* and *Across the River and into the Trees.* But they will claim that it yields only misleading information about the personality of the creator of a work of art, that its subjective readings deal with a bundle of unassimilated material already pressed into a design for completely other purposes, and that it is ignorant of the multitude of sensations that are a part of the artist's personality and that are never made manifest in his work. Dealing with Hemingway in particular, a man whom we have seen to pride himself on his role playing, such critics will remind us that we can see only what he chooses for us to see, and that he is not beyond "hoaxing" the reader for his own sense of satisfaction. Other critics, while owning that psychoanalytic criticism can be bunglingly used, argue that it can illuminate even great works of art, can unearth hidden information about the personality of an artist, can discern unconscious and counterintended designs in a bundle of unassimilated material, can glimpse latent meanings and significance in the manifest details of an artist's work. They will claim that even with such a role-playing author as Hemingway, he too has only limited control over what he consciously chooses for us to see; indeed, his "hoaxing" is a symptom that psychoanalytic criticism can deal with.[18]

Regardless how one regards psychoanalytic criticism, its discovery of concealed meanings does not at all negate other equally valuable meanings in the interpretation of a fiction. Moreover, it can be useful as one among many tools in hypothesizing a direction or a focus of examination in which the concealed springs of the creative fountain may show themselves. The single point that seems worth the discussion is the evidence suggesting that Hemingway's fiction is consistently concerned with the metaphors of his own consciousness; that his characters are intensely felt, partial projections of his own internal war, that their conflicts are less the actions of human beings in society contending with one another, than a delicate recording of the wracking ambiguities that always verge on rending man asunder. Hemingway, in short, is a writer of romances; perhaps the most realistic writer of romances of all time, but a romancer nonetheless. And the value of his metaphors depends on his ability to make his poetic vision move his readers toward discovering truths about themselves. This point is worth retaining because it allows us to approach his fictions for what they are and not for what even he may have pretended them to be.

NOTES

1. Hemingway's poetry is collected in Gerogiannis, 88 *Poems*.

2. For a more thorough explication of this subject see Earl Rovit, "The Shape of American Poetry," *Jahrbuch für Amerikastudien* 6 (1961): 122–33.

3. Philip Young's chapter "The Hero and the Code," in his *Reconsideration*, 55–78, is an excellent introduction. For other studies of the code, see Delmore Schwartz, "Ernest Hemingway's Literary Situation," *Southern Review* 3 (1938): 769–82; rpt. in McCaffery, *The Man and His Work*, 99–113, and in Meyers, *Heritage*, 243–56; Warren, "Ernest Hemingway," 1–28; rpt. in Wagner, *Five Decades*, 80–118; and James B. Colvert, "Ernest Hemingway's Morality in Action," *American Literature* 27 (1955): 372–85.

4. Ernest Hemingway, "The Denunciation," *Esquire*, November 1938, 112; rpt. in *The Fifth Column and Four Stories of the Spanish Civil War* (New York, 1969), 97.

5. Baker, *Hemingway*, 131. For additional commentary on Nick Adams, see Philip Young, "'Big World Out There': The Nick Adams Stories," *Novel: A Forum on Fiction* 6 (1972): 5–19; rpt. in Benson, *Short Stories*, 29–45, and Joseph M. Flora, *Hemingway's Nick Adams* (Baton Rouge, 1982).

6. One could argue that the bull in "The Undefeated" and the lion in "The Short Happy Life of Francis Macomber" are perfectly representative "tutors" in action. In Hemingway's renditions, their thoughts are as intelligent as those of Manuel.

7. Young, *Reconsideration*, 64. See also Robert P. Weeks, "Wise-Guy Narrator and Trickster Out-Tricked in Hemingway's 'Fifty Grand,'" *Studies in American Fiction* 10 (1982): 83–91.

8. Two excellent discussions of this phase of modern fiction are Ihab Hassan, *Radical Innocence* (Princeton: Princeton University Press, 1961) and R.W.B. Lewis, *The Picaresque Saint* (Philadelphia: Lippincott, 1959).

9. A possible exception to the rule is Schatz in "A Day's Wait."

10. Baker's discussion in *Hemingway*, 283–87, is especially valuable on this subject.

11. A survey of such studies includes Isaac Rosenfeld, "A Farewell to Hemingway," *Kenyan Review* 13 (1951): 147–55; rpt. in Meyers, *Heritage*, 385–93; Richard Drinnon, "In the American Heartland: Hemingway and Death," *Psychoanalytic Review* 52 (1965): 5–31; David Gordon, "The Son and the Father: Patterns of Response to Conflict in Hemingway's Fiction," *Literature and Psychology* 16 (1966): 122–38; rpt. in his *Literary Art and the Unconscious* (Baton Rouge: Louisiana State University Press, 1976), 171–94; Richard B. Hovey, *Hemingway: The Inward Terrain* (Seattle, 1968); Irvin D. and Marilyn Yalom, "Ernest Hemingway—A Psychiatric View," *Archives of General Psychiatry* 24 (1971): 485–94; Richard E. Hardy and John G. Cull, *Hemingway: A Psychological Portrait* (Sherman Oaks, Ca.: Banner Books, 1977), especially 47–56 and 81–92; Brenner, *Concealments*; and

Jeffrey Meyers, "Lawrence Kubie's Suppressed Essay on Hemingway," *American Imago* 41 (1984): 1–18.

12. *To Have and Have Not* (New York, 1937), 221; hereafter cited in the text as *TH*.

13. There is actually a further confusion in the end of the novel in which Henry identifies with his stillborn son: "Poor little kid. I wished the hell I'd been choked like that" (*F*, 327); he also rejects himself as father, claiming that he has no feeling of fatherhood. The most interesting detail is his looking into a mirror with his white gown and beard: "I looked in the glass and saw myself looking like a fake doctor with a beard" (*F*, 319). Dr. Clarence Hemingway and, presumably, Dr. Adams as well wore beards.

14. Baker, *Life Story*, 198–99.

15. The dates of the publication of *To Have and Have Not* are a little confusing because the first two sections of the novel had been previously published as stories, "Part One: Harry Morgan (*Spring*)" as "One Trip Across" in *Cosmopolitan*, April 1934, 20–23, 108–22; "Part Two: Harry Morgan (*Fall*)" as "The Tradesman's Return" in *Esquire*, February 1936, 27, 193–96. Although he published these as stories, as early as 1933, Hemingway had conceived of them as part of a novel, as a letter to Archibald MacLeish, 27 February 1933, indicates (*Selected Letters*, 381). The novel was published in October, 1937, the third part apparently drafted as early as the summer of 1936, for Hemingway showed some 30,000 words of it to Arnold Gingrich in early July, 1936 (*Selected Letters*, 447–49). For Hemingway's own estimate of the novel and of his having cut some 100,000 words from it, see his letter to Lillian Ross, 28 July 1948, in *Selected Letters*, 648–49.

16. Critical studies of this story continue to pile up; see "'Macomber' Bibliography," comp. William White in *Hemingway notes* 5 (1980): 35–38, for a list of 101 items and articles. More recently see Bert Bender, "Margot Macomber's Gimlet," *College Literature* 8 (1981): 12–20; Geoffrey Meyers, "A Queer, Ugly Business: The Origins of 'The Short Happy Life of Francis Macomber,'" *London*, November 1983, 26–37; Mark Spilka, "A Source for the Macomber 'Accident': Marryat's *Percival Keene*," *Hemingway Review* 3 (1984): 29–37; and Roger Whitlow, *Cassandra's Daughters: The Women in Hemingway* (Westport, Conn.: Greenwood Press, 1984), 59–68.

17. Baker, *Hemingway*, 238–39n.

18. The value of psychoanalytic criticism to the study of literature is well argued by Frederick Crews, "Anaesthetic Criticism," in *Psychoanalysis and Literary Process*, ed. Frederick Crews (Cambridge, Mass.: Winthrop Publishers, 1970), 1–24; David J. Gordon, "Introduction" and "The Unconscious in Literary Art," in his *Literary Art and the Unconscious*, xiii–xxx, 3–51; C. Barry Chabot, "Psychoanalysis as Literary Criticism / Literary Criticism as Psychoanalysis" and "Groundings in Theory: The Cohesive Life, the Whole Story," in his *Freud on Schreber: Psychoanalytic Theory and the Critical Act* (Amherst: University of Massachusetts Press, 1982), 49–107; and Meredith Anne Skura, *The Literary Use of the Psychoanalytic Process* (New Haven: Yale University Press, 1981).

EDWARD F. STANTON

Of Bulls and Men

It is a long one to write because it is not to be just a history and text book
or apologia for bull fighting—but instead, if possible, bull fighting its-
self. As it's a thing that nobody knows about in English I'd like to take it
first from altogether outside—how I happened to be interested in it, how
it seemed before I saw it—how it was when I didn't understand it—my
own experience with it, how it reacts on others—the gradual finding out
about it and try and build it up from the outside and then go all the way
inside with chapters on everything. It might be interesting to people
because nobody knows anything about it—and it really is terribly
interesting—being a matter of life and death.... I think a really true book
if it were fairly well written about the one thing that has, with the
exception of the ritual of the church, come down to us intact from the
old days would have a certain permanent value.

—EH to Maxwell Perkins, 6 December 1926

Even before *The Sun Also Rises*, Hemingway had probably begun taking
notes for a work on the art of toreo. In the spring of 1925 he was already
speaking of a "bull book on bullfighting" with photographs and illustrations
by Picasso, Juan Gris, and others. That project turned out to be a bubble, but
Hemingway was determined to compose a work that would open the world
of toreo to the English-speaking public as Doughty's *Travels in Arabia Deserta*
had opened the uninhabited Middle East. Many other foreigners, especially

From *Hemingway and Spain*. © 1989 by the University of Washington Press.

English, had written about the bullfight. Out of religious prejudice or moral squeamishness, all had failed to present toreo integrally. Even the British painter-writer Richard Ford, one of Hemingway's favorite authors on Spain, had admitted that "we turn away our eyes during moments of painful detail which are lost in the poetical ferocity of the whole." Hemingway wanted to write a book (and he did) with his eyes wide open, which would tell what he actually saw and felt at the corrida, not what he was supposed to see and feel. This was the well-known sequence of fact-motion-emotion-word he was striving to get in his writing and he had gotten it most consistently from the bullfight, leading to the creation of his rhythmic, ecstatic prose.

When Hemingway finally completed his book on toreo in 1932, it had been nearly eight years in gestation and some two-and-a-half in the writing—more than *The Sun Also Rises*, *A Farewell to Arms*, or any other work he would publish in his lifetime. Not his best book, *Death in the Afternoon* was his most personal, and the most important for understanding his views on the corrida, Spain, art, life and death. So much that is hopelessly wrongheaded has been written about this work that one despairs of being heard among the chorus of owls and popinjays. Hemingway himself put all future commentators on guard by warning them against too much abstraction and an "overmetaphysical tendency in speech," commonly known as horseshit. Anyone who wants to discuss *Death* feels afraid, almost as much as a torero smoking his last cigarette in the *patio de caballos* before a bullfight. But the trumpet sounds, the matadores stride into the ring, and there are a few practical things to be said.

First of all, why did Hemingway spend nearly three years writing his only real book of nonfiction, one which he himself and most critics have considered inferior to his novels and short stories? Like Doughty, he realized his subject was one that "nobody knows about in English," in Britain or America. The situation was similar in France: Mérimée had included toreo amid the local color of Andalusia in *Carmen* (1845), but it was only with Henri de Montherlant, Hemingway's contemporary, that bullfighting entered the mainstream of French letters. Even in Spain, serious writers did not turn to toreo as a subject worthy of literature until the late nineteenth and early twentieth centuries—Blasco Ibáñez, Ramón Pérez de Ayala, García Lorca, Rafael Alberti, José Bergamín.

Hemingway was correct when he said, in his "Bibliographical Note" at the end of *Death in the Afternoon*, that there had been no book in English or Spanish that explained the spectacle "both emotionally and practically." Such a book was especially necessary in the Anglo-Saxon world, where people approached bullfighting burdened with centuries of prejudices born from the

Black Legend, portraying Spain as the country of religious hypocrisy, oppression, and brutality. In his own manner, Hemingway, who had "converted" to Catholicism in 1927 in order to marry his second wife, Pauline, rewrote the legend and gave a new view of toreo from the Anglo-Saxon perspective, but with a deep understanding of Hispanic culture. The bullfight could exist only in the Catholic countries of the Western world, where there is a clear distinction between human beings with immortal souls and soulless animals. Since the bulls who die in the plaza do not have souls according to the Church, it is not morally wrong for men to kill them, nor to allow horses to suffer from goring by the bulls. In the Protestant world by contrast, the line between human and animal life is less neat; only there could the people Hemingway mockingly calls "animalarians" have originated. He realized from the beginning, with his almost unfailing instinct, that the corrida could not be judged by the notions of sport and fair play—in large part creations of the English-speaking peoples. He knew that the only way to appreciate toreo was to see it as a tragedy uniting many arts: music, dance, painting, sculpture. The very word "bullfight" is of course a misnomer ("corrida" literally means "running" of bulls), implying an adversarial relation between man and animal rather than a mutual participation in a prescribed ritual, or as some matadores have suggested, a kind of lovemaking between toro and torero. Although Hemingway's original intention was not to write an apology of toreo, *Death in the Afternoon* evolved into a subtle, implicit defense of the spectacle and the mentality that makes it an acceptable form of public entertainment among the Hispanic peoples alone. In this way, what had begun as a book on the bullfight grew outward to include Spain, Spaniards, Spanish life, and the whole culture. Like his partly autobiographical protagonist of *For Whom the Bell Tolls*, Robert Jordan, Hemingway wished his book to contain "what he had discovered in Spain in ten years of travelling in it, on foot, in third-class carriages, by bus, on horse- and mule-back and in trucks."

The bullfight had been the magic key that unlocked many of the secret things in Spanish life for Hemingway. Although the so-called *fiesta nacional* involves only a small minority of Spaniards directly, and some detest the spectacle as an embarrassing, degrading relic of a primitive and "African" past, innumerable aspects of Spanish culture are tied to images, memories, and idioms of the bull and toreo. Antonio Cala, a Spanish writer known more for his dramas and love of animals than for his afición, could still write in 1980: "In Spain, from its centuries-old traditions to its very geographical shape in the form of a bull's hide; from its racial virtues to the joyous impudence of its language, almost everything is connected ... to the attributes and the figure of the bull. There is no other totem that grips us so tightly. In its double mode, cultured or popular, almost all our creations are steeped in that theme and its related expression." Hemingway had learned for himself what Queen María Cristina had advised her son, later Alfonso XIII and King of Spain during the novelist's early trips to the peninsula: one must go to the bullring in order to understand the Spanish nation and her people.

The Culture of Death

Hemingway's original interest in bullfighting extended to all of Spain, her inhabitants and their ways of life. The best example of this process in *Death in the Afternoon* is the proverbial Spanish concern for death. Contrary to what Hemingway once said, the bullfight is not always a tragedy—in modern times the bulls and the toreros often do not have the dignity required by tragedy—but it always contains death: of the bulls inevitably, of the horses sometimes, of the men occasionally. *Death in the Afternoon* can be seen as the culmination of Hemingway's absorption with mortality, made more immediate by his father's suicide about a year before he began to write the book. The reader who is unaware of the proximity between the doctor's death and the composition of the book must be taken aback by its apparently gratuitous references to suicide—and in particular to that of one's father. The discussions of death (as in "A Natural History of the Dead" inserted in Chapter Twelve), of killing (Clarence Hemingway had taught his son the virtues of killing animals cleanly), of doctors and bullfight surgeons must have brought memories of his father teeming into Ernest's mind. The writing of *Death in the Afternoon* was his own peculiar way of overcoming the shock of his father's suicide and of approaching the Spanish concern for death through the corrida. Hemingway's personal experience, his afición for bullfighting, and his fascination with Spain all coincided and overlapped in the composition of the book.

Ernest's father was the one parent he really "cared about." He resented his mother because of the way she had raised him and because he believed she was partly responsible for Dr. Hemingway's suicide. In the bullfight book, he metamorphosed her to an extent into the wacky, despised "Old Lady" whose conversations with the author-narrator provided comic relief from the tragedy of the corrida and from all the technical material. As H.L. Mencken noted with more accuracy than he may have guessed, the reader to whom Hemingway seemed to address his book was "a sort of common denominator of all the Ladies' Aid Societies of his native Oak Park, Ill." This kind of reader, embodied in the Old Lady, could be scandalized by the more visceral elements of bullfighting and provide a foil to the world-weary, cynical aficionado who is the narrator and to a large degree the author himself.

One of the problems of *Death in the Afternoon* is in fact the confusion between Hemingway's public and private personalities, and the beginning of what Carlos Baker calls the "Narcissus principle"—the writer's assumption that the details of his life could engage the reader's interest as they engaged his own, and that they could be incorporated in his books without the same amount of invention he had used in *Sun, Farewell,* and the short stories until 1932. Although there is no doubt that the Narcissus principle is one of the major flaws in Hemingway's later novels, it might be argued that it contributes to the unique, idiosyncratic appeal of *Death,* which after all is a nonfiction book where the personality and opinions of the writer need not be transformed as in a work of fiction. It could also be argued that Hemingway's need to join his private and his public images, his life and his writing, was comparable to the recurrent tendency in Spanish culture called "integralism" by Américo Castro. It can be found in the works of such diverse figures as Cervantes, Lope de Vega, Velázquez, Goya, and Picasso, where there is usually no clear separation of the creator's life from its expression in artistic form.

So Hemingway's afición for bullfighting and the memory of his father's recent suicide converged in the typically Spanish preoccupation with death. The corrida is only one example of what the poet and critic Pedro Salinas has termed his country's culture of death. Other manifestations are the religious processions on Holy Friday in most Spanish towns and cities, and the moving *saetas* or songs addressed to Christ on the cross during Easter week in Andalusia. El Greco and Goya in painting and Jorge Manrique, Quevedo, and Lorca in literature are examples of the phenomenon; all of these artists were known and some of them admired by Hemingway. When he speaks of the culture of death, Salinas does not mean a kind of Thanatophilia or obsession with mortality as the Black Legend would have it—a morbid dwelling on the gruesome details of the grave or on the afterlife at the expense of life on earth. He refers rather to a vision of man and his existence in which the awareness of death is a positive force, a stimulus to living and acting which enables us to understand the full meaning of our lives. An existence in which the awareness of death is hidden or suppressed is lacking in the dimension that gives life its edge, its intensity and drama. "Man can only understand himself, can only be entire, by integrating death into his life; and every attempt to expel death, to take no account of it, in order to live, is a falsification, a fraud perpetrated by man on himself."

Hemingway recognized immediately that the Spaniards' refusal to ignore death was in actuality a way of sharpening life, of living more intensely. In the important chapter on the killing of the bull in *Death in the Afternoon*, he explains the Spaniards' commonsensical acceptance of mortality as part of the life process and mocks the hypocritical English and French attitude of living for life alone—only to discover death too late, when it arrives. Hemingway could have mentioned America too, where more than anywhere in Europe, discussion of dying was considered to be in bad taste. He found the Spaniards' attitude much wiser and more consistent with his own experience during and after the war.

The cardinal difference between Hemingway's tragic vision of life and death and that of most Spaniards lies in their virtually opposite views of immortality. For example, in the work of Unamuno—the modern Spanish writer who has written most trenchantly on the theme—the inevitability of death leads to a hunger for life beyond the grave and to a hope for the resurrection of the body and the individual personality according to Catholic doctrine. In spite of his conversion to Catholicism, Hemingway never mentions this kind of personal immortality in his published or unpublished work. In an important sentence deleted from *Death in the Afternoon*, he says "Men search consciously or unconsciously for some sort of immortality." In contrast to Unamuno and most Catholic thinkers, immortality for Hemingway does not mean an eternal life in heaven, but rather a feeling of timelessness transported to life on earth, such as the matador feels when he deals death to the bull, and this feeling is communicated to the public. Hemingway's achievement was to give death and immortality the religious overtones of the great Catholic writers like St. John of the Cross and the less orthodox Unamuno without mentioning God, heaven, or an afterlife. *Death in the Afternoon* and his other works on toreo have retained their freshness largely because they are not burdened with religious, historical, and cultural references. One critic has noted that Montherlant, the only other major author with a comparable knowledge of the bullfight, "ransacks anthropology and comparative religion for references to bulls, a violation of which Hemingway would have been incapable." When one of Ernest's matadores goes in over the horn for the kill, he does not think of Mithra's sacrifice, like Montherlant's toreros, but of where to place the sword with the right arm and how to cross the muleta in the left hand so that the animal passes out and away from his body. Hemingway had a few practical things to say.

The very title of *Death in the Afternoon* reflects the author's preoccupation. The letters he wrote during the composition of the book also contain frequent allusions to mortality and cite appropriate lines from writers like Andrew Marvell and Baudelaire. When the typesetter for Scribner's slugged the galley proofs of the book with the abbreviation "Hemingway's Death," the writer wired and wrote angrily to Max Perkins, asking him to "raise hell with the son of a bitch." Ernest's reaction showed his superstitiousness, a characteristic of his personality reinforced by years of close contact with bullfighting, where the constant potentiality of wounding and death makes virtually all toreros religious and sensitive to good or bad omens.

The title of *Death in the Afternoon* should warn us, even before we begin reading, that this book was intended to be much more than a manual on the modern Spanish bullfight. By calling his book in this way, Hemingway conveyed not only his vision of toreo as a matter of life and death, but also the subjective, emotional, and symbolic approach he would use, working both from the "outside" and from the "inside," as he put it. Let us see how this method functions in the book.

"Secret Things": Blood, Wine, and *Duende*

With the deaths of some 1,000 bulls in his memory, and the general assumptions of the work clear in his head, Hemingway began to write in his usual spontaneous way. He allowed the prose to create its own momentum, to find its own way without formal divisions; only later did he go back and divide the material into the chapters of the published version. In general, Hemingway followed his intention, announced to Perkins in the prescient letter of 1926 (epigraph to this chapter), of taking the bullfight first from the outside—how he came to be interested in it, his preconceptions and initial reactions—building it up until he finally went "all the way inside." But this process was not a steady one and the author made many digressions, some of them triggered by unconscious associations of images and ideas that give the work a vital, organic structure and its unique, compelling nature. This is in many ways his most poorly organized, confusing book, but it also possesses a strangely living quality that makes it his most revealing work.

During its largely sporadic, improvised composition, *Death in the Afternoon* acquired a loose structure which Hemingway was oddly reluctant to rework, as he had revised the first draft of *The Sun Also Rises*, for example. The real structure of the book is to be found deep below its surface, in a profound, irrational undercurrent of primordial images and symbols embedded in the rhythmic, ecstatic prose. It is useless to expect here an orderly progression of well-organized chapters which might have been called for by the bullfight itself—an extremely orthodox art whose three *tercios* or acts are almost as rigidly codified as the liturgy of the Mass. In fact the great Andalusian poet and playwright García Lorca called the corrida a liturgy, an "authentic religious drama in which a God is worshiped and sacrificed in the same way as in the Mass." The bull has been sacred among the Hispanic peoples from the earliest times; research has shown that the remote origins of the animal's sacrifice probably lay in nature and fertility rituals. Hemingway was intuitively aware of the mythic, religious dimension of the bullfight, but his training as a writer of fiction, his iceberg theory, and his anti-intellectual temperament led him merely to suggest this dimension rather than state it openly.

In the first chapter of *Death in the Afternoon,* for example, Hemingway begins by taking bullfighting from the outside: how he happened to be interested in it, how it helped him as a writer, his expectations before seeing his first corrida and his reactions afterwards; the most sensational aspect of the spectacle for most foreigners, the goring and killing of the horses; the definition of the bullfight as a tragedy strongly disciplined by ritual. So far nothing seems unusual about the book, except perhaps the narrator's very personal tone and his emphasis on the one aspect of the corrida whose significance he is attempting to deny (he protesteth too much)—the suffering of the horses. After this visceral introduction to the bullfight, the narrator makes a long digression about wine drinking, which he admits is "far-fetched"; yet he goes out of his way to justify it. Wine, he intimates, offers a great range of enjoyment and appreciation for the palate, as the bullfight does for the eye; a trained palate wants its wine unwatered and unsweetened, as the eye of the true aficionado wants his bullfights unadulterated by fancy tricks or protection of the horses by the *peto* (quilted mattress).

It must be confessed that part of Hemingway's motivation for including several extensive paragraphs on wine probably derived from the Narcissus principle—his unwillingness to exclude his minor passions from his writings; also from his constant urge to prove himself an insider—on wine, food, bullfighting, fishing, shooting, war, loving, etc. But there is a deeper, secret justification for this passage: the country where bulls are fought and killed in the ring is also wine country, and the libation of wine is an integral part of the whole ritualistic world of bullfighting. At the *tientas* or testing of calves for bravery on bull-breeding ranches, there is always much eating accompanied by wine. At the *sorteo* or sorting of the bulls in the corrals at noon on the day of a corrida, sherry is often served; afterwards one goes to the café to drink an aperitif in order to whet the appetite for lunch. Before entering the bullring in the afternoon, one may visit a bar for a glass of sherry brandy, wine, beer, or coffee with aficionado friends. At the corrida itself, leather wine bags make the rounds, especially on the sunny side of the plaza. Afterwards, the cafés are filled once more with aficionados drinking and discussing the performance of bulls and men.

Due to the amount of liquor, especially wine, that is imbibed as a necessary part of life in and around the bullring, alcoholism can be one of the occupational diseases of toreros. Hemingway discreetly silences this fact, perhaps from having known personally several cases of careers destroyed by the sauce. (Cayetano Ordóñez, Niño de la Palma, is the most obvious example.) To live in the tradition-bound, masculine world of bullfighting and not to partake of wine would be considered odd and unnatural. At a deeper level, wine is connected to the religious dimension of the bullfight, as in ancient rituals of sacrifice and fertility. The body of the slain god—bull or Dionysus—was torn to pieces by the worshipers, who then ate the raw flesh. There are still survivals of this kind of totem banquet in many parts of Spain, such as the celebration of Midsummer or the *Día de San Juan* in Soria, where the dead bull's meat is cooked and eaten. A Catholic writer like Anthony Burgess, never an aficionado, has admitted feeling an emotion of sacramental participation, as valid as communion in the Church, after eating the roasted meat of a fighting bull. If the bullfight is a liturgical sacrifice, then wine corresponds to the blood of the animal as it stands for the blood of Christ in the Catholic Mass. This association between wine and blood is reflected in the popular imagination by the name of the famous wine-punch sangría (the word also means "bloodletting") and by the well-known red wine "Sangre de Toro."

Hemingway's apparent digression on wine drinking may not be defensible on the surface, but we can see how it begins to build, from the inside, the deep, irrational, mythic dimension of the bullfight. Of course the author does not tell us so; the reader must make this perception from the association of words and images. It does not matter if the reader does this consciously, because Hemingway himself may have been working unconsciously here, making an intuitive connection between wine and blood after his visceral discussion of horses in the preceding pages. In the first paragraph after the passage on wine drinking, he creates, with a long sentence of rhythmic, ecstatic prose, the emotion of a slow, sculptural faena by the gypsy Cagancho, which produces a kind of drunkenness and ecstasy in the bullfighter and in the public. This passage was added to the original draft of the manuscript, as if Hemingway realized that something was missing from the first chapter—the bullfight "its-self," what makes his book different from all others on the subject.

So after evoking the hidden, religious depths of the corrida with the passage on wine in the first chapter, he shows the irrational, Dionysian ecstasy of a faena by Cagancho—an emotion as profound as any religious experience, he will tell us later. This emotion is related to the Spanish word and feeling of *duende*, a power nearly everyone can feel but nobody can explain satisfactorily. Its basic meaning is inspiration in the root sense, yet no foreign word can convey the wealth of connotations evoked by the Spanish. It may refer to a bullfight; to the singing of *cante jondo*, the traditional song of southern Spain; or to any moment charged with feeling and enveloped in grace. Duende should not be confused with mere artistic skill or technical competence: the catalyst of inspiration must be present. In the most lyrical treatment of the subject by any writer, the poet Lorca says that duende is not rational, but is linked to the dark realm of the unconscious. It does not descend from Aristotle but from the Dionysian Greeks, later from Nietzsche. Literally a spirit or demon, it cannot be summoned at will. When it does arrive, it shakes the man it possesses like an electric charge. Duende reveals itself most readily in the temporal arts—music, dance, spoken poetry, bullfighting. It depends on an actual present, being a perpetual baptism of the moment. Its appearance is received with a kind of religious ecstasy. In Arabic music, Lorca says that the participants cry "Allah! Allah!"—an exact parallel to the "*Olé!*" shouted by the public in spontaneous acclaim of a bullfighter. At this instant, those who are present feel a kind of communion with the supernatural through the senses.

Hemingway knew all about this experience, and he may have been familiar with Lorca's beautiful description of the phenomenon (written about 1929–30), which in fact uses Cagancho as an example of a bullfighter who performs with duende. In *For Whom the Bell Tolls*, duende is expressed as "La Gloria." Robert Jordan says, as his creator suggests in the bullfight book, that he is no mystic, but to deny the mystic experience would be "as ignorant as though you denied the telephone or that the earth revolves around the sun or that there are other planets than this." *Death in the Afternoon* evokes the sense of duende or gloria through the mythic dimension of the bullfight buried in the secret structure of the book.

Secret Things: Sun, Sacrifice, *Cojones*

After the discussion of wine and the feeling of Dionysian ecstasy produced by a great faena, Hemingway concludes his first chapter with another apparently gratuitous passage, this time about the sun. Like the evocation of Cagancho's magical faena, this passage was added to the typescript in longhand by the author. Rather enigmatically, the narrator says that the best bullfight for a beginner to see would be on a hot, sunny day, because the entire spectacle has been built on the assumption that the sun will shine. If it does not, "over a third of the bullfight is missing." Of course the other two thirds are the matador and the bull, completing the triad of man, animal, and nature. Hemingway does not attempt to explain his cryptic words, allowing the sun, like the blood and wine earlier, to reverberate in the reader's mind. Here his prose begins to resemble lyric poetry in its preference for showing over telling, for image over explanation, for implication over statement.

The absolute importance of the sun in the bullfight is well known to anyone who has attended corridas. The ring itself is divided into two halves, *sol y sombra*, sun and shade. The bullfight season in Spain, from April through October, corresponds to the warmest, sunniest part of the year. Every plaza de toros is oriented so that about half of the arena will be in the light, the other half in the shade at the hour when most bullfights begin—usually sometime between four and seven in the afternoon. As Montherlant has noted, Spaniards have an acute sense for the subtleties of sun and shade. In his novel *Les Bestiares* (translated as *The Bullfighters*), probably checked out by Hemingway at Sylvia Beach's lending library in Paris in 1926, Montherlant related the bull to the ancient worship of the sun. In the plaza, the sun or the life-principle illuminates the giving of death by the man and the loss of life by the animal. The substance of the bull's life-force, his blood, is also the sign of his wounding and death. Without the sun, the bull's blood—dual symbol of life and death—does not shine on the animal's neck. It has been said that one of the few times the sight of blood does not repel human beings is when it streams from the hump of muscle in the bull's neck during a corrida. In fact, far from being repulsive, the blood may even have an esthetic quality for the aficionado as it flows and gleams in the sunlight, the bright red against the black of the bull's hide.

So in the first chapter of his book, Hemingway has approached the bullfight from the outside through an explanation of facts, but more important, from the inside through an apparently arbitrary evocation of three fundamental images or symbols—blood, wine, sun. They are important elements in most religions, from primitive nature worship and fertility rituals to Catholicism, in which the eucharistic wine represents the blood of Christ and the host recalls the solar circle. All three symbols converge around the potent, central figure of the bull, whose blood is spilled inevitably, and to a lesser extent around the matador, who will perhaps shed his own blood in the sacrifice of the animal that was worshiped as a god for thousands of years.

The spectators, like the public at the performance of an ancient Greek tragedy or the community of the faithful at the celebration of a Mass, will participate in the rite through their necessary presence, and ideally will achieve a sense of ecstasy, catharsis, and renewal. The remainder of *Death in the Afternoon* will develop this symbolic, mythic undercurrent through the subtle use of primordial symbols expressed in rhythmic prose. This is the deep, hidden structure of the book, the source of its originality, power, and meaning.

Now that we have seen Hemingway's secret method in the opening chapter, let us follow it briefly through the most significant parts of the book. The beginning of the next chapter reverts to the tone of a treatise on bullfighting, defining the spectacle again as a tragedy, not a sport or equal contest in the Anglo-Saxon tradition. In contrast to the corrida, sports do not deal with death but with victory; they replace the bullfight's avoidance of death with the avoidance of defeat. The narrator says that it "takes more cojones" to be a sportsman when death is part of the game. This is the book's first mention of testicles or *cojones*, a word that frequently interlards the discourse of Spaniards (as it did Hemingway's, whether he was speaking in English or Spanish). The valor of a matador is popularly believed to reside in his testicles, like the fierceness of the fighting bull. When castrated, the bull becomes a *manso* or mild, tame animal. The manso is concerned only with avoiding danger, while the great fighting bull actually prefers danger and even death to escape or surrender. Thus Hemingway associated cojones not only with courage, daring, and masculinity, but also with a sense of death. He once called critics the mansos or eunuchs of literature because they do not have or understand the writer's tragic sense of life and death. Cojones, whether the bull's or the man's, are another one of the recurring images in the deep structure of *Death in the Afternoon*.

Since the technique of toreo is more readily discernible in a state of imperfection, Hemingway now advises novice aficionados to attend a *novillada*, or apprentice fight, before they see a corrida with fully grown bulls. Accordingly, he launches into an apparently logical description of a novillada he saw one very hot Sunday in Madrid. The clumsy Basque *novillero* Hernandorena suffered a massive horn wound that day because of his suicidal insistence on receiving the bull's charge from a kneeling position. The declared purpose of this lengthy description is to give the reader an instructive example of faulty technique at a novillada, yet a paragraph inserted into the original typescript of the book, preserved in the final printed version, reveals a more subtle, deeper purpose. In this paragraph Hemingway tells how he awoke in the night, trying to remember what it was that he had really seen in Hernandorena's goring that was significant and eluded his memory. Then he got it: it was the dirtiness of the man's breeches and underwear and "the clean, clean, unbearably clean whiteness of the thigh bone that I had seen, and it was that which was important." In other words, Hemingway denies his own proclaimed purpose for including this episode here—to show how a bullfighter's imperfect technique can be instructive for a novice spectator. The real purpose of this passage is not pedagogical but esthetic and psychological: the problem was one of the writer keeping his eyes wide open, looking unflinchingly at the act, preserving it in his memory somewhere between the conscious and the subconscious, and depicting it truthfully in words. Hernandorena's bloody wound, revealing the depth of bone beneath the surface of clothing and skin, belongs to that irrational undercurrent of the book which attempts to reach the deeper layers of the mind.

As if he were testing the reader's stomach, Hemingway proceeds with a discussion of the *capeas*, informal bullfights or bull-baitings in village squares; they usually contain more violence and cruelty than formal corridas. If the village or town can afford to buy the bull, the animal may be killed by the male populace swarming over him with rocks, sticks, daggers, and knives until he sways and goes down. This kind of collective brutality is disappearing from most of Spain, but still survives in some rural areas.

If a town or village cannot afford to purchase the bull, an older animal who has been fought before is used; he may be so knowledgeable of men on foot that he is said to know Latin. Hemingway tells the story of one such bull in the province of Valencia who killed sixteen men and boys and wounded over sixty. In order to avenge the death of their brother who had been killed by the animal, a gypsy boy and his sister followed this bull for two years, hoping to assassinate him in the village capeas. When bull baiting was temporarily abolished by government order, the animal's owner sent him to the slaughterhouse in Valencia. The two gypsies followed him there, and the boy was given permission to slay the bull that had killed his brother. While the animal was still in a cage, the boy dug out the bull's eyes, spitting into the sockets, and killed him by severing the spine with a dagger between the neck vertebrae. He then cut off the bull's testicles, which he and his sister roasted on sticks over a small fire "at the edge of the dusty street outside the slaughterhouse."

The anecdotes of the village capeas and of the bull in Valencia round out Hemingway's introduction of the ancient, sacrificial dimension of the bullfight. The capeas are the closest modern survivals of the primitive rituals of sacrifice in which the god, horned or human, was slain and eaten by his worshipers. The gypsy boy and girl who slay the bull and eat his testicles are responding to the same primordial instinct as the participants in the ancient mysteries of sacrifice and communion with the dead god. It is not by chance that the brother and sister are gypsies, a people who have managed to preserve the old ways of life more than any other in Europe. We can be almost certain that Hemingway invented or at least embellished this anecdote; he gives no source and tells the story from the point of view of an omniscient narrator in a work of fiction. By having the gypsy boy and girl consume the bull's testicles, the author implies that they absorb the animal's life-force as the worshipers in remote sacrificial rites supposedly acquired the strength of the dead god, bull, or man. If Hemingway awakens echoes of ancient religions here, these are always masculine and pre-Christian: the bull represents the generative, male power. The ancient cults of bull-gods in the Mediterranean basin were replaced in Christianity by the worship of the lamb and the Virgin Mary, symbols of meekness and femininity. Unlike other twentieth-century artists who believed the creative instinct was mainly feminine—Joyce and D.H. Lawrence come to mind—Hemingway, at this stage of his career, expressed the male principle.

The first two chapters of *Death in the Afternoon* form a kind of rite of passage for the reader. The visceral accounts of horses slain by bulls, the stories of Hernandorena's terrible goring, the bloody village capeas, and the brutal assassination of the bull in Valencia by the gypsy boy are so many tests of the reader's fortitude. If he has survived the trial, he is prepared to learn the technical facts of the corrida. He has proved his mettle and he knows that the bullfight is not sport but a tragedy demanding blood and death. He has passed through a labyrinth, a subtle initiation into the irrational, mythic ritual of the corrida, revealed through a secret structure of primordial symbols—blood, wine, sun, cojones.

Secret Structure: From the Bullfight to Spain

After describing the plaza de toros and the sorting of the animals in the corrals, Hemingway tells the reader where and when to see bullfights in Spain. He ends up by following the book's general trajectory from toreo to Spain and Spanish life. When he says that Aranjuez would be a good place in which to see one's first corrida, for example, he soon forgets about bullfighting and proceeds to recreate the town's life and scenery. Although he has been accused of sounding like a cross between Baedeker and Duncan Hines in these sections, he does much more than merely describe the monuments and cuisine of Spain. In a wonderful, revealing passage on

Aranjuez, Hemingway does not call it the Spanish Versailles as so many travel writers have done, nor does he depict the royal palaces and gardens. On the contrary, he reduces all of the historic and cultural background of the town to one magnificently scornful sentence: "You can find the sights in Baedeker." Instead of describing the sights, he tells us how to live in Aranjuez and penetrates directly into the actual, present life of the town—its swift river, tall trees, and rich gardens, the succulent strawberries and thumb-thick asparagus for which the area is famous in spring, the booths where chickens are roasted and steaks are grilled over charcoal fires and washed down with Valdepeñas wine. But all is not pleasure in Aranjuez; the author remembers to include the Goyesque army of cripples and beggars who follow the ferias throughout the peninsula. Hemingway's Spain: a land of contrasts.

The sensual atmosphere in Aranjuez is deepened by an evocation of the beauty of Spanish women, observed in the "girl inspection" with opera or field glasses at the bullring in Aranjuez, or during the evening *paseo* in the town square. Here once more there is a spontaneous association of ideas—between the sensual imbibing of food and wine and the sexual attraction of women, all related to the erotic undercurrent of the bullfight. In the original manuscript of this section, Hemingway wrote a telling passage which he later deleted, perhaps because it was too personal and may have offended his wife Pauline (who often typed for him during this period):

> I have seen at least six girls in Spain so beautiful that it would tear
> your heart out and let you realize your life had been wasted to see
> them. I saw a girl one evening at Escorial ... who was so beautiful
> it made the ribs in back of your lungs ache to see her....

In his myth-making fashion, Ernest concludes the passage by suggesting, ever so ambiguously, that he might have spent the night with this beautiful girl.

Under the pretense of telling the reader where to see bullfights, Hemingway continues his search for the deepest core of Spanish life with an evocation of Madrid. Although some of his favorite bullfighters—Maera, Juan Belmonte, Cayetano Ordóñez—were from Andalusia, by this time he had acquired a predilection for the heartland of the Iberian Peninsula: Castile and the capital of Spain, Madrid, located in the precise geographic center of the country. While nearly all other foreign writers on Spain have preferred the sunnier, more "exotic" Andalusia, Hemingway detested the picturesque costumes, local color, and exploitation of tourists in southern Spain; he did not feel as comfortable with the facile Andalusians as he did with the more austere Castilians, Navarrese, Basques, and Aragonese. He also favored the higher average elevation of central and northern Spain, the invigorating contrasts of heat and cold, and the mountain climate of cities like Madrid and Pamplona. If the Navarrese were his favorite people in Spain, he also felt that the *madrileños* were fine and that Madrid alone contained "the essence" of Spain. With its tonic climate of high cloudless sky and clear mountain air (polluted by smog since Hemingway's death), some of the best bullfights and the most knowledgeable afición in the world, the Prado museum, and the city's proximity to such good towns as El Escorial, Toledo, Ávila, Segovia, and La Granja, "it makes you feel very badly, all questions of immortality aside, to know that you will have to die" and never see Madrid again.

When he first traveled there in 1923, Hemingway did not understand the city because it had none of the picturesque look he had expected to find. Everything seemed too simple and unadorned. He compared the Prado, for example, to a naked woman, because of the accessibility of the paintings and the simplicity with which they were hung; he thought there had to be a catch somewhere. Hemingway was also befuddled by the madrileños' habit of staying up most of the night, then rising from bed late in the morning—the reverse of his own daily habit of waking at dawn. But as he returned to Madrid each summer, he began to be accustomed and to acquire an affection for this "strange place." By the time he wrote *Death in the Afternoon*, it had become one of his favorite cities, a good town for working and living. In his imagination, Madrid was related to the sun because of its cloudless skies and dry heat, and because so many of its inhabitants stay up most of the night in the summer "until that cool time that comes just before daylight." This thought triggered Hemingway's memories of postwar Constantinople, where people also exhausted the night then drove out to the Bosphorus to see the sunrise. One memory awakened another, more recent, of the time he was driving in the country late one night near Kansas City and saw the glow of a great fire on the horizon. He drove toward the fire, only to discover that it was the sunrise. By following his memories, writing spontaneously with a free association of images, Hemingway thus expressed the nature of Madrid—the "essence" of Spain—through images of the night, heat, fire, and sun.

It was appropriate that he concluded this section on Madrid with a condemnation of those overwritten, one-visit books with a false epic tone, like Waldo Frank's *Virgin Spain*. In a letter several years earlier, Hemingway had said that Spain lost its virginity before any other country. By this he did not mean that it had been spoiled by the forces of modernization and progress, like America and other Western European countries. On the contrary, Spain had lost its virginity in the sense that it was the most ancient, sensual, "pagan" country in Europe despite its official veneer of orthodoxy and Catholicism. To know Spain, one cannot use the "bedside mysticism," the "pseudo-scientific jargon," and the "false epic quality" employed by intellectual authors in a state of sexual frustration and sublimation— Hemingway called their work "erectile writing." In order to know Spain one must use all the senses, the cojones and the whole body as well as the mind: one must immerse himself in the life of the fiesta, imbibe the wine of the country, eat the abundant fruits of the earth and seas, exhaust the night, love women, participate in the ritual of sacrifice in the bullring beneath the sun in the high cloudless skies. And to write about this experience, Hemingway tells us that an author should use clear, unadorned language. By implication, we can add that the writer should prefer a lyrical to an epic tone, using the expressive rhythms of prose and concrete images to imply rather than declare his meaning, much like a poet.

Hemingway, *Torerista*

By now the author assumes that his reader has seen a bullfight, and the tone of the book changes. Instead of continuing directly with a formal description of the corrida, Hemingway introduces the Old Lady, who will serve as a foil to the narrator. First he goes back in time to recall the golden age of toreo during the competition between Joselito and Belmonte (1914–20), which led to the present state of the spectacle. Then he recalls the young "phenomenons" who raised great hopes but ultimately failed to regenerate bullfighting. This section of the book is chatty and journalistic, dropping enticing details about the matadores' private lives; it would have benefited from intelligent editing. Here Hemingway commits the sin of which he was very critical in other aficionados—being a *torerista* or worshiper of bullfighters rather than a *torista* or admirer of the fighting bull as the center of the fiesta. In a sentence deleted from the manuscript, he had said that there are two loose groupings of aficionados: "those who care most for the bull fighters and those who care most for the bulls." The situation is similar if not identical to horseracing, where the most knowledgeable and passionate are those who love the horses, not the jockeys, trainers, or owners. The deterioration of toreo derives from human beings, not from the animals. For his part, the matador soon learns from experience that the real beast in the plaza is not the animal but the public, as in the famous ending of Blasco Ibáñez's *Blood and Sand*. Because the danger of painful wounding and death is always on the points of the bull's horns, toreros, their managers, the breeders, and all the supernumeraries of the taurine world have customarily done as much as their cunning, influence, and power have enabled them in order to lessen risk and increase profit. For this reason, many of the best aficionados have normally reserved their greatest interest, respect, and admiration for the fighting bull and not for the man, who is often a mere intermediary, like the priest in a Mass. Hemingway tried to emulate such aficionados, but tended inevitably to fall back into an almost puerile adulation of matadores which became more dominant as he grew older. The reasons for this tendency may have lain in his original identification with the torero as a man who must learn to live with fear and death, as the young ambulance driver in Italy had been forced to learn; in his recognition of the terrible solitude of the matador with the bull before the implacable crowd, as a parallel to the writer's loneliness with a sheet of paper before the unpardoning judgment of history.

So in these middle chapters of *Death in the Afternoon,* Hemingway prattles on about bullfighters who have nearly all been forgotten, while the figure of the bull practically disappears. This part of the book has aged more than any other. The overemphasis on the personalities of toreros is a major flaw relieved occasionally by a memorable portrait, like the one of Hemingway's greatest hero at this time of his life, Maera. The writer paid this matador the highest compliment he would ever offer to any man: "Era muy hombre." In a curious sentence deleted from the manuscript, he went even further in his praise by saying that after Maera's death, "I felt the worse I've felt after any man dead so far." Since Dr. Hemingway had died by this time, we can understand the force of the writer's statement and his reasons for removing it from the book. Most bullfight critics and aficionados who were around in the 1920s believe that Hemingway exaggerated Maera's value and importance in toreo, perhaps because he knew the man personally and because the matador died in 1924, before the young, impressionable Ernest had become an experienced connoisseur.

Hemingway goes on with his treatment of the "personal element" in bullfighting, turning to a pair of toreros who had appeared early in his fiction—Nicanor Villalta and Cayetano Ordóñez. Describing Ordóñez's short, happy life as the new messiah of toreo, and his shameful fall into ignominy after his first serious goring, the author is led by an association of ideas to discuss the theme of honor in and out of the bullring. When Cayetano showed cowardice truly and unmistakably, he lost his honor. Pride is the strongest characteristic of the Spaniard, Hemingway tells us, and it is a matter of pride to keep one's honor. Here he confuses two Spanish words, *honor* and *pundonor*. *Honor* is an inner, moral quality or virtue, while *pundonor* is a point or state of honor which involves one's reputation and depends to an extent upon the opinion of others—as in the hundreds of classic Spanish plays by Lope de Vega, Tirso de Molina, Pedro Calderón de la Barca, and other dramatists of the sixteenth and seventeenth centuries. Although he gets the words wrong, it is clear that Hemingway is always concerned with the inner quality, not with its social manifestation. As in so many aspects of Spanish life, he goes directly to the heart of his subject.

Only a few years earlier, in the famous passage of *A Farewell to Arms*, the narrator Frederic Henry had said that "abstract words" like honor, glory, and courage sounded obscene beside the concrete names of villages, roads, and rivers where soldiers had fought and died. Unlike his creator and his fictional brother Jake Barnes in *The Sun Also Rises*, Henry was not able to heal his wounds after the war in Spain, nor to meet bullfighters and other men for whom courage, honor, and glory were real qualities to be lived by, not empty slogans of chauvinistic propaganda and wartime rhetoric. For a Spaniard, no matter how dishonest, Hemingway tells us, honor "is as real a thing as water, wine, or olive oil." *Death in the Afternoon* and later works, like *For Whom the Bell Tolls* and *The Old Man and the Sea*, are the stories of men and women—toreros, guerrillas, or a fisherman—who succeed or fail in various degrees to keep their sense of honor in times of stress and danger.

Hemingway, *Torista*

After all the gossipy chatter on toreros, Hemingway dedicates the following, central portion of his book to *El Señor Toro*, the real protagonist of the bullfight. The fighting bull, he tells us, comes from a strain that descends directly from the wild bulls that used to range over the peninsula, and is as different from the domestic bull as a wolf from a dog. The bravery of the bull is the root of the whole corrida; it is "unearthly and unbelievable." People who have not been close to the fiesta, or have never faced an animal with brave blood in a ring, find it difficult to understand the seemingly preternatural speed, power, and ferociousness of the fighting bull. Unlike nearly all other animals, he will attack and destroy even when not motivated by hunger. He is more fierce than predators and also more deadly, as was proven in barbarous spectacles of former times when bulls confronted elephants, lions, and tigers in the plaza. Hemingway tells anecdotes of bulls who have charged motor cars and stopped trains, slaughtered as many as seven horses in a single corrida, jumped the barrera and maimed or gored spectators to death.

The purpose of these taurine horror stories is to build up the undercurrent of fear that flows throughout the book; the bull is surrounded by such an aura of terror that he nearly comes to represent all of the dark, destructive forces of nature, as in much of Picasso's work. Yet the true fighting bull also possesses a quality, called nobility in Spanish, "which is the most extraordinary part of the whole business." Unlike the lion and the tiger, for example, he does not use stealth against his enemies: he is frank, simple, and straight in his charges, and thus easily deceived. Because of his nobility we could say of the fighting bull, more truly than of the lion, that he is the king of beasts. This quality, combined with his fierceness and power, give an atmosphere of seriousness, dignity, and fear to the corrida which justifies its tragedy of necessary death.

The description of the bulls' potency awakens the Old Lady's curiosity about their "love life." Animals destined for the ring are not allowed to breed, the narrator tells her, but a seed bull can service more than fifty cows. The very first photograph at the end of *Death in the Afternoon* shows a mighty seed bull who has fathered 822 sons for the ring; his "hind quarters are light as a calf's," the author says in the caption, "but all the rest is built into the bull's own monument" of his penis and testicles. The Old Lady's frivolous question leads to a development of the book's underlying themes of sexuality and the traditional religious dimension of the bull, long worshiped as a male divinity.

Amid his treatment of the breeding, raising, testing, and fighting of the bull, Hemingway inserted his "Natural History of the Dead," which has always been a source of confusion to readers and critics. In it the author describes, with the cold detachment of a naturalist describing animals or plants, the gore and cruelty of war, especially during the bloody Austrian offensive of June 1918. Why did Hemingway include this extensive piece— without a single reference to bullfighting—in a book about toreo? As we have seen, *Death in the Afternoon* is a work about death anywhere, not only in the plaza de toros. As Hemingway had observed the corrida with his eyes wide open, he wished to observe and describe warfare with the same forthrightness. The various references to Goya, in the sections of the book on both bullfighting and war, show that Hemingway was attempting to do in words what the Spaniard had done in the etchings of *La Tauromaquia* and *The Disasters of War*. "A Natural History ... " would also be included in Hemingway's collection of short stories, *Winner Take Nothing* (1933), yet he preferred to print it first in the bullfight book for a good reason. In a letter written between the publication of the two works, he said that he used the piece not "directly, but indirectly ... to make a point." The point was that war is far more terrible and cruel than bullfighting. While death is partial to bulls, horses, and men in the plaza, it is indiscriminate in war—as shown by Hemingway's paragraph on the explosion of a munitions factory whose employees were women. Even outside of war, most humans die like animals. In spite of Hemingway's intention of not writing an apology for the corrida, the point of "A Natural History of the Dead" was in fact to show the relatively unimportant amount of cruelty and bloodshed in bullfighting when compared to modern war.

In the last pages dedicated to the bull in this central portion of the book, Hemingway gives the best treatment I have ever read of the querencia, or the place in the ring where the fighting bull tends to go and where he feels most comfortable. The writer was intrigued by the mentality of animals and considered himself somewhat of an expert on the subject. To him the development of querencia was the most interesting change in the bull's brain during the unfolding of a corrida. The animal can develop a querencia for a cool spot in the ring on a hot day, for a place where he has enjoyed success or can smell the blood of a wounded horse, for a location where he feels secure—like the *toril* from which he entered the plaza, or the barrera where he has a back-to-the-wall sense of protection. From his love and understanding of the fighting bull, I believe Hemingway himself began to sympathize with the animal's feeling for a querencia or a place where he felt secure and confident. From his experience as a fisherman and hunter and as a soldier with a knowledge of tactics and terrain, he had already acquired a feeling for the importance of location. Spaniards always have a knack for detecting whether or not a place has *ambiente*—the complex, indefinable balance of light and shade, comfort and naturalness, visibility and inconspicuousness, human presence or absence which makes a location habitable at a given moment or at any time. A place either has or does not have ambiente, and Hemingway knew this as intuitively as the Spaniards. All the places where he lived and worked had it; his favorite bars, cafés and restaurants had it, and within those locales, his favorite stool, table, or window. There he was just as strong, confident, and dangerous as a fighting bull in his querencia.

Secret Structure: Appearances versus R*eality*

After the well-placed discourse on the fighting bull in the center of his book, Hemingway defines his own stance in relation to the decadence of modern bulls and toreros. If an aficionado makes the error of placing himself in the bullfighters' position, he will condone their disasters and their failures to work with all kinds of animals, as some of the old matadores could do. By seeing the fiesta from the toreros' point of view, the aficionado becomes an accomplice to the decay in standards that characterizes the modern spectacle. On the other hand, if he is more of a torista than a torerista, if he stands for the real fighting bull and for the complete bullfight, the individual spectator becomes a kind of moral arbiter who knows what is good and what is bad, who lets nothing confuse his standards. A bullfighter, Hemingway says, will not be superior to his audience for long. If complete toreros are to return to the ring, there must be a nucleus of spectators who prefer honesty to tricks, real danger to the appearance of danger, the integral corrida to partial brilliance of cape or muleta. Of course Hemingway's definition of the true aficionado could also serve as a code for the reader of literature or the spectator of drama, cinema, and television.

The true aficionado must learn how to distinguish between what is real and what seems to be real; he must be both an esthetic and an ethical witness. Like so many aspects of Spanish life, the corrida has an attractive, official exterior which often conceals a seamy side. One example is bullfight journalism, which frequently reports the fiesta with inflated rhetoric while sustaining itself on the gratuities given by toreros to the newspaper critics. The venality of journalists and the pervasive use of the *propina* or baksheesh at every level of the business are two examples of the economic corruption of the bullfight. Hemingway knew it from the inside, since he used to prepare the envelopes, containing money and the torero's card, from his friend Sidney Franklin to the critics of the Madrid papers. (He did not admit this in *Death*, but in a passage deleted from his last work, "Dangerous Summer.") As he once said, a corrida is not always art, but "it is always business."

In the final chapters of the book, leading up to the epilogue, Hemingway treats in an orderly way the progressive *suertes* of toreo from the time the bull enters the ring to his death by sword, always telling the reader how to distinguish between real and simulated danger. After the technical sections, he lightens the tone with digressions. In one of the last, the Old Lady asks the narrator to tell another story, this time about the living, not the dead. As before, she shows her preference for erotic stories and requests a tale of homosexuals. The narrator complies by telling her what he called, in a marginal note to himself in the manuscript, a "Story of 2 fairies...." In Paris, a newspaperman friend of his had met two "fine, clean-cut looking" American youths. The older of the two forced the other to comply with his sexual advances, perhaps because of superior strength and certainly because of his money. From a distraught victim, the younger man quickly became a willing accomplice, a kind of male prostitute maintained by his wealthy friend.

In order to understand the meaning and function of this story within the context of *Death in the Afternoon*, we should remember that for Hemingway, homosexuality was a kind of ultimate in degradation. Partly because he had rejected his mother and the artistic, cultural qualities she represented for him, he detested men in whom feminine aspects prevailed. This story of people who are alive makes an indirect point, like the "Natural History of the Dead": the cruelty of man to man is immeasurably greater than the cruelty of man to animal in the bullring. The Paris story carries the point even farther, because the psychological suffering inflicted by the wealthy homosexual on his helpless friend—we remember the younger man's sobs and despairing scream—surpasses even the terrible physical pain portrayed in the piece on wartime Italy. Hemingway knew from his own experience at Fossalta that death and the actual wounds of war cause less suffering than the aftermath of nightmares, insomnia, and the feeling of nada. He called death "a sovereign remedy for all misfortunes"; the agony of the living is more prolonged, and it lacks the finality, the dignity of death.

Finally, the Paris story develops the important theme of appearances versus reality. When the narrator (possibly Hemingway himself here) saw the two youths sitting on the terrace of the Café des Deux Magots, wearing well-tailored clothes, they looked as clean-cut as ever except that the younger man "had had his hair hennaed." After this story representing the extremity of sexual and moral corruption, Hemingway threw the Old Lady out of his book.

Since his foil was gone, the narrator had to create his own digressions now. He took advantage of the opportunity to answer a recent criticism of his work by Aldous Huxley in an essay entitled "Foreheads Villainous Low," where the English novelist accused Hemingway of consciously avoiding the appearance of education and culture in his work. The accusation was largely true: Ernest's rejection of his mother included the values she represented—formal education, socially respectable art, high culture. In his reply to Huxley, Hemingway did not admit this; perhaps he was not entirely aware of how much his mother had influenced his life and writing. Instead, he defends his own method in fiction and implicitly in *Death*. He accuses Huxley of being a solemn intellectual writer who creates his characters out of his head alone, while a greater novelist projects the people in his work "from his head, from his heart and from all there is of him"—including his cojones, we could add with Hemingway's approval no doubt. Unlike the intellectual author who overanalyzes experience, the great novelist writes so truly that he can leave out things that he knows and yet give the reader a feeling of those things: the iceberg theory. In a famous sentence, Hemingway says that

"Prose is architecture, not interior decoration, and the Baroque is over." Although he is ostensibly discussing fiction, his words are even more applicable to *Death in the Afternoon* than to his novels and short stories. The bullfight book is architecture because its meaning is revealed more by the deep structure than by the surface decoration. The work is like an iceberg whose tip consists of a manual on the bullfight and whose submerged body contains the deeper levels of life, death, sacrifice, and renewal, expressed in primordial symbols and rhythmic prose.

The final digression in *Death* is Hemingway's best piece of prose on Spanish art. After so many allusions to the Prado and to Goya, it was only a matter of time before he compared this painter to the other classic Spanish artists, Greco and Velázquez, whose major works are also housed in that museum. Hemingway recognized the greatness of all three, but preferred Goya for reasons consistent with his own personality and art. Ever since he had first seen the artist's hundreds of oils, cartoons, etchings, and lithographs at the Prado in 1923, Ernest had been under a spell. He perceived the parallels between his own life and the painter's: both were born in the provinces and gravitated to metropolitan centers of artistic activity—Madrid or Paris; both were self-educated men who felt uncomfortable in the intellectual circles of the court or city. Each was a revolutionary in his art, defying the accepted rules and working against the grand manner of his predecessors. Both Goya and Hemingway were anticlerical and liberal in politics, and supreme lovers of the bullfight. One of the Spaniard's nicknames was "Don Francisco de los Toros"; he was the first man to consider the corrida worthy of treatment by a serious artist. In the etchings of his *Tauromaquia*, he portrayed what he saw and felt, as Hemingway would do in the later miniatures of *in our time*, with a similar taste for the more violent, visceral aspects of the fiesta. Both Spaniard and American lived in periods of crisis and were profoundly marked by the great wars of their times, of which they were two of the most honest, moving witnesses. The wartime interchapters of *in our time*, like *A Farewell to Arms*, "A Natural History of the Dead," and *For Whom the Bell Tolls*, were Hemingway's equivalent of the *Disasters of War*.

More than almost any modern painter, Goya was a "narrative" artist who held a natural attraction for a writer of fiction: with the exception of his portraits, his works tend to depict episodes caught at the moment of maximum tension. His subjects are usually drawn not from classical or Christian tradition but from the life and events of his time, like Hemingway's. If Velázquez painted from the head and Greco from the spirit, Goya painted from all the senses, his body, heart, head, spirit, and cojones.

In one of the fullest, most revealing sentences he ever wrote, the writer offered this personal tribute to his favorite painter:

> Goya did not believe in costume but he did believe in blacks and in grays, in dust and in light, in high places rising from plains, in the country around Madrid, in movement, in his own cojones, in painting, in etching, and in what he had seen, felt, touched, handled, smelled, enjoyed, drunk, mounted, suffered, spewed-up, lain-with, suspected, observed, loved, hated, lusted, feared, detested, admired, loathed, and destroyed.

If we substitute "writing" for "painting" and "etching," we would have Hemingway's most forceful expression of his own artistic convictions and methods in *Death in the Afternoon*.

The Art of Killing

The last regular chapter of *Death in the Afternoon* deals with the final suerte of the bullfight; it is the longest and one of the most significant chapters in the book. The actual kill used to be considered the supreme action performed by the torero in the ring, as indicated by the very name of matador. But since the golden age and the later decadence of bullfighting, with its almost exclusive emphasis on the esthetic use of cape and muleta, the art of killing has declined. Hemingway shows his adherence to the old ways and to the integral bullfight by granting more space to the sword than to any other aspect of toreo.

The kill is the most dangerous part of the corrida. If he is performing properly, the man must expose himself to the bull's horns more than at any other moment: this is the *momento de la verdad*. The true killer must have more courage, pride, and honor than the ordinary torero. As a soldier and hunter, Hemingway identified himself with the strong, manly swordsmen more than with the graceful, "feminine" artists of cape and muleta. When a man is still in rebellion against death, he tells us, he has pleasure in taking to himself the divine power of giving death. A man kills from pride—a pagan virtue but a Christian sin. It is pride that makes the bullfight.

Hemingway was one of the few writers with the courage to discuss the "spiritual" qualities of killing. Since most of those who enjoy the kill have been simple men, and those who do not enjoy it have been more articulate, there has been little fair treatment of the subject. Hemingway, who was both simple and articulate, makes one of his most eloquent statements on the esthetic enjoyment of killing in this section of *Death in the Afternoon*. His father had taught him to kill cleanly and never to kill more than he could use to eat. Since Ernest was in rebellion against death more than Dr. Hemingway, he did not always follow the second part of his father's advice. Although he never went in over the horn for the kill himself, he witnessed the deaths of hundreds of fighting bulls in his lifetime, caught countless fish in rivers and seas, and shot thousands of animals ranging from jack rabbits to lions and water buffaloes. His indiscriminate killing of animals is difficult to excuse; it will not be pardoned easily by future generations more aware of life's fragility. Hemingway walked across the earth like a giant, leaving behind a trail of blood and carcasses. His need to kill was a measure of his pride, anxiety, and unhappiness. He killed well, with enjoyment but also with desperation, as if the giving of death postponed his own mortality.

After describing the technique of the kill in the bullring, Hemingway ended this last regular chapter with a treatment of the culture of death in Spain. Whereas most foreign writers on the country lump all Spaniards together when attempting to analyze the national character, Hemingway knew the peninsula too well to make that mistake. For him, the Spaniards' interest in death was based on a common sense as hard and dry as the plains of Castile, and he believed that common sense diminishes in hardness and dryness as it moves away from Castile. The Castilian peasant lives in a country with a severe climate: *Nueve meses de invierno y tres de infierno*, as the proverb has it ("Nine months of winter and three of hell"). He lives austerely, with little comfort and few possessions. He knows that death is an unescapable reality, and he has a religion that says life is much shorter than death. Therefore he can afford to risk his life with an impracticality that would be difficult to understand in the countries of northern Europe. In his lucid analysis, Hemingway coincided with other modern Spanish writers such as Unamuno and Lorca, who saw the Castilian as a man with an acute sense of death and a tragic sense of life.

The Navarrese and Aragonese in the north of the peninsula also have a bravery that comes from pride and honor. The Andalusians, who have given the country many of her best toreros and fighting bulls, have a strong sense of death too. But unlike most foreigners, Hemingway did not worship the *andaluces* as being the wittiest, most daring, and characteristic Spaniards. Although he revered the name of Joselito, admired Belmonte, and worshiped Maera, he believed that southern Spain was becoming less important as a center of toreo; his belief turned out to be mistaken. He thought the bravery of the Castilian to be tragic and that of the Navarrese and Aragonese "romantic," while the southerner's is "picturesque." Bullfighters from the south, especially those who follow the Sevillian school of toreo, tend to have a varied, flowery style that gives more importance to cape, banderillas, or muleta than to the kill. Many of the gypsy toreros are Andalusians, and Hemingway was not a great admirer of the *gitanos* either in or out of the ring. (El Gallo, Joselito, and Cagancho were notable exceptions.) While they could be brilliant with the right kind of bull, he believed they did not have the simple, steady bravery nor the sense of duty to the public possessed by the fighters from central Spain whom he preferred, like Marcial Lalanda and Nicanor Villalta.

For one reason or another, the peoples from the remaining areas of the country do not have the special feeling for death required by the bullfight, according to Hemingway. In Galicia on the Atlantic coast, death is not "a mystery to be sought and meditated on"—as in central Spain—but rather a daily peril to be avoided. In Catalonia, life is too practical and businesslike for there to be much feeling about death.

As we would expect, there is a direct proportion between the sense of death in the various regions of Spain and Hemingway's admiration for the inhabitants. The Basque-Navarrese and the Castilians were his favorite peoples in Spain, followed by the Aragonese and Andalusians. In this as in so many other things, he was different from most of the foreigners who have traveled in the Iberian Peninsula over the last several hundred years.

The Tragic Sense

In a sentence deleted from an earlier chapter of *Death in the Afternoon*, Hemingway said: "To get Spain into a book is very hard." He believed his friend Joan Miró had managed to get Spain into a painting, *The Farm*, which the writer had purchased in 1925 and considered one of his most cherished possessions. Since nearly everything in his Spain had to do with bullfighting in one way or another, Hemingway tried to get the whole country into his book. Of course he failed, but in Chapter Twenty—his epilogue or coda, one of the best things he ever wrote—he would try to condense all of his thronging memories of Spain into a few pages. He knew that if you could see one part of the world clearly and wholly, it would stand for the rest.

The secret structure of *Death in the Afternoon* culminates in the last chapter. Since most of the epilogue does not deal directly with the bullfight, we realize that this has been a book about many things besides the corrida. In a letter to Arnold Gingrich, written soon after the publication of *Death*, Hemingway said:

Am glad you liked the last chapter in the last book—it is what the book is about but nobody seems to notice that. They think it is just a catalogue of things that were omitted. How would they like them to be put in? Framed in pictures or with a map?

What the book is about is of course Spain, its land, peoples, food, drinks, ways of life and death of which the bullfight is a supreme example; it is also about the writer's experience in a country he loved very much. As Robert W. Lewis has said, *Death* is really about Hemingway and "his love affair with Spain and all that passed between them."

In the epilogue, the secret structure of the book reveals itself in some of the primordial images and symbols that have been embedded in its prose—sun, heat, wine, blood, sacrifice, death, woman, sex. To take only one of these symbols, wine or alcohol in general, Hemingway recalls the year everyone drank so much at Pamplona (1924); drinking wine on picnics along the Irati River during San Fermín; the leather wineskins of Navarre; a boy carrying wicker-bound jugs of wine and everyone getting drunk on the train from Pamplona to Madrid (1925); the sweatbeaded pitchers of cold beer in Valencia; hard Asturian cider; "the beer place on the cool side of the street" beneath the Hotel Palace in Madrid; the earthen wine jars, twelve feet high, each with a different vintage, set side by side in a dark room of Miró's house at Montroig, then drinking the wine of that year (1929) and of the year before and so on; whisky in an earthen crock at Sidney Franklin's house; the cafés where the saucers pile up and drinks are tallied in pencil on the marble tabletops; riding back from Toledo in the car at night, washing out the dust with Fundador.

The sacramental use of wine or alcohol is accompanied by related images of death, blood, and sacrifice. For example, there is a cryptic reference to the death of the novillero Pedro Carreño, killed by a bull in 1930 (Hemingway was not in Spain at the time). According to some friends of the writer, people carried the dead torero's body through the streets, surrounded by torches, into the church where they put him naked on the altar. There are references to other gorings and deaths of bulls, horses, and men, but they are absorbed in the overwhelming affirmation of life contained in these pages: the fertility, abundance, and beauty of the Spanish earth, evoked just as powerfully here as in *The Sun Also Rises;* the immersion of all the senses in the fiesta sense of life embodied by the ferias of Pamplona, Madrid, Valencia, and so many other towns; the warm camaraderie of friends and aficionados, like the bullfight critic Rafael Hernández and the owner of the hotel in Pamplona, Juanito Quintana ("Que tal Juanito? Que tal, hombre, que tal?"); the sexual presence of women, always in the background. *Death in the Afternoon* is a book about tragedy and death, but even more, it is a book about a still greater mystery, life.

The last chapter of the work is a symbolic trip through Spain and through time—all of Hemingway's experience there between 1923 and 1932. The trip begins where it should: at the Prado in Madrid, the heart and essence of Spain. With the same organic, spontaneous association of images, memories, and ideas that has guided him in the body of the book, the narrator moves back and forth from Madrid to the provinces, and backward and forward in time from the past to the present. He remembers the places he loved most in the capital: the Prado, the streets and cafés full of people after midnight, the bullrings, the old Pensión Aguilar, the bare white mud hills looking toward Carabanchel from Luis Quintanilla's house, the Manzanares River along the Pardo road where he and Franklin swam with the toreros and their cheap whores. Then the towns near and around Madrid: Toledo; La Granja where they practiced capework on the gravelled paths between the shadows of the trees; Barco de Ávila with storks nesting on the houses or wheeling above the mountains.

From Madrid, Hemingway's memory naturally leads him to his other main querencia in Spain—Pamplona. He recalls the first two ferias of San Fermín when he had such a good time and "no one was nasty"; the cafés on the main plaza with all the bootblacks and the fine girls walking by; the Hotel Quintana with its friendly owner, good food, and all the rooms full. Then outside of Pamplona toward the Pyrenees, the landscapes of *The Sun Also Rises:* the countryside the color of ripe wheat; villages with churches and pelota courts; clouds coming across the mountains from the sea; the beech forests of the Irati with "trees like drawings in a child's fairy book"; the water of the river as clear as light; the hot days of summer and the cold mountain nights; the early morning smells and always trees with shade. Then there were all of the simple, natural things with the nobility of objects in a still life painting—the loops of twisted garlic, leather wineskins and saddlebags, rope-soled shoes, earthen pots, wooden pitchforks with branches for tines. If you had all of that, Hemingway said, "then you would have a little of Navarra."

Although Madrid and Navarre dominate this symbolic trip through Spain, other favorite places also appear: Valencia with its ice-cold beer and *horchata*, the smell of burnt powder, the flash and explosion of the *tracas* or fireworks during the feria each July; Saragossa at night on the bridge over the Ebro, the hills of baked clay, the red dust, and the small shade beside the dry rivers in Aragón; Santiago de Compostella in the rain, fishing for trout in the Tambre, the hills and pines of Galicia; the green country of the Basque provinces. Among the major regions of Spain, only Andalusia, Asturias, and Extremadura shine because of their absence.

Since the technical part of the bullfight has been dispatched, the prose of the final chapter is liberated: the sentences become longer and freer, the language more rhythmical and poetic. It is not by chance that portions of the epilogue to *Death in the Afternoon* have been included in an anthology of modern verse, since its language is as concrete, lyrical, and musical as a poem's. Entire sections of the prose can easily be arranged in metrical units. The language is tied together by the repetition of certain key phrases functioning like refrains: "If I could have made this enough of a book," "If it were more of a book," "it should have ...," "There ought to be ...," "Make all that come true again." These refrains bind together the dozens of memories from the past, evoked in an actual present. Hemingway "makes" the country by recreating all of the specific, sensual images in a living present, as if they would never change; this is the eternal Spain of *The Sun Also Rises*. As in the novel, human beings act out their brief lives against the enduring background of the Spanish earth.

By using the present tense predominantly to recall the past, Hemingway makes it "come true again" for himself and for the reader—in the same way he had recreated the movement and emotion of cape, banderillas, and muleta earlier in the book. Whereas he employed his rhythmic, ecstatic prose to make the bullfight itself in the previous works and in the main chapters of *Death in the Afternoon*, he uses it now to create the emotion of time. Nearly ten years had passed between Hemingway's first visit to Spain and the writing of the epilogue. He had gone through one marriage and a divorce, remarried, begotten two sons, lost his father, grown from an unknown young journalist to a famous, mature writer. Through a few subtle references, the narrator suggests that things have changed in the world and for him. He admits that he could not get all of the people and places he knew into his book, "nor all of us ourselves as we were then." Pamplona has changed for the worse; modern apartment buildings block the view of the mountains. Some of the trees in the forest of the Irati have been cut down by loggers, polluting the streams and killing the fish. The writer's friend Rafael Hernández says things are so changed that he won't return to Pamplona. Hemingway is wiser than his friend when he says toward the end of the epilogue: "Pamplona is changed, of course, but not as much as we are older." After a drink, things get much the way they were before.

Neither Hemingway nor any other writer can capture all of the complexity of life and death in a single work: "No. It is not enough of a book...." He accepts the limitations of art and the inevitability of change in his own life and in Spain. Although the past can be recreated—in Miró's *Farm* or the epilogue he is writing—it cannot be erased. He, his friends, and family will grow and change, and they will "all be gone before it's changed too much." Even when they are dead, it will rain again in the summer in the north and hawks will nest again in the Cathedral at Santiago. The author will be gone, but the Spanish earth will last; the sun will also rise. Individuals pass on, the species and nature endure. Life does not end; it renews itself.

In the epilogue, the tragic emotion of the bullfight, always related to death, becomes the more universal emotion of human life, whose law is also mortality. The elegiac rhythm of the prose slows to a decrescendo. *Death in the Afternoon* has been transformed, by the music and rhythm of its language, into Hemingway's most personal expression of the tragic sense of life.

NOTES

Epigraph: *Letters*, pp. 236–37.

EH probably began notes for bullfight book before *SAR:* MS #295 ("Bullfighting Manuscript Notes"), JFK. See also Robert W. Lewis, "The Making of *Death in the Afternoon*," in James Nagel (ed.), *Ernest Hemingway: The Writer in Context* (Madison: University of Wisconsin Press, 1984), pp. 36–37; Susan Beegel, "The Death of El Espartero: An Historic Matador Links 'The Undefeated' and *Death in the Afternoon*," *Hemingway Review* (Spring 1986), pp. 12–23.

EH's project for bullfight book (1925): EH to Dos Passos, 22 Apr. 1925 (Dos Passos, 22 Apr. 1925 (Dos Passos Collection, Univ. of Virginia). EH denied the rumor about this book in a letter to Carlos Baker, 1 Apr. 1951 (*The Writer as Artist*, p. 145n).

EH and Doughty's *Travels in Arabia Deserta:* EH to Perkins, 15 Apr. 1925 (*Letters*, p. 156).

R. Ford on bullfight: *Gatherings from Spain*, p. 339.

Robert Jordan on Spain: *FWBT*, p. 248.

Antonio Gala on bullfight: *Charlas con Troylo* (Madrid: Espasa-Calpe, 1981), p. 164.

EH said bullfight always a tragedy and tragedy requires dignity: "Bullfighting, Sport and Industry," *Fortune* (Mar. 1930), p. 83; *DIA*, p. 159.

References to suicide in *DIA:* pp. 3, 20, 122.

Dr. Hemingway and killing cleanly: M. Hemingway Sanford, *At the Hemingways*, p. 81.

EH "cared about" his father: EH to Perkins, 16 Dec. 1928 (*Letters*, p. 291).

Mencken on *DIA:* "The Spanish Idea of a Good Time," *The American Mercury* (Dec. 1932), pp. 506–7; reprint in Robert O. Stephens (ed.), *Ernest Hemingway: The Critical Reception* (New York: Burt Franklin, 1977), p. 123.

EH and "Narcissus principle": Baker, *The Writer as Artist*, pp. 385–86, 388. Baker sees *TFC* (1938) as the first indisputable example of the principle in EH's work, but I believe it is already evident in *DIA*.

Américo Castro and "Spanish integralism": see *Sobre el nombre y el quién de los españoles* (Madrid: Taurus, 1973), p. 321.

Salinas on culture of death: "Lorca and the Poetry of Death," in Manuel Durⁿ (ed.),

Lorca: A Collection of Critical Essays (Englewood Cliffs, N.J.: Prentice-Hall, 1962), pp. 102–4, 106.

Hemingway, death, and immortality: see Sean O'Faolain, *The Vanishing Hero: Studies in Novelists of the Twenties* (Boston: Little, Brown, 1957), p. 127; John McCormick and Mario Sevilla Mascareñas, *The Complete Aficionado* (Cleveland: World, 1967), pp. 236–37.

Unamuno on immortality: *Del sentimiento trágico de la vida en los hombres y en los pueblos* (1913), tr. Anthony Kerrigan, *The Tragic Sense of Life in Man and Nations* (Princeton: Princeton University Press, 1972).

Deleted sentence from *DIA* on immortality: MS, p. 272 (Humanities Research Center, Univ. of Texas).

Montherlant compared to Hemingway re bullfight: McCormick, *The Middle Distance*, pp. 71–72; Mario Praz, "Hemingway in Italy," in Baker (ed.), *Hemingway and His Critics*, pp. 117–18.

EH on death during the composition of *DIA*: EH to Fitzgerald, 13 Sept., c. 24 or 31 Oct. 1929; EH to Archibald MacLeish, 30 June 1930, 14 Mar. 1931; EH to Waldo Peirce, 15 Apr. 1932 (*Letters*, pp. 306, 310, 326, 338, 359).

EH and typesetter for *DIA*: EH to Perkins, 28 June 1932 (*Letters*, pp. 361–62); Baker, *Life Story*, p. 229.

EH's improvised composition of *DIA*: see MS (Univ. of Texas), where it is obvious that EH divided his material into chapters afterwards.

Lorca on bullfight as religious drama: "Teoría y jucgo del duende," *Obras completas*, 1:1077.

Origin of bullfight in nature rituals: see Angel Álvarez de Miranda, *Ritos y juegos del toro* (Madrid: Taurus, 1962); McCormick and Mascareñas, *The Complete Aficionado*, p. 27.

Survival of totem banquet in Spain: Pedro Caba, "A Half-Philosophical Theory," in *Los toros/Bullfighting* (Madrid: Indice, 1974), pp. 38–39.

Burgess and eating meat of bull: *Ernest Hemingway y su mundo* (Madrid: Ultramar, 1980), p. 71 (trans. of *Ernest Hemingway and His World* [London: Thames & Hudson, 1978]).

"Sangre de Toro" wine: produced by Torres vinters, Catalonia.

Passage on Cagancho's faena added to original draft: MS, pp. 9ff. (Univ. of Texas).

Lorca on duende: "Teoría y juego del duende," *Obras completas*, 1:1067–79.

Robert Jordan on "La Gloria": *FWBT*, p. 380.

Montherlant on sun and shade: *Chaos and Night* (New York: Macmillan, 1964), p. 44.

Montherlant's *The Bullfighters (Les Bestiares)* checked out by EH: Richard Layman, "Hemingway's Library Cards at Shakespeare & Co.," *Fitzgerald/Hemingway Annual* (1975), p. 192.

Blood, wine, sun in the cucharist: I am indebted to Fernando Claramunt for the association between the host and the solar circle. See his "Los toros desde la psicología," in Cossío, *Los toros*, 7:20.

EH on cojones and sense of death: "Chroniques: And to the United States," *The Transatlantic Review* (May–June 1924), p. 355.

EH on critics as eunuchs: Rodrigo Royo, "Las pequeñas confesiones de Hemingway," *Arriba*, Madrid (5 Oct. 1956), n.p. In a poem beginning "Little Mr. Wilson . . .," published posthumously, EH spoke of "All the ball-less critics / All their cuntless wives." Gerogiannis (ed.), *EH: 88 Poems*, p. 97.

Christianity replaced cults of bullgods with worship of lamb: Claramunt, "Los toros desde la psicología," p. 20.

EH accused of sounding like Bacdeker *cum* **Duncan Hines:** Young, *EH: A Reconsideration*, p. 96.

Aranjuncz as Spanish Versailles: see for example Gerald Brenan, *The Face of Spain* (New York: Pellegrini & Cudahy, 1951), pp. 285–88.

Deleted passage on beautiful Spanish women, *DIA*: MS, p. 54 (Univ. of Texas).

Spain lost its virginity before any other country: EH to Isidore Schneider, 23 Mar. 1926 (JFK).

EH divides aficionados in two groups *DIA*, MS, p. 8 (Univ. of Texas).

EH on Maera's death: *DIA*, MS, p. 109 (Univ. of Texas).

"Personal element" in bullfight: *DIA* MS, p. 121 (Univ. of Texas).

Honor vs. pundonor **in Spanish:** see *Diccionario de la lengua española* (Madrid: Real Academia Española, 1970), p. 1082; Capellán, "Hemingway and the Hispanic World," pp. 293–94.

Frederic Henry on "abstract words": *FTA*, pp. 184–85. See also Keneth Kinnamon, "Hemingway, the *Corrida*, and Spain," *Texas Studies in Literature and Language* (Spring 1959), p. 55.

EH used "A Natural History of the Dead" indirectly in *DIA:* EH to Everett R. Perry, c. 7 Feb. 1933 (*Letters*, p. 380).

EH admits complicity in paying off bullfight critics: "DS," MS #354a, p. 10 of insert to p. 14 (JFK).

EH on "Story of 2 fairies" for *DIA:* MS, p. 218 (Univ. of Texas).

Huxley, "Foreheads Villainous Low": in *Music at Night and Other Essays* (New York: Fountain Press, 1931), pp. 111–15.

EH and Goya: see EH to Breit, 21 June 1952 (*Letters*, pp. 767–68); José Luis Castillo-Puche, "Hemingway, peregrino en España," *ABC* (25 June 1984), p. 3: "Hemingway y los toros a través de Goya," *Diario de Navarra* (7 July 1984). pp. 16–17; "La influencia de Goya en la obra de Hemingway," lecture delivered by Sr. Castillo-Puche at the International Hemingway Conference, Madrid, 26 June 1984.

Goya's nickname, "D. Francisco de los Toros": Mario Lepore, *The Life and Times of Goya* (New York: Curtis Books, 1966), p. 42.

Dr. Hemingway taught son about killing: M. Hemingway Sanford, *At the Hemingways*, p. 81.

EH not great admirer of gypsies: evident from several passages in *DIA*, and from the portrayal of the cowardly, irresponsible Rafael in *FWBT.*

"To get Spain into a book is hard": *DIA*, MS, p. 73 (Univ. of Texas).

EH to Gingrich on last chapter, *DIA:* 4 Dec. 1932 (*Letters*, p. 378).

Lewis on *DIA* **as a book about EH and his love affair with Spain:** "The Making of *DIA*," in Nagel (ed.), *EH: The Writer in Context*, p. 39.

Death of novillero, Pedro Carreño: see Cossío, *Los toros*, 3:174–75.

Epilogue to *DIA* **included in anthology of verse:** Selden Rodman (ed.), *100 Modern Poems* (New York: Pellegrini & Cudahy, 1949), pp. 66–67.

Prose of *DIA* **as poetry:** Donald Junkins, "Hemingway's Contribution to American Poetry," *Hemingway Review* (Spring 1985), p. 22; "Hemingway's Bullfight Poems," *Hemingway Review* (Spring 1987), pp. 38–45.

MARK SPILKA

A Retrospective Epilogue:
On the Importance of Being Androgynous

My text for this retrospective epilogue is an item taken from the Sunday *New York Times* "Arts & Leisure" section for April 24, 1988, entitled "Reading Hemingway with One Eye Closed." It begins with a brief account of Hemingway's animadversions against biographers and selects from those unkind observations a summary remark: "Imagine what they can do with the soiled sheets of four legal beds by the same writer."[1] The remark is chosen by way of introducing still another object of animadversion, the recent television mini-series called "Hemingway," which "focuses on the women in Hemingway's life," his four wives and two of his many wished-for sweethearts. As the title of the article indicates, its author, James R. Mellow, himself a Hemingway biographer in the making, takes issue with the narrow focus on Hemingway's relations with women to the exclusion of his relations with men: "What one misses in this dramatized portrait," says Mellow, "is a real sense that there were men who were equally as important as the women in Hemingway's personal life and certainly more important to the literary career."[2]

Though Mellow's observation seems just and speaks to the Hemingway that many people—myself among them—admire, it may be that it speaks also to a kind of growing anxiety that such admirers are about to lose him. As indeed we are. The anxiety registered here, in the name of biographical

From *Hemingway's Quarrel with Androgyny.* © 1990 by the University of Nebraska Press.

inclusiveness and literary value, is actually being registered in the name of hat male camaraderie which the *Times* copyeditor highlights with a boldface insertion—**"The author's sense of male camaraderie gets little prominence in the mini-series"**—and which Mellow himself proceeds to apotheosize in no uncertain terms:

> At the age of 19, for instance, Hemingway, a wounded hero of the Italian Campaign in World War I, had attracted a small circle of male friends—significantly three to five years older than he— for whom he was the leader and the authority on subjects ranging from sports to sex. None of them objected to his role. It was Hemingway who made the plans for the summer fishing and camping expeditions on the Black and the Sturgeon rivers in Michigan, plotted the itineraries, fussed over the arrangements with a ritual insistence. It was more than the cultivation of a machismo image (though it was that, too). By then Hemingway had developed a sense of male camaraderie that verged almost on the mystical. It would haunt his fiction (most notably his Nick Adams stories) and his personal life.[3]

Never mind that Hemingway clobbered most of his male friends with surprising regularity, or that he was more wounded than heroic in the Italian campaign, or that he had little or no sexual authority at the age of 19, or that Nick Adams is more nearly a loner than a comrade in his stories, to the point where D.H. Lawrence might comfortably call him "the remains of the lone trapper and cowboy."[4] What matters here is the loving transcription of that mythical sense of mystical camaraderie that Hemingway has indeed created in his fiction and above all in his personal life. This is indeed the Hemingway who early wrote a group of tales called *Men Without Women*, the Hemingway who gave us male definitions of manhood to ponder, cherish, even perhaps to grow by. The machismo problem, so lightly touched on here, has everything to do, nonetheless, with those relations with women the perusal of which Mellow so anxiously calls "Reading Hemingway with One Eye Closed." For surely the point should be that critics have been reading Hemingway with one eye closed for years, that his peculiar world of men without women was in fact founded on relations with women that we are just now beginning to understand, and perhaps more importantly, on relations with himself, or on a sense of himself in relation to women, that we are also only recently and I think alarmingly just beginning to understand. It is this side of Hemingway, his secret and continuing dependence on women, now not so secret after all, and his own curiously androgynous makeup, that threaten to deprive his admirers—myself still among them—of that one-eyed myth of mystical camaraderie we have all more or less embraced.

There are changes in the offing, then, that might prove hard to take. There is reason to be uneasy, if not to despair. It is not simply the new feminism that asks us to judge more carefully Hemingway's dubious (i.e.; abusive, triangulated, exploitive) relations with women, and with the more feminine aspects of himself, or the androgynous aspects that, like so many men, he found so hard to cope with. It is his own central role in the creation and perpetuation of cultural myths and codes that are now under scrutiny from many angles, chief among which is the myth of men without women.

He did not invent it. It began, rather, in imperial England when the code of the stiff upper lip first openly replaced the possibility of manly tears in schools for boys—schools for the instruction of future servants of the Empire; it received its first American impress after the Civil War in the fictions of Mark Twain and other celebrants of postpioneer nostalgia; and from imperial British celebrants like Marryat, Kipling, and Masefield, as well as from Twain himself, it passed into the life and fiction of Ernest Hemingway. It is his role as the receiver, transmuter, and perpetuater of such myths that requires us to judge him now in terms of his continuing cultural role as what Edmund Wilson once called our "gauge of morale."[5] And if the gauge seems singularly low in these days of professional cynicism and distrust, all the more reason to give it our serious attention.

Let us turn, then, to Hemingway's oft-quoted justification for the title of a new collection of his stories in a letter to his editor at Scribner's, Maxwell Perkins, dated February 14, 1927: "Want to call it Men Without Women [because] in all of these [stories], almost, the softening feminine influence through training, discipline, death or other causes [is] absent."[6] Hemingway was twenty-seven at the time and about to marry his second wife, Pauline Pfeiffer. His divorce from his first wife, Hadley Richardson, had become final only two weeks before, and he would delay the marriage with Pauline only a few months more so as to join his friend Guy Hickok on a bachelor tour of fascist Italy, an excursion the disgruntled Pauline acidly called his "Italian tour for the promotion of masculine society."[7] Her remark seems apt enough. Masculine society was something Hemingway would always pursue from within the confines of marriage or near-marriage. From 1921 to his death in 1961 he was consecutively married to four wives without any significant pause between marriages. He literally never lived alone for as much as a year in his life. From the cradle to the grave he was himself never free of "the softening influence of women through training, discipline, death or other causes," though he certainly did his best to think and write otherwise, and with enormous success. Until recently, at least, none of his critics and admirers have made much of the fact that—like so many of us— he was extremely dependent on women.

In *A Literature of Their Own* Elaine Showalter offers a useful clue to Hemingway's desire to free himself of that dependence by literary fiat. While discussing how British women novelists in the nineteenth century created model heroes as projections of how they might act and feel if they were men, or of how they felt men should act and feel, she compares these projections of wished-for power and authority with those of male novelists of the day like Thomas Hughes, author of *Tom Brown's School Days at Rugby*: "The love of sport and animals, the ability to withstand pain, the sublimation of sexuality into religious devotion, and the channeling of sexuality into mighty action are traits the model heroes share. In Hughes' novels, however, manliness is achieved through separation from women; in the women's novels, mothers, sisters, and wives are the sources of instruction on the manly character."[8]

It was the precedent of imperialist writers like Hughes, Marryat, Kipling, and Stevenson, then, whom he had read and admired in his childhood, that Hemingway was trying to extend when he wrote the tales that comprise *Men Without Women* and described them as free of those "softening influences"—those female "sources of instruction on the manly character"—that he too wished to avoid. Yet those influences would soon recur, as we can see in *A Farewell to Arms*, and would crop up periodically thereafter, as in *For Whom the Bell Tolls* and *Across the River and Into the Trees*, until their amazingly predominant resurgence in manuscripts of his final years like *The Garden of Eden* and "The Last Good Country," both now posthumously published in selective forms.

For Hemingway was never really free, as I have said, of those "softening influences." Their presence in his childhood and adolescence was in fact deeply formative. He was raised androgynously by parents peculiarly steeped in the conflicting codes of manhood that were vying for sway in the late nineteenth century and that would continue to press their rival claims upon him throughout his lifetime. His mother's early interest in feminism, her pursuit of a musical career with parental encouragement, her mother's admonition that she should stay out of the kitchen as much as possible, were matched by his father's early interest in Indian lore and his cultivation of the skills of camping, as in that famous expedition to the Smoky Mountains in his youth when he served proudly as camp cook. Her genteel feminism and his postpioneer nostalgia blended readily when it came to questions of rearing their six children, at least during the infant years and shortly after, when the children were schooled by their father in the outdoor skills of swimming, fishing, hunting, and cooking, and exposed by their mother to the arts of music, literature, and painting. It was no accident that the Hemingways' firstborn son at the age of two years and eleven months both loved to sew and to shoot his gun in target practice; or that he could hit the bull's-eye by four and still loved his mama kitty; or that he wore Dutchlength hair like his sister Marcelline's and was often dressed in similar smocks and frocks, or, alternately, in straw hat and Tom Sawyer rags while going barefoot.

The Fauntleroy craze that swept England and America in the 1890s helps in some ways to explain this peculiar blend of male and female definitions of manhood. For Frances Hodgson Burnett's controversial little hero was a kind of last-ditch representation of the claims of genteel feminism to "instruct the manly character" at an early age. His competitor on the best-seller lists of the mid-1880s was Huckleberry Finn, then entering the lists as America's contribution to the new imperial definitions of future manhood in England, its postpioneer equivalent of the new British belief that manliness is best achieved through separation from women. These vying codes could for a time blend in American households because they shared a common belief in the stoic virtues—courage under stress, the ability to withstand pain, the love of outdoor sports and animals—and differed only in their stress on consideration of women and of women's feelings about the nature of manliness. Hemingway was in fact raised by a blend of these then relatively compatible codes. The interesting point about his boyhood is his gradual separation of their hold upon him, his crossing over from one to another as he broke with his mother's and his older sister's influence, shifted his emotional allegiances to his younger sisters, and began to model himself upon the prevailing example in his turn-of-the-century culture of Teddy Roosevelt and Huckleberry Finn, the imperial and postpioneer representatives, respectively, of the new male codes.[9] The Fauntleroy impress would never, however, wholly leave him; and the androgynous impress of his early years would return to haunt him in his final years, even as it now begins to haunt us all.

From his peculiarly androgynous parents, then, Hemingway had received a mixed impress of blending and conflicting definitions of manhood. His father, Dr. Clarence Edmonds Hemingway, had tried to raise him as the frontier scout he had always wanted to be himself; yet he had also taught him the naturalistic lore that he had learned from his own college-educated mother, and had impressed upon him as well the importance of his own nurturing and healing profession, which Ernest would in effect follow when he joined the Red Cross ambulance corps in World War I and was wounded, not as a soldier in battle, but as a canteen worker at the front, serving food, cigarettes, candy, and postcards to men in the lines. His father was also a deeply religious man, a muscular Christian like his mother, and with a damp susceptibility to prayers and tears that his supposedly more toughminded son seems to have found embarrassing.[10] His mother, Grace Hall Hemingway, had named him Ernest Miller Hemingway after the two Christian businessmen she most admired, her father and uncle, Ernest and Miller Hall; and beyond the going androgynous fashions, she had curiously twinned him with his older sister Marcelline in his infant and boyhood years. In these ways she seems to have been projecting upon him her own fantasies of how she might act and feel if she were a man; for there is every evidence that her stake in his future was very much like that of nineteenth-century women novelists in their model male heroes. Indeed, one such novelist, Dinah Mulock Craik, had written a novel in the mid-nineteenth century called *John Halifax, Gentleman*, which served as the Hemingway family bible. It was about a heroic Christian businessman like Grace's father as well as her uncle, who had married an aristocrat named Ursula March after whom Hemingway's next younger sister Ursula was named, and who had brought his family to live on a country estate called Longfield, after which Grace would name the farm across from the Hemingway cottage on Lake Walloon in northern Michigan where she would eventually build herself a music studio. What Grace wanted for her son Ernest, then, was very much what she wanted for herself; and when she twinned him with his older sister, Marcelline, and began experimenting with their hairstyles, first Dutch-length in infancy, then close-cut when Ernest began school and received his first boy's haircut, she was telling her firstborn son something about the gender she favored in creating such twinships. For Marcelline too would receive her first boy's haircut at this time and would be punished when it grew out unevenly and seemed even more unsightly after a girlfriend tried to trim it. And on two occasions Marcelline would also be held back in school until Ernest caught up with her.

In such odd ways, apparently, Grace Hemingway would express her own need to find a place for her considerable talents in a culture which encouraged men to pursue careers and encouraged women to choose motherhood over careers, or to attempt somehow to combine them, as she had done shortly after her mother's untimely death. As with Clarence, indeed as with many parents, what she wanted for her children she wanted for herself. It does not seem surprising, then, that Ernest too might be influenced by such desires, or by their personal consequences, in his adult years. We have no hesitation in saying as much where his father was concerned. Now it is Grace's turn. She wanted and she got a distinctly androgynous son; but then so in his own way did her husband Clarence.

We have long known the places in Hemingway's fiction where mothers and sisters may be said to have provided "sources of instruction" for the hero's manly character. In *A Farewell to Arms* the message of selfless love which the priest first intimates and which Lieutenant Henry manages to forget is given its hospital workout when the wounded and supine and therefore interestingly feminine Henry finally falls in love with the crazy nurse, Catherine Barkley, with whom he had previously temporized, and is thus instructed in a love so selfless that the lovers become one another at night, even as an earlier fictional couple, mad Catherine Earnshaw and her foster brother Healthcliff, had identified with each other ("I *am* Heathcliff") as romantic lovers in a novel Hemingway had read and admired in adolescence and would emulate several times thereafter. One of those occasions, surely, is *For Whom the Bell Tolls*, where the motherly and sisterly sources of instruction, tough Pilar and close-cropped Maria, may be said to have worked the same selfless lesson on the hero, Robert Jordan, who not only resembles Maria like a brother but identifies with her in mystical succession as his female survivor. The model for *Across the River and Into the Trees* is more clearly Italian, that of Dante and Beatrice, and the source of instruction more daughterly than sisterly, as dying Colonel Cantwell is softened from his military ragings by his selfless love for young Countess Renata, a nineteen-year-old female replacement for the author's World War I persona, particularly in her desire to become well-versed in her own turn in military lore and tough battle attitudes. But let us turn from these easy examples, and the various hair-cropping or hair-lengthening scenes that may be said to go with them, and turn to another mad Catherine, or more precisely, to another sisterly *ménage à trois*, in *The Garden of Eden* manuscript and the novel selected from it and published in 1986, after which all things may be said (in Yeatsian terms) to have changed utterly.

What seems remarkable about this amazingly self-reflexive novel, this story about opposing kinds of stories, is its reenactment of the conflict between male and female definitions of the manly character in ways invidious to both, and its establishment thereby of a wound-and-the-bow approach to androgyny that speaks profoundly to Hemingway's struggle with himself, or with the opposing female muses within himself, one hostile, the other supportive, against both of whom he seems to establish the terms for his own distinctly masculine artistry. The ambitiousness, the risk-taking, in this unfinished, many-sided novel, this experiment in self-reflexive psychodrama which Faulkner at least might have recognized as a clear instance of going beyond safe limits,[11] will make it an object of study for some time to come; and not the least among its ponderable treasures will be the theory of androgynous creativity that emerges most clearly from its manuscript rather than its published pages. The decision of Scribner's editor, Tom Jenks, to remove from the published version visits by two American couples to the Rodin statue of two women making love, along with the subplot about the Paris couple, Nick and Barbara Sheldon, who are equally implicated in the statue's resonant meanings, diminishes that printed version considerably, and of itself turns us to the original manuscript for clues to the author's fascinating intentions—his decision, that is, to present the Garden of Eden theme as an androgynous love bond, a lesbian coupling, as it were, the peculiar happiness of which—in his own mournful words—"a man must lose." It looks very much as if Hemingway were trying toward the end of his life to come to terms with his own androgynous leanings, especially as they might help to define his lifelong quarrel with them in both external and internal ways, and with his ultimate sense that androgyny might after all be the wound against which he had always drawn his masculine bow.

Within the original manuscript, then, there are repeated assertions by Hemingway's chief male persona, the young writer David Bourne, that the worse his life becomes, the more his character deteriorates, the better he writes. "All that is left entire in you," he muses in book 3, chapter 23, "is your ability to write and that gets better. You would think it would be destroyed. ... But so far as you corrupt or change that grows and strengthens. It should not but it has."[12] The corruption and change to which David refers involves his own absorption in the androgynous relations with his wife Catherine inspired by the Rodin statue. Thus, when making love at night, David accedes to Catherine's request, assumes her name, and imagines himself as the passive female partner in the statue; whereas Catherine assumes the active and dominant position and calls herself Peter. This role reversal is given a kind of public showing, moreover, when Catherine has her hair cut short to resemble his and persuades him to dye his hair blond like hers. The hair fetishism is the public expression, that is, of their private relations and of the new definition Catherine has given to David's male identity. For the first time in Hemingway's major fiction the female source of instruction on the manly character becomes, on romantic grounds, decidedly suspect.

To make matters worse, Catherine also encourages David to write a narrative account of their newlywed life on the French Riviera, much like that which Hemingway provides, so that the text itself becomes an expression of the author's stake in these suspect events. Thus David's narrative soon becomes a source of marital conflict. The jealously possessive Catherine prefers it to the tales of his African boyhood which David also attempts to write, as if trying to reclaim that world of men without women he once shared with his father. But the disillusionment with his father these tales record suggests that even exclusively male definitions of manhood are now suspect. The only way left for David to assert and reclaim his male identity is through the act of writing itself; it is there that he overcomes what seems to be the wound of androgyny. Thus, when Catherine destroys the African manuscripts, David is able to reassert that identity, and to overcome the corrupting effects of the androgynous wounding, by writing them again.

The parable that the novel offers on Hemingway's life is certainly instructive, and the novel virtually asks us to work it out, even as the supposedly impersonal Joyce asks us to extrapolate from Stephen Dedalus's experiences some implications about his own. The parallels with Scott and Zelda Fitzgerald are in this regard somewhat misleading. It is not so much Zelda's jealousy of Scott's writing that Catherine reenacts as that of Hemingway's several wives. One thinks of that suitcase full of manuscripts that Hadley left unguarded; or how impugned Pauline must have felt by "The Snows of Kilimanjaro" and the windfall approach to her rival, Jane Mason, in the Macomber story; or Martha's active rivalry as a novelist and foreign correspondent; or Mary's sacrifice of her own writing career to marriage. Similarly, one thinks of Pauline's refrain during the famous one hundred days of separation: "You and me are the same guy"; or of Mary's account of her androgynous relations with Ernest in *How It Was;* or of the sexual role reversals with the lost wife in *Islands in the Stream.* We have good reason to read this novel, then, as a revealing gloss on Hemingway's long adult quarrel with androgyny in his several marriages, and therefore as a revealing gloss on his own artistic struggles, his own self-definition as a writer with decidedly androgynous propensities.

That he presents David Bourne as the passive victim of those propensities is not surprising. Earlier male personas like Jake Barnes or the corrupt writer Harry in "The Snows of Kilimanjaro" are presented as passive victims of weaknesses or conditions which they nonetheless bear or struggle against with stoic courage. What is surprising here is David's strong attraction to androgyny, his fascination with the Rodin statue, and his attempt—like that of Hemingway himself—to do justice to Catherine in the main narrative, to create a sympathetic portrait of *her* painful struggles. It is the betrayal of those possibilities that makes this manuscript such a poignant record of Hemingway's ultimate failure to resolve his quarrel with androgyny—or better still, to continue it honestly rather than resolve it falsely. For if we take Catherine Bourne as she is ultimately meant to be taken—as an internalization of that fiercely independent creativity which Hemingway first recognized in his mother's prideful ways, including that twinning process which made him part of those ways from infancy onward and which he recognized again in the determination of his second wife, Pauline, to create an androgynous bond—perhaps a lesbian bond—between them, a bond at any rate with echoes and reflections in his other marriages— then the casting off of Catherine in favor of the supportive adjunct mate, Marita, whom like mother Grace with his younger sisters she thoughtfully provides for him, is like a casting out of his own creative strength, or of that secret muse within himself with whom he struggled to keep alive his own artistic pride, his own creative maleness as the author of wasteland narratives and assorted tales of boyhood disillusionments and of men without women. This, it seems to me, is the ultimate importance of Hemingway's lifelong quarrel with androgyny: that it was crucial to his creative strength throughout his life, and that he came remarkably, even heroically, close to affirming it before tragically betraying it as his life neared its grim conclusion.

NOTES

1. James R. Mellow, "Reading Hemingway with One Eye Closed," *New York Times*, April 24, 1988, H33.

2. Ibid.

3. Ibid., H38.

4. D.H. Lawrence, *Selected Literary Criticism*, 427.

5. Edmund Wilson, "Hemingway: Gauge of Morale," 92–114.

6. Hemingway, *Selected Letters*, 245.

7. Baker, *Ernest Hemingway*, 236.

8. Showalter, *A Literature of Their Own*, 136–37.

9. For the Fauntleroy-Finn conjunction, see Thwaite, *Waiting for the Party*, 95. For the Teddy Roosevelt impress, see Reynolds, *The Young Hemingway*, 16, 23–35, 27–30 ff.

10. For Ernest's father's embarrassing tears, see especially Baker, *Ernest Hemingway*, 45–46, and *For Whom the Bell Tolls*, 401–6.

11. See Baker, *Ernest Hemingway*, 585, for Faulkner's famous judgment in 1947 that Hemingway "lacked the courage to get out on a limb of experimentation," which Hemingway characteristically misread as an attack on his physical courage.

12. *The Garden of Eden* Manuscript, 3/23/9, Hemingway Collection, Kennedy Library, Boston.

HUBERT ZAPF

Reflection vs. Daydream:
Two Types of the Implied Reader
in Hemingway's Fiction

T he role of the reader in Hemingway's works had attracted the attention
of critics even before the rise of modern reception theory made such
attention part of a more or less established methodology of literary
scholarship. The strange emotional intensity of his fiction vis-à-vis the
objective, decidedly nonemotional quality of his style pointed to a
paradoxical tension in his writing which could be resolved only by
interpolating what was in effect the dimension of an "implied reader" in the
texts, whose "involuntary subjective response" was recognized as an essential
part of the author's literary technique.[1] The most conspicuous elements of
this technique were the use of emotional understatement; the extreme
reduction of language, style, and fictional world; and the deliberate strategy
of leaving out relevant information, that is, of providing blanks in the textual
surface that have an appellative function, calling upon the reader's activity to
supply the missing context.[2] Hemingway himself described his technique
metaphorically in the famous comparison of his writing with the movement
of an iceberg, of which only the smallest part is visible on the surface.[3]
Beneath the delusively factual surface of realistic description and objective
report there was recognized, especially after the reconsideration of
Hemingway as a symbolist and even expressionist writer, a deep structure of

From *New Critical Approaches to the Short Stories of Ernest Hemingway*, edited by Jackson J.
Benson. © 1990 by Duke University Press.

potential significance which required the intense imaginative participation of the reader in the constitution of the text.[4] This deep structure presented, in the language of reception theory, an implicit dimension of indeterminacy which allowed for a great variety of symbolic, ironic, emotional, or reflective realizations of the text.

However, the iceberg metaphor and similar concepts for describing the specific mode of communication between text and reader in Hemingway designate only one aspect of the implied reader in his fiction. This aspect could be called "vertical," as it considers the texts primarily from the vertical tension expressed in the spatial metaphor of surface vs. depth. The other equally important aspect is the "horizontal" aspect of the text as a temporal process in which the expectations of the reader are built up, modified, fulfilled, or disappointed in successive steps in the course of the text. Little attention has been paid in criticism to the psychodynamic structure of this process, although it is highly operative in producing the strong emotional effect that Hemingway's works, perhaps because of their carefully controlled surface realism, communicate to the reader.

These two aspects of reception (the vertical aspect of the implied reader as defined by the indeterminacy of a suggested deep structure of the text and the horizontal aspect of the implied reader as defined by the process of experience inscribed into the text) represent *two different types* of appellative structure in Hemingway's fiction. The first appeals to the reader's sense of discovery and cognitive coherence, to his ability to detect, connect, and interpret implicit, ambiguous, or incomplete textual information. It therefore involves a predominantly mental, reflective activity of the reader. The second type appeals to the reader's sense of empathy with significant human fate, building upon the psychic tension of expectation vs. result, desire vs. reality, hope vs. disappointment. It involves a predominantly emotional, psychological activity. The first reception type is essentially spatial and circular, the second essentially temporal and linear. The one is characterized by the structural simultaneity of opposing elements of meaning, the other by the dramatized succession of opposing phases of psychodynamic development. The one leads to reflective distance, the other to emotional identification. In many texts, of course, these types occur in mixed form and with varying emphasis. But they nevertheless can be distinguished as two contrasting, ideal-typical variants of the implied reader in Hemingway which mark the range of possible responses evoked by his works.

Type I will be exemplified here by *The Sun Also Rises* and "Big Two-Hearted River." Type II will be exemplified by some of the best known works of Hemingway's middle and late periods of composition—"The Short Happy

Life of Francis Macomber," "The Snows of Kilimanjaro," *A Farewell to Arms*, and *The Old Man and the Sea*.

Before going to concrete textual analyses, however, it seems useful to determine on a theoretical level what is meant here by the vertical and the horizontal axes of Hemingway's texts and how they are related to "reflection" and "daydream" as predominant reader-responses. For clarification of these concepts it is helpful to consult two of the most influential theories of reader-response, Wolfgang Iser's phenomenological reception theory and the psychological theory of Sigmund Freud.

Iser, who introduced the implied reader as a critical category, defined it not in the sense of a concrete, historical reader but as the characteristic *activity* of reading as it is generated by and inscribed into what he calls the "appellative structure" of literary texts.[5] How is this structure conceived in Iser's theory? A guiding assumption of his reception aesthetics, which has become widely popular in recent criticism, is the idea of the indeterminacy of the literary text. The text presents itself to the reader not as a finished whole but only in the form of "schematized views,"[6] It consists only of reduced, incomplete outlines and "component parts" of an imaginary world which must be completed and put together in the reader's mind to be fully realized.[7] Because literature is a highly indirect, nonreferential mode of speech, there results a constant tension between the explicit statements on the textual surface and the implicit connotations, symbolic cross-references, ironic undercurrents which, though not directly formulated, make up the truly "literary" quality of the discourse. Literary communication is thus defined by the tension between what is stated and what is left out, between what is formulated and what is left unformulated in the actual text. And it is particularly the dimension of the unformulated that decisively stimulates the reader's activity. "Thus by reading," as Iser states, "we uncover the unformulated part of the text, and this very indeterminacy is the force that drives us to work out a configurative meaning while at the same time giving us the necessary degree of freedom to do so."[8]

It can be seen here that the underlying concept of literature in this theory is essentially a concept of negativity. Literature is defined by what it is, says, and does *not* say, by techniques and strategies that negate the reader's expectations of coherence and consistency. It becomes a medium that distances the reader from immediate experience, that subliminally counteracts his tendency of illusion-building and emotional identification. It defamiliarizes the familiar and thus irritates any affirmative views of man and the world.

What kind of receptive activity does this model imply? In the final analysis it turns literature into a medium of *reflection*. The typical activities of Iser's implied reader remind one of an aesthetical version of the reflective consciousness which philosophy distinguishes from the naive consciousness and its "natural attitude" toward reality.[9] In the act of reflection the subjective consciousness "turns back" upon itself, distancing itself from immediate experience and questioning all apparent certainties and determinacies of the everyday world. By radically suspending habitual values and "prejudgments,"[10] the reflecting consciousness becomes aware of its own constitutive role in the structuring and interpretation of the "objective" world. One need only replace the "world" by the "text" to see that Iser's implied reader, in a similar way, is conceived as an all-pervading critical consciousness which explicates itself in progressive acts of (self-)reflection. Indeed, the very negativity that Iser attributes to literature, as well as the emancipatory effect that this negativity assumes in the sense of an increased self-awareness and thus self-realization of the reader's subjectivity, corresponds to the most distinctive features of reflection as it has been defined in philosophy. According to Walter Schulz, "It is the interest and intention of all reflection to negate the given as the substantial, to suspend its objective validity, and to incorporate it into one's own subjectivity."[11]

Sigmund Freud's theory of reading is quite different from Iser's. Indeed, one could say that Freud emphasizes precisely those aspects of the reading activity that are neglected in Iser's reception aesthetics. To Freud the reading of fictional literature is not an act of hermeneutic (self-) reflection but like the enactment of a symbolic *daydream*.[12] Reading—like writing—is the fictive realization of a wish-fulfilling fantasy, which to Freud is the primary motive and content of all daydreams. "Wish-fulfillment" should not be understood here in any fixed, narrow sense—such as referring only to sexual fantasies or to a regressive reenactment of primal childhood scenes— but in the sense of a basic anthropological desire for idealization, for the imaginative correction of a deficient reality, which manifests itself in many different forms.[13] The scenarios of fictional daydreams can range from more simple forms of heroic self-aggrandizement and of all sorts of erotic, professional, and other success fantasies to more elevated fantasies of moral greatness and humane self-realization.

Instead of Iser's emphasis on the negativity of literature, then, Freud's emphasis is on its "positivity"—in a thematic as well as in a structural sense. What induces the reader's reaction is not what is "left out" or remains indeterminate but what is "put in" and is determined by the immanent logic of the world of the text as the author has symbolically projected it. Literature here is not primarily a means of criticizing or negating existing systems of sociocultural reality but an imaginative counterworld which offers a possible escape from or alternative to reality. The act of reading is not conceived as the cognitive enactment of a highly mediated, secondary form of experience but as the emotional enactment of an immediate, lifelike form of primary experience. Instead of the self-reflective detachment of the reader from the narrated world, Freud postulates the reader's psychological involvement in it.

Although at first sight these two models appear to be contradictory, they should nonetheless be seen as complementary. Instead of universal concepts which can be applied to all texts indifferently, they should be viewed as specific, analytical concepts which describe two different dimensions of the act of reading and, correspondingly, two kinds of appellative structure in literature. The response-patterns of reflection and daydream should not be considered primarily as projections of the reader's subjectivity but as inherent possibilities of fictional texts.[14] They gain hermeneutic value only if they are viewed as dimensions of the *implied* reader, that is, of the dynamics of response as it is inscribed within the structure of the narrative itself.

As stated, these theoretical models can serve to illuminate two characteristic types of reader-appeal in Hemingway's works. In which sense, then, can the first type be called vertical, the second horizontal? The two types refer to two fundamental aspects of narrative composition, and they specifically emphasize one of these aspects in the communication between text and reader: the aspect of the text as a *system* of potential meaning and the aspect of the text as a *process* of potential experience. In the first case we tend to get a vertical effect in that the explicitly formulated surface of the narrative must be constantly related to the unformulated implications of the narrative to figure out its "deeper" meaning and significance. What happens on the level of narrated events is no more important than what these events signify, how they are to be interpreted and related to other elements and layers of the text. If, as in Hemingway's *The Sun Also Rises*, we have an almost pathological distance from, and indifference of the narrator toward, the narrated world, and if this world is furthermore presented as a world of stasis and futility where human action loses any meaningful direction and teleological purpose, the focus of the reader's attention is all the more turned away ("re-flected") from the reported facts toward an inner, subjective world beneath the external surface world of appearances. Of course, this reflective activity is in itself a temporal process. In reading we cannot but react to one sentence after another, following the lines of the written text. But what matters here is that the reading process in the reflective response pattern is not simply defined by the progress of fictional events but also by the gradual accumulation of interpretive data about these events. Reflection essentially occurs in a timeless mental space, because by its very nature of "turning back" upon itself it breaks up the objective flux of time and suspends the laws of temporal linearity and irreversibility, making past and present simultaneous in the potentially infinite space of subjective thought.

This is different in Type II of the implied reader. In the daydream pattern of response the reader, instead of being confronted with his own interpretive subjectivity, is drawn into the imaginative world of the text. His psyche is brought to experience the fictitious world under the simulated conditions of "real life." He is not primarily led to question the premises of this world but to follow the immanent logic of the developing narrative. What this means is that above all he is psychically subject to the temporal process of the fiction, to the changes and the promising or disappointing turns of events on the horizontal axis of the text. The reader is not put in a reflective position "above" the narrative (in an indeterminate mental space where each step is potentially reversible) but is implicated in its horizontal unfolding in time, which is inscribed in successively determined, irreversible steps into the narrative sequence of the text. In Hemingway's "Macomber," for example, the reading process is characterized not by the static wasteland effect of sterility and monotonous repetition but by sharp changes of mood and highly emotionalized climaxes of the narrative. The story dramatizes the daydream of Macomber's rise from utter humiliation to heroic self-affirmation. This daydream is gradually built up in the reader's expectation, is almost miraculously fulfilled in the course of the text, and is destroyed in the shock of Macomber's unexpected death at the end of the story.

The following analysis of selected texts demonstrates the validity of this distinction between two types of the implied reader in Hemingway; and it examines the way in which they help to shape the narrative composition of his works.

In *The Sun Also Rises*, which will serve here as chief example of Type I of appellative structure, the reader experiences the world as from a painfully insurmountable distance. He is informed early in the book of Jake Barnes's impotence which, as the physical manifestation of his psychic war trauma, becomes a more general metaphor for his inability to participate fully in the life that is going on around him. Jake's paralysis is like a silent center of indifference, an ever-present principle of negativity which inhabits all potentially positive and meaningful experiences in the novel and taints them with the same color of a controlled but extreme disillusionment. The surface of the text is above all characterized by Jake's desperate attempt at composure and self-control and at rigorously suppressing all signs of his wounded subjectivity. In his obsession with objectivity, he restricts his narrative largely to a neutral, almost monotonous registration of external facts, actions, and dialogues. The inner world of his subjectivity, however, which is responsible for this reduced perspective, is almost entirely excluded from the explicit text. It thus forms a kind of central indeterminacy in the novel which undermines the apparent determinateness of the textual surface as an element of constant irritation and uncertainty and puts the reader at a skeptical distance to the narrated world. As Jake Barnes mistrusts "all simple people, especially when their stories hold together,"[15] the reader is led to mistrust the facade of controlled matter-of-factness and naturalistic certainty that the narrator strives to establish. No real change, no development is possible in such a constellation, neither in the external world, whose activities appear as a pointless *circulus vitiosus* in the light of Jake's disillusioned subjectivity, nor in Jake's subjectivity itself, which is imprisoned, as in a gloomy inner exile, in its paralysis. The expectation of the reader of such change and the psychodynamic potential of the temporal-horizontal tension it would create is therefore neutralized early in the novel, and what is left is a reflective, vertical tension between different levels of meaning and reality that are interrelated in a sort of negative coexistence, simultaneously defining and denying each other.

Only at some points in the novel does Jake's suppressed subjectivity come to the surface, creating short moments of intensity that interrupt the overall sense of objective control and frustrated emotion—for example, when in chapter 4 he lies awake in bed at night thinking of Brett and, as the strain of his depression is getting too strong, starts to cry (31); or when in chapter 17 he goes up to the hotel room of Robert Cohn—who has had a psychic breakdown—and remembers a blow on his head which he suffered when playing football in his youth. This experience is a parallel to his later war wound, as well as to the desperate situation of his weaker alter ego, Robert Cohn (192ff.). But these are only short moments in the book, signals from the deep structure of the text which do not really shape or substantially change the reading experience. They are flashlights illuminating an internal reality which is largely concealed beneath the surface of external events and which appears as a deep-rooted feeling of self-alienation and of a traumatic division from life that goes back to Jake's earliest confrontations with the world. As the incident with Cohn is placed in the context of the bullfights in Pamplona, this psychic division from life is specifically emphasized, because the scenes of unbroken vitality at the fiesta seem strangely removed from the two isolated American expatriates, whose incommunicable emptiness and "impotence" stand in sharp contrast to the communicative celebration of life, and death, surrounding them.

Even the bullfights, which are seen by some critics as an authentic alternative to the world of social frustration and as a "climax of the entire novel,"[16] are undercut in their immediate effect by the distance and alienation implied in the novel's narrative perspective. It is certainly true that the bullfighting scenes create moments of great intensity in the novel, which transmit some sense of Jake's enthusiasm as an aficionado (who has projected what is left of his vital emotions into the bullfighting myth) to the reader. But they do not add up to an actualized *process* of experience for the reader, because the short moments of a ritualized coherence of life that they convey are sharply juxtaposed with the much longer scenes of the totally deritualized and incoherent life of the foreign group of bourgeois bohemians who, including Jake, seem strangely eccentric and out of place in the quasi-mythic world of the fiesta. The bullfights represent an idealized mythical counterworld, which we are allowed to glimpse, but which only increases our awareness of the fragmentation and disorientation of life in the real, modern world of the main characters—and of the reader. This is mirrored in the narrative focus which, with Jake Barnes, shows a contradictory tendency throughout the fiesta to move away from the center of the action to which it is simultaneously attracted, to seek some sort of mythic identity with the community of the fiesta, and yet compulsively to withdraw into an isolated outsider-position. Although Jake admires Romero as the natural man of action and archetypical bullfighter, he remains at an impersonal distance from him. It is rather that he finds Romero fascinating as an example of that original beauty and vitality of life from which he himself is forever separated. And it may in a sense be true, as has often been maintained, that Hemingway expounds his own principle of art in his description of Romero's art of bullfighting (167ff.). But that is only one, idealized side of his art, of which the other side is the irredeemable "break" between self and reality, consciousness and life, which through Jake's perspective determines the structure of the novel—and of the way in which Hemingway presents the fiesta.

As Paul Goodman has shown in an analysis of the bullfighting scenes, this is also true from a linguistic viewpoint. Through the "passive style" of descriptive objectivity, "the persons are held at arm's length, [and] there is no way to get inside them or identify with them"; indeed, "the effect... is like the Brechtian 'alienation,' which Hemingway achieves more consistently than Brecht."[17] In other words the text calls not for the identification of the reader but embodies a specific *resistance* to such identification. Hemingway's alienation effect, however, differs from Brecht's in that this resistance is not transformed into an epic meta-discourse with the audience—and thus dissolved into rational understanding—but points to a deeper structure of textual meaning which requires continuous interpretation of the presented reality without offering any finished version of that reality.

A similar "break" in the textual surface can be observed in the fishing episode at Burguete. As the scene is a particularly illuminating example of Hemingway's technique of reader-guidance in the novel, it should be looked at in some detail. Like the bullfights, the fishing prima facie suggests a meaningful alternative, a return from the spiritual wasteland of modern society to natural life, and thus promises a potential emotional change or even climax for the reader. Yet again a closer look reveals that this potential is not used but is in fact deliberately *counteracted* by the way in which the episode is related. The fishing excursion is the first real contact with nature that Jake and his friend Bill establish after their long travel from Paris and from the anonymous jungle of the city that it symbolizes. But other than Bill, who is full of eager ambition and wades deep into the stream to catch particularly great fish, Jake—and with him the focus of the reader's attention—again remains curiously detached from the fishing, avoiding any immediate involvement in the experience. He sits on a dam above the falls where the water "was deep" (99) and gets through with his fishing in a very economical, almost mechanical way, catching six identical trout in a row at the easiest place of the stream: "While I had him on [the first trout] several trout had jumped at the falls. As soon as I baited up and dropped in again I hooked another and brought him in the same way. In a little while I had six. They were all about the same size. I laid them out side by side, all their heads pointing the same way, and looked at them" (119).

With this Jake's fishing adventure is about over. Clearly, the effect here is anticlimactic, emphasizing not the dynamic element of action and experience but the static or, rather, circular element of recurrence of the same—note the conspicuous repetition of the word "same" in reference to Jake's activities, as well as to the "result" of these activities (the trout). This is even sharper brought to light in view of Bill's unreserved engagement in the fishing and of the far more impressive success of his efforts: "Bill sat down, opened up his bag, laid a big trout on the grass. He took out three more, each one a little bigger than the last, and laid them side by side in the shade from the tree. His face was sweaty and happy" (120). Bill has indeed had an experience, and the excited ambition and "climax" of his adventure are not only mirrored in his face but, in a nice bit of ironic imagery, in the increasingly bigger size of his trout. Yet again, the energy and adventure of active life which Bill's fishing symbolizes are distinctly removed from the novel's narrative center. His experience happens in absentia; it is not accessible to the reader as a subjective process but only as the "dead," objectified result of that process. This detachment from concrete experience is underlined by the fact that while Bill, outside the novel's narrative focus, is engaged in fishing, Jake has withdrawn under a tree to read. What he is reading is a story "about a man who had been frozen in the Alps and fallen into a glacier and disappeared, and his bride was going to wait twenty-four years exactly for his body to come out on the moraine, while her true love waited too, and they were still waiting when Bill came up" (120). This strange story of a love-relationship which contains the impossibility of its own realization, and which indicates a more general stalemate of human feelings and, indeed, of life itself, is an ironic-reflective comment on Jake's situation in the book. It emphasizes his unrealized, self-negating relationship to Brett Ashley, with which he continues to be preoccupied even in this pastoral scene (see the ensuing dialogue with Bill, 103–4), signifying once more his psychic alienation from active life and experience.

From the analysis of these key passages in the book, the implied reader in *The Sun Also Rises* clearly emerges as an example of Type I of the reader-appeal in Hemingway distinguished above. The emotive potential of fictional wish fulfillment is a priori neutralized here, because all potentially life-affirming experiences are undermined by the implicit negativity of the narrator's consciousness which distances the reader from any immediate involvement in the fictional world. The tension created in the reader's mind is thus not primarily dynamic but static, not primarily processual but simultaneous. Rather than an emotional tension between distinct and alternating phases of reception, it is a reflective tension between surface vs. deep structure, external vs. internal reality, explicit vs. implicit text.

A variation of this type of reader-appeal is represented by the story "Big Two-Hearted River." Placed at the end of *In Our Time*, it is significantly reduced in external action and conflict. All that happens is Nick's journey to a river in the country, his stay there overnight, and his trout fishing on the next day. At the same time, however, there are symbolic and linguistic signals in the formulated text which, in the sense of the iceberg theory, point to a constitutive dimension of the unformulated, to deeper and more problematical levels of meaning beneath the uneventful and apparently unproblematical surface of the explicit text. Examples of such signals are the interchapters with their horrifying scenes of death and violence that are placed before Part I and between the two parts like electrifying psycho-shocks; the wasteland motif of the burnt town at the beginning; the nervous control and intensity of Nick's activities, in which every detail seems to gain disproportionate importance; his overreaction to "deeper" areas of reality, as in the "shock" he suffers when he steps into the stream to fish[18] or in the characterization of the fishing of the swamp as a "tragic adventure";[19] the symbol of the swamp itself, which is an objective correlative of the unexplored depths of Nick's psyche. Nick's behavior thus appears as a compulsive attempt to remain on a safe, unproblematical surface of life and to avoid, for the time being, any conscious confrontation with the experiences which lie behind him, but which, as these signals show, in fact form a constituent part of his present situation. This discrepancy between the formulated and the unformulated dimensions of the text, between the manifest pastoral idyl of a man's ritual regeneration in nature and the latent crisis of his psyche which, in his overidentification with this idyllic pattern, he tries to suppress, creates a constant tension in the reader's mind, provoking him to reflect on those problematical, subconscious implications that Nick, like Jake Barnes, tries to exclude from consciousness and communication. Nick's effort to certify and (over-) determine the reality of his experience, by clinging to simplistic rituals and sensory details, on a level of unproblematical, "natural" action produces a paradoxical result, causing instead an irritating feeling of uncertainty and indeterminacy which all the more activates the reflective skepticism of the reader. The more Nick suppresses reflection, the more the reader is forced into it. Nick's psyche, like Jake's, marks a central indeterminacy of the text, a "black box" of the actions in the story which, at the same time that it motivates these actions, constantly threatens to undermine the attempt at a new life. Other examples of this type of reader-appeal are Hemingway's "static stories" such as "Mr. and Mrs. Elliot," "Cat in the Rain," "A Clean, Well-Lighted Place," "Hills Like White Elephants"—in all of which a similar effect of emotional deadlock and reflective distance is created.

A model example of the second type of the implied reader in Hemingway is "The Short Happy Life of Francis Macomber," but "The Snows of Kilimanjaro" or novels like *A Farewell to Arms* and *The Old Man and the Sea* are also distinctively shaped in their appellative structure by this type. As has been said, the second type, in contrast to the first, is very much defined by the horizontal aspect of reception, by the dynamic process of experience inscribed into the text. The two sides of affective reader-appeal—the daydream of an imaginative fulfillment of life and the shock of witnessing the destruction of that daydream—which are fused and mutually neutralized in Type I in favor of reflection, are separated in Type II and projected into a temporal sequence of distinct and successive phases of reception. The psychodramatic potential of this tension is fully released and pushed to the extreme here, involving the reader in a fictional experience characterized by sharp changes and contrasting climaxes of his emotional participation in the text. Indeed, the characteristic pattern of Type II quite distinctly follows the model of a daydream, which is developed as an idealizing counterfantasy out of the experience of a negative reality, is—sometimes almost miraculously—fulfilled in the course of the text and is inevitably destroyed in its clash with the reality from which it has tried to emancipate itself.[20]

This pattern can be seen in an analysis of "The Short Happy Life of Francis Macomber," one of the author's major stories, where it occurs in an almost ideal-typical form. Basically, the story can be divided into three parts, which correspond to different yet interrelated phases of reception.

(1) The situation at the beginning is one of utter humiliation for Macomber, who has behaved like a coward at a lion hunt and is now the subject of contempt among the hunting company. Because his cowardice is the implicit center of attention to which the other characters—Wilson, the guide, and Margot Macomber—react, the reader is involuntarily placed in Macomber's position and is made to feel, indirectly but all the more painfully, his frustration and isolation.[21] This feeling is enforced and at the same time charged with an aggressive undertone by Margaret's behavior, who demonstrates her disdain of her husband to a degree that she provokes not only Wilson's but the reader's sharp antipathy (16ff.). However, there are already some first signals in the text that direct the hopeful attention of the reader to the buffalo-hunt of the following day, which is repeatedly mentioned in the dialogue and is associated with the intense but diametrically opposed expectations of the couple. To Margaret it means the promise of another defeat for her husband and thus of another triumph for herself: "You don't know how I look forward to tomorrow" (16). To Macomber it represents the desperate hope of rehabilitating himself: "Maybe I can fix it up on buffalo" (15), and "I would like to clear away this lion business" (17). Clearly, the reader is with Macomber here, although the vague hope of a reaffirmation of his virtually annihilated self that is evoked here may still seem rather unrealistic at this point. This is especially true as there follows, first of all, a further intensification of Macomber's feeling of (self-) humiliation and a retrospective exploration of the reasons for his crisis within his own subjectivity. As he lies awake at night, he becomes aware of the extreme shame and the "cold, hollow fear" (20) which entirely dominate and paralyze his psyche. In a reconstruction of the events of the preceding day, his act of cowardice is retraced in its successive steps and is

communicated to the reader in all the nightmarish intensity it gains through Macomber's fear-ridden perspective. It is retold as a process of inevitable failure which results from his lifelong fear of death and which culminates in the scene when he runs away in panic as the wounded lion charges: "they had just moved into the grass when Macomber heard the blood-choked coughing grunt, and saw the swishing rush in the grass. The next thing he knew he was running; running wildly in the open, running toward the stream" (25). This is the first, *negative* climax in the reading process which is inscribed into the story. Though rendered retrospectively, it is brought alive through scenic dramatization and is thus conveyed to the reader not as a finished event of the past but as a concrete emotional experience, which is actualized in his consciousness as a determining part of the present situation. And when afterward Margaret, who has been absent from the tent during Macomber's painful recollections, returns from Wilson's tent, provocatively admitting her adultery, this appears as an act of final humiliation which makes Macomber's defeat complete. At the same time, however, it psychologically prepares the reader for the dramatic change of emotion that takes place in the second part of the story.

(2) For on the morning of the next day, Macomber's mood is conspicuously altered. The negation of his whole personality has been pushed to a point where his self-destructive despair has been transformed into a feeling of violent aggression, which finds its first object in Wilson. "At breakfast they were all three at the table before daylight and Francis Macomber found that, of all the many men that he had hated, he hated Robert Wilson the most" (28). Macomber is in an explosive mood, in which he throws off all restrictions of social appearances. All at once, anything can be expected of him, as his paralyzed, fear-ridden state of crisis has turned into an irresistible impulse to action: "'Going shooting?' he [Wilson] asked. 'Yes,' said Macomber, standing up. 'Yes'" (30). The reader's identification increases as Macomber more and more seems to fill the heroic role of fearless self-affirmation that has been built up as a counterfantasy to his preceding crisis in the reader's expectation. Indeed, the nightmare of cowardice and fear, which dominates the first part of the story, is transformed in the second part into a trancelike triumph of self-assertion, in which Macomber, as the reader's fictional second self, feels a "drunken elation," a moment of supreme happiness: "In his life he had never felt so good" (33). From the reader's point of view, then, the hope of Macomber's rehabilitation which is raised *ex negativo* in the first part is fulfilled in the second part in the form of a wish-fulfilling daydream which, as the *positive* climax of the implied reader-response, forms a symmetrical counterpart to the negativity of the preceding experience.

(3) All the more shocking to the reader is the sudden, new turn of events shortly afterward when Macomber, boldly confronting the wounded buffalo, is shot in the head by his wife:

> he shot again at the wide nostrils and saw the horns jolt again and fragments fly, and he did not see Wilson now and, aiming carefully, shot again with the buffalo's huge bulk almost on him and his rifle almost level with the coming head, nose out, and he could see the little wicked eyes and the head started to lower, and he felt a sudden white-hot, blinding flash explode inside his head and that was all he ever felt. (39)

As the narrative focus is entirely on Macomber, the shot hits the reader, metaphorically speaking, as if "from behind," disillusioning, like a *vis a tergo*, the euphoric fantasy of his heroic daydream. With this unexpected anticlimax, the reader is left in shock and bewilderment and is forcefully lead back to a problematical reality from which his heroic daydream has promised to take him away. Mrs. Macomber's (accidental?) shot creates a central indeterminacy in the story that retrospectively invalidates the attempt of determining modern human reality in terms of direct, physical action which Macomber—like Wilson before him—has undertaken. Her shot thus becomes the pivotal point in the text, whose interpretation largely decides about the interpretation of the story as a whole. It forces the reader to reflect on the fictional experience he has gone through and possibly to recognize the problematical implications, the narrowness and one-sidedness of that experience.[22]

This is roughly the psychodramatic pattern inscribed into the activity of the implied reader in "Macomber," and this pattern is to a considerable extent responsible for the high degree of emotional involvement which the story provokes and which is reflected in the particularly passionate critical controversies it has set off. The reader's reaction to the story is characterized by extreme contrasts and sharp changes of emotional mood. His participation in the text is not, as in Type I, primarily evoked by structural-reflective ambiguity but by the immediacy of a psychic experience which only *afterward*, after Mrs. Macomber's shot has wakened him from his fictional daydream, is subject to the retrospective and, potentially, (self-) critical reflection of the reader. Instead of the static effect of simultaneous, largely unchanging, mutually obstructing emotions as in Type I, we have here the dynamic effect of a process of sharply alternating, mutually intensifying emotions which are transmitted through the temporal sequence of contrasting climaxes marked by the wish-fulfilling daydream vs. the shock of disillusioning reality.

This pattern recurs more frequently in Hemingway than one would think, especially since he is a writer often labeled a naturalist and a clinical realist. In it an element of hope and affirmation of life manifests itself, as well as a high degree of sensibility for the resistance that this hope encounters in the modern world. In fact a closer look reveals that some of the author's major works follow this or a similar model. Thus in "The Snows of Kilimanjaro" Harry's hopeless situation is transformed near the end of the story into the dream of his miraculous rescue by an airplane. To the reader, as to Harry, this waking dream, which at first is presented quite realistically and which only later, during the flight to the top of the mountain, becomes recognizable as a mere fantasy, quite explicitly resembles the structure of a wish-fulfilling daydream. And as in "Macomber"—though in a temporally much more condensed form—the daydream is developed out of a desperate death-in-life situation, dramatizing in the reader's psyche the rise of the wounded hero to symbolic self-fulfillment, before he is forced to witness his destruction in the shocklike clash with the disillusioning forces of reality (Harry is discovered to be dead on his cot by his wife). *A Farewell to Arms* also draws on the appellative potential of the daydream structure. Here it is the dream of peace and love that is evoked as a counterfantasy to the experience of war. It begins to materialize in Henry's relationship to Catherine in the first part of the novel, is built up further in his desertion and his idea of a "separate peace," and is fulfilled in an idealized way in the symbiotic union of the two lovers in the Utopian sphere of the Swiss mountains, before it is all the more mercilessly destroyed with Catherine's death at the end of the book. A paradigmatic example of the structure is *The Old Man and the Sea.* From the very beginning the reader's expectation is directed, by the exceptionally luckless situation of the old man (he "was now definitely and finally *salao*")[23] and by his wish for an all the more triumphant compensation for his humiliating lack of success, toward the Great Fish.[24] With Santiago's sailing out to sea, and with the increasing size of the fish he encounters, this expectation if further intensified finds its first climax in the actual appearance of the Great Fish, whose gigantic size borders on the fantastic, and is after a long, fierce struggle, marvelously fulfilled in the eventual defeat of the Fish. And again the reader is made to feel all the more painfully the relentless disillusionment which follows, on the way back to the harbor, with the attacks of the sharks, against whose ever-growing number the old man is powerless and who finally have left only the skeleton of the fish when he reaches home. Quite clearly, the reader's participation in the novel is shaped by the daydream pattern, which is employed here, as in other texts, to increase the psychic intensity of the fictional experience and to activate the life-affirming tendencies in the reader's consciousness in order to make him even more acutely aware of—and, possibly, also better able to cope with—the disillusioning facts of reality.

As has been said, there are of course overlappings between the two types of implied reader here distinguished. The vertical tension between surface and depth, between the formulated and the unformulated dimension of the text, is also part of the reader-appeal in "Macomber" or *The Old Man and the Sea;* and there is the indication of a horizontal tension, of an at least symbolic development of the hero, in *The Sun Also Rises* and in "Big Two-Hearted River."[25] But what matters here is that one or the other of these aspects more or less clearly dominates in the texts, giving the role of the reader a distinctly different character. They represent the two basic forms of appellative structure in Hemingway that mark the endpoints of a whole range of possible combinations and variations. At the same time, they illustrate different phases in the literary development of the author in that Type I more frequently occurs in his earlier work and Type II in his middle and later work. All that can be done here is to indicate the main characteristics of these two types and to demonstrate their realization in a few selected works. A much more extensive and systematic study of the reader-appeal of Hemingway's fictions would be necessary to arrive at a more differentiated typology, involving the careful analysis and comparison of many more texts.

NOTES

1. Earl Rovit, *Ernest Hemingway* (Boston, 1963), p. 31.

2. See especially Julian Smith, "Hemingway and the Thing Left Out," *Journal of Modern Literature* 1 (1970): 169–82. The connection between literary styles and certain kinds of reader-responses was investigated by Walter J. Ong in "The Writer's Audience Is Always a Fiction," *PMLA* 90 (1975): 9–21, where he comes close to the conception of an "implied reader" in that he discusses several writers, among them Hemingway, in the way they "fictionalize" the reader in their texts, that is, induce the real, historical reader to let himself become part of the fictional world, actively participating in its imaginative construction.

3. *Death in the Afternoon* (New York: Scribner's, 1932), p. 192.

4. See, for example, Raymond S. Nelson, *Hemingway: Expressionist Artist* (Ames, Iowa, 1979).

5. See Wolfgang Iser, *The Implied Reader: Patterns of Communication in Prose Fiction from Bunyan to Beckett* (Baltimore: Johns Hopkins University Press, 1978), and *The Act of Reading: A Theory of Aesthetic Response* (Baltimore: Johns Hopkins University Press, 1979).

A useful introduction to Iser's theory is his article "The Reading Process: A Phenomenological Approach," *New Literary History* 3 (1971): 279–99.

6. This notion of "schematized views," as well as of the "indeterminacy" of literature, derives from Roman Ingarden's phenomenological theory of literature: *The Cognition of the Literary Work of Art* (Evanston, Ill.: Northwestern University Press, 1974).

7. Iser, "The Reading Process," 282ff.

8. Ibid., 292.

9. See, for example, Edmund Husserl, *Cartesianische Meditationen: Husserliana*, vol. 1 (The Hague, 1950), p. 73. Here the principle of reflection is formulated as the basic principle of human consciousness and knowledge. Engl. trans, *Cartesian Meditations* (Boston: Kluwer, 1977).

10. For this term see Hans-Georg Gadamer, *Truth and Method: Basics of a Philosophical Hermeneutics* (New York, 1975).

11. Walter Schulz. "Anmerkungen zur Hermeneutik Gadamers" ["Notes on Gadamer's Hermeneutics"] in *Hermeneutik und Dialektik I*, ed. R. Bubner, K. Kramer, R. Wiehl (Tübingen, 1970), pp. 305–16.

12. Sigmund Freud. "Der Dichter und das Phantasieren" ["The Poet and Fantasy"] *Sigmund Freud: Studienausgabe*, vol. 10, *Bildende Kunst und Literatur* [*Visual Art and Literature*] (Frankfurt, 1969), pp. 171–79.

13. Thus, for example, in Norman Holland's 5 *Readers Reading* (New Haven, Conn., 1975), p. 127.

14. Thus when N. Holland has the reader project any fantasy into the text "that yields the pleasure he characteristically seeks": *Poems in Persons: An Introduction to the Psychoanalysis of Literature* (New York, 1973), p. 77, or in David Bleich's classroom experiments with his "subjective criticism," *Readings and Feelings: An Introduction to Subjective Criticism* (Urbana, Ill., 1975).

15. Ernest Hemingway, *The Sun Also Rises* (New York: Scribner's, 1970), p. 4. All subsequent references to the text are to this edition and are given in parentheses after the quotation.

16. Beoncheong Yu, "The Still Center of Hemingway's World" in *Ernest Hemingway: Five Decades of Criticism*, ed. Linda W. Wagner (East Lansing, Mich., 1974), pp. 109–31.

17. Paul Goodman, "The Sweet Style of Ernest Hemingway," in *Ernest Hemingway: Five Decades of Criticism*, pp. 153–60.

18. "Big Two-Hearted River," *The First Forty-nine Stories* (London: Jonathan Cape, 1944), pp. 165–85.

19. Ibid., p. 183.

20. This shows that while Freud defines literature in undialectic opposition to reality, Hemingway dramatizes the collision between daydream and reality *within* the literary work itself.

21. "The Short Happy Life of Francis Macomber," *The First Forty-nine Stories*, pp. 11–40.

22. These problematical implications, especially with regard to Mrs. Macomber's role in the story and to the male-chauvinist distortions created by Wilson's simplistic "code," were first pointed out by Warren Beck in his article "The Shorter Happy Life of Mrs. Macomber," *Modern Fiction Studies* 1–2 (1955): 28–37, where he argues for a much more positive view of Margot Macomber than most critics before him. The article set off a controversy with Mark Spilka which continued over more than twenty years.

23. *The Old Man and the Sea* (New York: Scribner's, 1952), p. 9.

24. On pp. 16, 18, 20, 23, 30 of *The Old Man and the Sea*, this hope of a great fish is explicitly expressed.

25. See the rebirth motif of Jake's bathing in the sea at the end of the novel and Nick's gradual, if slow, approximation of the deeper levels of reality in "Big Two-Hearted River."

EARL ROVIT

On Psychic Retrenchment in Hemingway

> We sat close against each other. I put my arm around her and she
> rested against me comfortably. It was very hot and bright, and the house
> looked sharply white. We turned out onto the Gran Via.
>
> "Oh, Jake," Brett said, "we could have had such a damned good time
> together."
>
> Ahead was a mounted policeman in khaki directing traffic. He raised
> his baton. The car slowed suddenly pressing Brett against me.
>
> "Yes," I said. "Isn't it pretty to think so?"

These well-known last lines of *The Sun Also Rises* provide a convenient
starting place to talk about what appears to be the almost obsessive policy of
exclusion in Hemingway's work and, perhaps, his life as well. That is, a
consistent tactic of pushing away, warding off, editing out everything that
can be considered extraneous—everything that is "not me"—seems to
characterize Hemingway's celebrated code of morality, his quasi-Draconian
division of the world into those who are "one of us" and those multitudinous
others who fail to qualify, his consistent aesthetic techniques; it even
permeates his well-chronicled life-style with its global safari-like
peregrinations as he breaks one camp after another, leaving behind resentful
loved ones, soured friendships, and, ultimately, everyone outside of the
shotgun-blasted front foyer of his Ketchum ranch. From the viewpoint of the

From *Hemingway: Essays of Reassessment.* © 1991 by Oxford University Press.

survivors, suicide is necessarily—and healthily—synonymous with "self-slaughter," an act of personal eradication which solely concerns the actor in cruel relationship to himself. It is not illogical to imagine, however, that from the suicide's viewpoint, the act may be externally directed—a deliberate attempt to eliminate the world, the desperate equivalent of ultimate editorial deletion.

There has been some small controversy over the final dialogue in *The Sun Also Rises*, but whether one reads Jake's last line as a bitter, subtly hostile rejoinder or a mildly ironic agreement, there can be no question of the final effect. If Jake, in fact, concurs with Brett's sentimental gushiness, he does so in such a way as to keep her at heart's, although not arm's, length. At the end of the novel, Jake is more firmly alone in the universe than he was at the beginning, and in some perverse way this establishment of his own isolation is presented as a kind of moral success, if not triumph. Further, one notes that this position of fortified isolation is replicated throughout Hemingway's fiction—Frederic Henry in the rain; Jordan in prone firing position on the pine needles; Santiago dreaming of the lions; Harry free from the fetid lowlands, the hyena, and Helen his wife; all the Nick or Nick-like stories that recede into silence with the protagonist either alone or protected by nuanced barriers of ambiguity and irony. One might almost suppose that the crucial function of plot in a Hemingway story is to stake out a significant space where the protagonist can be separate from and palpably superior to the rest of the world.

Again, from the quoted excerpt, one can argue that Jake's willed isolation as he distances himself from Brett is also something of a repudiation of those he has seemed to have accepted and approved of, along with those whose credentials obviously fall short. If Woolsey and Krum, the Dayton pilgrims, and the Pamplona wastrels—most spectacularly Robert Cohn—are patently not "one of us," one can conclude that Jake's surgical excision of Brett also signals a kind of judgment on Pedro Romero and Count Mippipopolous as well. In this respect, Montoya's cold formality toward the American who has betrayed his *afición* is repeated by Jake toward his entire human world. "One of us," that exclusive membership echoed in Colonel Cantwell's secret society, turns out to be comprised of *only* one of us—namely me. Or, to put a more generous interpretation on these acts of blatant or more gentle rejection—this effort to find things one cannot lose—if Jake and the reader can keep a positive admiration for both the count and the young bullfighter, it is only by so defining their achieved prowess as to consider each of them as fundamentally unencumbered by human commitments as Jake is.

But once more to the excerpt. It seems reasonably representative of Hemingway's prose at its best—ten short, syntactically unadorned, declarative sentences; a sequence of understated periodic rhythms which may evoke resonances of meaning through the studied impersonality of what is not said, not described, and, in fact, not even showily implied. The few graphic details that are included are so severely outlined and highlighted as to nearly disconnect themselves from both the narrative texture and the source of perception that renders them. Paradoxically, the effect of this style is to implicate the sensitized reader into a more actively participating role of shared authorship than he would otherwise assume.

The sexual connotations of the "mounted policeman" who raises "his baton" in ironic contrast to the necessarily quiescent Jake—and this at the moment when Brett is pressing herself upon him—have been generally recognized. The only other detail that offers a potential comment upon the situation is the statement that "the houses looked sharply white." At this culminating point in the novel, since the reader is urgently searching for a key to Jake's frame of mind, the tendency to overinterpret details is almost inevitable. Here, the statement seems to support only two possibilities. First, it can be read as an innocuous perception which serves merely to buttress the narrative illusion of reality. Spanish houses *are* frequently white, and Jake has been lunching in the restaurant out of the sun, drinking large quantities of wine which increases intraocular pressure, causing the pupils of his eyes to dilate. The sudden exposure to the bright daylight, the contraction of the pupils, the reflected glare of walls and roofs—these are surely sufficient causes to make the houses look "sharply white." Second, beyond this, however, the detail may attest to Jake's deliberate separation from the scene of sentimental self-pity that Brett is playing out with him. While she uses his shoulder to weep on, his hunter's eyes are sweeping the landscape, and a substantial portion of his attention has already severed itself from her and from her plight of self-indulgence. If the latter is the case, Jake's final sentence is a little more chilling in its effect than is often thought.

I wonder whether we have accurately weighed the abundance of partings, departures, and fractured relationships that Hemingway's stories register. Because of the paramount importance he ascribed to his variety of individualism, it is to be expected that his plot situations will be contrived to place his protagonists in positions where they are alone. Still, his way of accenting that individualism characteristically asserts selfhood by excluding others rather than by absorbing creatively from others to strengthen that self. From "Up in Michigan" and "My Old Man" through "A Canary for One," "Homage to Switzerland," and "The Snows of Kilimanjaro," the

Hemingway protagonist is either forced involuntarily into solitude (*A Farewell to Arms*) or chooses that position for his own purposes (*Across the River, The Old Man and the Sea*). Once, perhaps, in *For Whom the Bell Tolls*, the choice is made in terms of a higher altruistic good, "self-sacrifice," but the typical denouement of isolation is the result of an implacable fate (designed, of course, by the author) or the deliberate preference of the character himself.

It seems likely to me that the nexus of circumstances that led Hemingway to aggrandize his fictional heroes by excluding everyone else from their centers of being must also be behind the compulsion that resulted in the development of a pared minimalist prose style, a doctrine of narrative omission, and a moral code heavily dependent on judgmental exclusions. And, further, as we have noted in the quoted excerpt, the kinds of unresolved ambiguities that his use of irony and the withholding of explanatory information produce—do these not work to hold the reader at bay in the same way that Jake establishes a measured distance between Brett and himself? In other words, we ought to consider the curious possibility that a significant source of Hemingway's appeal to his audience may be secured by strategic devices that exclude the reader from Hemingway's heroic world even as they beguile and seduce him into admiring its austerities of courage and integrity.

Assuming that this perspective is worth pursuing, we are then faced with two formidable questions. First, obviously, is why Hemingway would come to harbor such powerful, if somewhat concealed attitudes of defensive hostility. And second, why would a culture of supposedly democratic ideals and aspirations embrace so wholeheartedly a body of work that virtually flaunts the reader's inherent incapacity or unworthiness to be more than an uninformed spectator of heroic high jinks and derring-do incontrovertibly beyond his ken? Clearly these are enormously complex questions, dealing as they do with two traditional mysteries: the secret of Hemingway's psychic structure and the secret of audience response. Although I don't expect to shed any radically new light on areas already exhaustively inspected and speculated on, I will try to indicate some places that we may have ignored or viewed a little askew.

With the accumulation in the past twenty years of the vast bulk of primary and secondary source materials (manuscripts, letters, the secondhand memoir testimony of those who knew him well or ill), scholarship has edged closer and closer to the ultimately impenetrable enigma of not only how Hemingway transacted his life and his art, but how life conspired to shape his character. For my purposes it is sufficient to accept the tentative broad hypothesis that as an adolescent, Hemingway—the second oldest and for a long time the only male child surrounded by sisters—found himself twisting between a rueful contemptuous love for his father and a furious contemptuous love for his mother and—for reasons unknown—was emotionally incapable of accepting or rejecting wholeheartedly either or both of them. I do not at all understand the etiology of this process, but it seems likely to me that the deep-seated consequences of this intolerable position was a lifelong strategy of escape and evasion which led him to exclude not only his parents but his whole family, his childhood religion, his hometown, friend after friend who entered his life with familial intimacy, and—during his most productive years—his country itself.

Curiously enough, just as Hemingway's deceptively simple but evocative prose style tempts the reader to search for meanings and run the risk of overinterpretation, so the jarring contradictions between his public and private personae and the deliberate confusion of autobiographical fact and invention in his fictions tempt the reader to sinful speculation in a psychoanalytical direction. Willing but unqualified to do much in the way of this sin, I would simply note an odd fact. For an American Protestant of his generation, and especially for a writer unusually addicted to scraping at the psychic scabs of presumably unhealable childhood wounds, Hemingway and his work seem astonishingly free of guilt. Instead, I have the impression that shame—or the overwhelming fear of being placed in a shame situation—is, rather than guilt, the most cogent motivating force in his psyche. His compulsive work habits, his inordinate need to demonstrate that he will stand up to any physical test with courage and stamina, his forceful advocation of a code of honor in which achievement is measured by the ability to best one's competitors in a rule-defined ordeal—these things suggest that it was not so much compensatory success that Hemingway lusted after as it was a desperate urgency to avoid the humiliation of failure.

The three-year-old boy who shouts with gusto that he is "fraid of nothin" strikes me in retrospect as a personality normally susceptible to fear and—more than that—abnormally fearful of being exposed as afraid. Granted the difficulties of making clear distinctions between shame and guilt, especially when shame is internalized; still, some sense of what I mean may be seen in the respective antonyms of these concepts. The automatic opposite of *guilt* is *innocence*—a condition generally conceded to be endangered-species-rare in Protestant American culture. And yet innocence seems relatively congruent with my sense of both Hemingway and the fictional world he made. (Think for a moment of some Hemingway characters who behave badly: Macomber, Cohn, Pablo. None of them appears particularly guilt-ridden, not even Jake after he betrays Montoya's trust.) The opposite of *shame*, on the other hand, is *pride*; for my purposes, neither the religious cardinal sin nor that democratic virtue which is the concomitant of self-reliance. What I have in mind is pride as a more rigid, externally validated quality which I associate with exclusionary codes of honor and which are nicely summed up in medals, awards, and documentable achievements. Accordingly, I wonder whether in our zeal to investigate oedipal pressures, homosexual latencies, and dark depressive morbidities, we may have overlooked the role of shame and, perhaps, its equally coercive function in Hemingway's personality.

Shame differs from guilt, of course, in being socially engendered. Most commonly, it seems to be a by-product effect of stringent toilet training, and we have ample knowledge about the Armageddon-like militancy with which Protestants of Hemingway's parents' class regarded the subject of santitation and filth and especially personal cleanliness. I can cite no data about young Ernest's possible problems in learning to control his bowels, but I am struck when looking at his childhood pictures by the difficulties of keeping those crisply starched white dresses unsoiled. Admittedly, I have only speculation to rely on, but exclusion, after all, is a logical reflex formation to develop as a way of cleaning up or eradicating that shame-causing extraneous which is considered to be filth. And I would note in passing Hemingway's oft-proclaimed pride in possessing a first-class "shit detector"—something almost identical in his case to an active Christian conscience as well as an aesthetic censor. If Hemingway's morality is what you feel good after, it may be a sense of cleanliness that is a concern less of the shriven spirit than of the debrided body. (What you feel bad after, on the other hand, is typically referred to in Hemingway's letters as "black-ass" moods.) And, finally, the accumulation of laboriously counted and painstakingly winnowed words may be viewed as the triumphantly offered gifts of that residual small boy in him, eager to please, loath to be humiliated, and exuberantly proud of his labored accomplishment.

In conclusion, let me touch on the special class consciousness which Hemingway shared with so many of his Lost Generation fellows. A full-fledged member by birth of that upper-middle professional class that had dominated American culture and society from its inception, Hemingway imbibed most of his social prejudices and frustrations with his mother's milk. As a different kind of political power broker and business entrepreneur ascended to rapid hegemony in the early years of the twentieth century, Hemingway's once dominant class was left with the least essential—although the most durable—of culture's prizes, namely a control over taste and opinions. The assumed superiorities of the genteel tradition—a casual racist, anti-immigrant, anti-Semitic, antiurban sex chauvinism—become allied with a sentimentally disillusioned nostalgia for a preindustrialized America that was, in reality, merely a fantasy of childhood. These "new" alien Americans—immigrant, working-class, or bourgeoisie—were patently "not one of us." The country was now "a bloody mess," Hemingway declared in *Green Hills:* "Let the others come to America who did not know that they had come too late. Our people had seen it at its best and fought for it when it was well worth fighting for. Now I would go somewhere else." And thus this despiser of American cities found Paris, Venice, Madrid, and Havana compatible with his hieratic standards of taste when he was not living the life of a respected *padrone* among the earthy and worshipful peasantry. And when we check the roster of his exemplary heroes, it is no surprise to discover that, with the exception of the more or less autobiographical characters, Americans are strictly excluded.

Exclusion, then, becomes for Hemingway an instinctive psychic response, a social creed, an aesthetic principle. In time, as his energies became depleted, the circle in which he stood at the center of his exclusions—the clean well-lighted place—became smaller and smaller until it reached a vanishing point. And that out of this extraordinary melange of bitter resentment, intense self-discipline, and perverse courage should emerge the luminous work which is his heritage is nothing less than the kind of miraculous act that makes the earth move. Or, at least, it's pretty to think so.

> *He woke and was pleased that it was not yet light and he was happy, as always, with the early morning. Then he remembered the night with distaste and went into the bathroom to shower and brush his teeth. He was angry when he put on his shorts and left the room and he was still angry when he started to write; hardly able to see the handwriting on the lined page and feeling the anger clamped against his temples.*
>
> *His anger was against himself and against emotion and against the disorder of his life; but as he went on writing it relaxed and left him alone with what he had to do. It had helped him to start and once he was going, it left him as un-noticed as anyone who had pushed a car on a cold morning and fallen behind instead of passing when the motor started. He wrote with precision, good judgement, a delicate understanding of seeming callousness and a comprehension of evil that distilled from the ill smelling mash of his own recent life and he could smell the mash as sour smelling as the native brew at the Shamba where this other evil had begun....*
>
> (*Eden* manuscript, box 3, Chap. 25, p.3)

DEBRA A. MODDELMOG

The Disabled Able Body
and White Heteromasculinity

It is impossible to explore the intersections of mobility and desire without
also examining the body and its capacity for being mobile and desirable. In
mentioning Hemingway's mobility, one undoubtedly recalls some famous
images and stories of his attractive and capable body in action, for example,
Hemingway hunting, boxing, fishing, running with the bulls, swimming,
skiing, supposedly carrying an injured soldier to safety during battle, or
busting his way out of a crashed and burning airplane.[47] Always, one sees
Hemingway walking—through the streets of Paris, across the plains of East
Africa, in the woods of Upper Michigan, up the snow-covered mountains of
Switzerland and Austria. But Hemingway's active life took a toll on his body
as well, and almost as famous as the images of his body in motion are images
of his body in pain.[48] Some idea of the pain Hemingway endured—and of
the legendary status his body in pain has acquired—can be found at the end
of Jeffrey Meyers's biography of Hemingway where a three-page appendix
lists Hemingway's accidents and illnesses. The appendix begins with a
childhood accident in which Hemingway fell with a stick in his throat and
gouged his tonsils and concludes with a 14-item list of ailments suffered
during the last two years of his life, everything from skin rash to hepatitis to
severe depression. Another measure of both Hemingway's body in pain and
the legend surrounding it appears in a letter Hemingway wrote while he

From *Reading Desire: In Pursuit of Ernest Hemingway.* © 1999 by Cornell University.

recuperated from two plane crashes in Africa in 1954 and after he had read
the obituaries erroneously announcing his death. "Ruptured kidney (much
blood and pieces of kidney in urine). The hell with the rest of it. It goes on
from there. It is all much better but it hurts and people aren't indestructible
even if the journalists say so" (2 February 1954; *Ernest Hemingway: Selected
Letters*, 828).

Of course, both desirability and mobility are culturally and historically
determined. What one culture finds beautiful, another finds repulsive; the
body that one society views as blessed with special powers, another labels
crippled, deformed, or retarded. In regard to modern Western nations,
Lennard Davis argues that Western Europe and the United States have
formed their identities upon a notion of normalcy that is "intricately tied up
with eugenics, statistical proofs of intelligence, ability, and so on."[49]
According to Davis, this hegemony of normalcy is the driving force behind
Western imperialism which has evolved standards of normal behavior and
normal bodies based on the white, able (and, I would add, heterosexual)
body. Indeed, Davis claims that this hegemony of normalcy is so pervasive in
modern Western culture that it shapes our literature as well. For example,
the form of the novel tends to be normative, "ideologically emphasizing the
universal quality of the central character whose normativity encourages us to
identify with him or her" (41). Most novels, Davis contends, rely upon
characters with disabilities, characters who are "lame, tubercular, dying of
AIDS, chronically ill, depressed, mentally ill, and so on" to reinforce the
normalcy of the primary characters (44). As Rosemarie Garland Thomson
states, "main characters [in literature] almost never have physical
disabilities."[50]

Given that Hemingway assumed this ideology of normalcy and that he
had first-hand experiences with all kinds of illnesses and injuries, we can
construct him as having intimate knowledge of the culturally determined line
separating the able body from the disabled body. His fiction supports such a
portrayal, filled as it is with characters who suffer illness, accidents, and, most
of all, injury in the line of duty, especially duty related to military service,
hazardous occupations, and sporting events. Contrary to Davis's and
Thomson's assertions about the physical normalcy of main characters in
literature, Hemingway's disabled characters are not secondary, deviating and
deviant characters; they are the central characters, Hemingway's male
heroes. As Philip Young insisted years ago, rare is the Hemingway novel
whose white male protagonist lacks experience with serious injury, usually
injury related to his participation in war-time activities.[51] Not surprisingly,
given the masculine arenas in which these characters sustain their injuries,

their scars or disabilities do not detract from their masculinity or their ability to perform successfully. Peter Lehman notes that in the cinema, a scar on a man's face "frequently enhances rather than detracts from his power, providing a sign that he has been tested in the violent and dangerous world of male action and has survived. He is not easily defeated or killed."[52] Such an observation can be extended to Hemingway's work as well. But as I argue in this section, the scarring of Hemingway's heroes, which occurs more often on their bodies than their faces, operates in several ways. Not only is it an index of their toughness, their ability to endure a harsh and cruel world (a common characterization of Hemingway's male protagonists), but it also serves as a visible marker of their white, masculine heterosexuality, as if the white male body were incapable of doing that work by itself. However, as I will also show, the wound ultimately increases rather than appeases the anxieties it was meant to deflect, moving the heteromasculine body into the realm of the female, the feminine, and the homosexual.

Let us begin with a simple inventory of the injuries, accidents, and health problems suffered by the male heroes of Hemingway's novels. Jake Barnes has lost his penis during World War I, a "rotten way to be wounded" (*The Sun Also Rises*, 31). While delivering food to Italian troops in that war, Frederic Henry endures "Multiple superficial wounds of the left and right thigh and left and right knee and right foot. Profound wounds of right knee and foot. Lacerations of the scalp . . . with possible fracture of the skull"; he also gets jaundice and has recovered from gonorrhea.[53] Harry Morgan is shot and loses his right arm while running liquor between Cuba and Key West but continues to transport contraband and revolutionaries until he is fatally shot (*To Have and Have Not*). Robert Jordan is healthy for the first two days of *For Whom the Bell Tolls*; on the third day, he breaks his left thigh bone while fleeing Fascist soldiers in Spain and determines to make a final stand, disabled but armed, in order that his Loyalist compatriots and lover, Maria, might escape. Colonel Richard Cantwell (*Across the River and Into the Trees*) admits to having had ten concussions, has a bad leg which hurts him always, takes medicine for a bad heart, and has a misshapen right hand (the result of his hand being shot twice during war).[54] Santiago of *The Old Man and the Sea* has skin cancer and "deep-creased" scars on his hands from handling heavy fish on the cords, and his lower leg was once paralyzed by a sting ray.[55] While battling the enormous marlin that makes up the bulk of his story, he suffers a cut below his eye, rope burns on his hands, and a painful cramp that temporarily disables his left hand. Patrolling for German submarines off the shore of Cuba during World War II, Thomas Hudson (*Islands in the Stream*) is shot in his left leg, a wound that eventually causes his death. The only

Hemingway male who seems to be without injury is David Bourne, at least in the published text; the manuscript of *Garden* reveals that David was wounded and trepanned during World War I.[56]

The obvious explanation for the recurrence of the wounded hero in Hemingway's work is that the wound marks a character's inner worth, especially his virility. We can hardly miss this meaning of the wound since these men or members of their circle repeatedly assert it. For instance, after speaking to Arnaldo, "the glass-eyed waiter," Richard Cantwell comes to the following understanding about himself: "He only loved people ... who had fought or been mutilated. Other people were fine and you liked them and were good friends; but you only felt true tenderness and love for those who had been there and had received the castigation that everyone receives who goes there long enough. So I'm a sucker for crips.... And any son of a bitch who has been hit solidly, as every man will be if he stays, then I love him" (*Across the River*, 71). Expressing a similar philosophy, Thomas Hudson refuses to intervene when his son, David, attempts to catch a huge fish, even though David's feet and hands are bloody: "there is a time boys have to do things if they are ever going to be men. That's where Dave is now."[57] If David catches this fish, "he'll have something inside him for all his life and it will make everything else easier" (131). In *To Have and Have Not*, Harry Morgan, a man who has stayed and been hit solidly, determines that a lost arm signals no loss of manhood: "You lose an arm you lose an arm. There's worse things than lose [*sic*] an arm. You've got two arms and you've got two of something else [testicles]. And a man's still a man with one arm or with one of those."[58] As a final example, when Brett Ashley brings Count Mippipopolous to Jake Barnes's room, the count displays scars on his ribs and back, the result of being wounded by arrows while on a business trip to Abyssinia at age twenty one. Jake is impressed, and Brett proudly asserts, "I told you he was one of us. Didn't I?" (*Sun*, 60).

Given the wound's function as a measure of character worth and manhood, it is no surprise that the wound never prevents Hemingway's male heroes from leading active lives, except when it kills, and even then, the character never dies immediately but performs one or more acts of heroism before dying. Hemingway's wounded heroes ski, fish, hunt, ride bicycles, walk, swim, row themselves and their lovers to safety, lead troops, get into fights, play tennis, and do their work. Moreover, with important exceptions (i.e., when the wound is fatal or in the case of Jake Barnes's destroyed penis), the injury does not obstruct the hero's ability to make love, but can actually improve it. Even though Hemingway's leading men often worry, especially when older, that their wounds might make them less sexually desirable, the women they take up with assure them otherwise. Renata is practically obsessed with Richard Cantwell's misshapen hand, wanting to touch it and dreaming about it, telling him, "I love your hand and all your other wounded places" (*Across the River*, 141). When Harry Morgan asks his wife, Marie, whether she minds his amputated arm, she replies, "You're silly. I like it. Any that's you I like. Put it across there. Put it along there. Go on. I like it, true" (*Have*, 113). Marie sexualizes Harry's disability, asking him as they make love to "Put the stump there. Hold it. Hold it now. Hold it" (114). Here disability enhances ability, the ability to please a woman. The disabled hero's body performs as an able one, as "normal."

The full meaning of this normality, its status as "the norm," becomes clearer when we recognize that the men in Hemingway's novels who are identified as men of color or as homosexual generally lack the wound or react to it in despicable ways. For instance, Mr. Sing, the Chinese man who engages Harry Morgan to transport unfortunate Chinese "compatriots" (32), is about "the smoothest-looking thing" Harry has ever seen, an observation that applies to Mr. Sing's dress and English manner but also implies unblemished features. Similarly, the white homosexual men who accompany Brett to the bal musette in *The Sun Also Rises* are distinguished by newly washed white hands, wavy hair, and white faces (20). These are men who are unmarked by the effects of dangerous situations, hard work, or even the sun—and thus are to be read as unmasculine.

When a man of color or a homosexually identified man *is* wounded, he generally responds in a weak and cowardly way or his bravery is undercut. For instance, as Toni Morrison emphasizes, when Wesley, the black crewman in *To Have and Have Not*, is wounded, he whines and calls attention to his pain, a reaction that contrasts sharply with the impassive response of the more critically wounded Harry (Morrison, 74–75). More conventionally heroic is "the great negro from Cienfuegos" who arm wrestles Santiago until blood comes out from under the fingernails of both men. However, this wound is temporary, superficial, and Santiago not only defeats this black man but also breaks his confidence (*Old Man*, 76–78). In David Bourne's elephant story in *The Garden of Eden*, the native African guide, Juma, keeps his "pain in contempt" after he is mauled by an elephant (200), but because David despises him for killing this animal, his stoic response never achieves the status of bravery associated with Hemingway's wounded white heroes. Finally, in *Across the River and Into the Trees*, Renata points out "a boy with [a] wave in his hair" who is a very good painter but has false teeth in front "because he was a little bit *pédéraste* once and other *pédérastes* attacked him." The boy, she concludes, "is a man now, of course, and goes with very many women to hide what he is" (96). Here the wound is a brand that announces what the character seeks to hide, his lack of heterosexuality and virtue.

In delineating the structure of war and how nationality and nationalism become insignificant at the moment of the soldier's injury, Elaine Scarry notes that the wound "is empty of reference, though its intended referent can be inferred by the uniform over which the blood now falls, or by some other cultural insignia, a symbol and fragment of disembodied national identification."[59] Although Hemingway's protagonists typically receive their wounds during war, the inferences to the nation and its politics that Scarry mentions are often unavailable to readers since the male protagonist either does not wear the uniform of the state (e.g., Robert Jordan, Thomas Hudson) or renounces the patriotism that motivated his military participation (e.g., Frederic Henry). Through such actions, the wound loses its connections to state politics and becomes a vehicle for signifying the virtue of the body it marks. But as I pointed out, these virtuous bodies are all white, male, and heterosexually identified. Such men are the only ones in Hemingway's fiction who consistently respond with bravery and integrity to injury (besides Hemingway's protagonists, one thinks also of many of his Spanish bullfighters). The wound can thus be read as a way of asserting the physical and moral superiority of white normative masculinity and heterosexuality. At the same time, the need to repeat this pattern reveals an underlying hysteria about this superiority. It is as if white heteromasculinity requires some kind of physical mark to confirm its identity and affirm its dominance.

Clearly, the wound in Hemingway's fiction is overdetermined. One clue to understanding Hemingway's obsession with the wound and its meaning lies in the portrayal of his heroes' bodies. In most Hemingway novels, the male hero's injury is described in more detail than are the features of the man who endures it. One tries in vain to develop a mental picture of the bodies and faces of first-person narrators such as Jake Barnes and Frederic Henry. A reader might have more success in imagining Richard Cantwell, Thomas Hudson, Robert Jordan, and Santiago, but not much more. All these men are described at some point, but their portraits are vague generalities: suntanned skin, streaked hair, a thin or big body, steel eyes, an occasional broken nose. This information marks these men as outdoor types and as Anglo—their skin and hair are colored by the sun—but the details that might individualize them are scanty and, significantly, often mixed in with references to their scars.

For instance, the only information we get about Thomas Hudson's features is that he is "a big man and looked bigger stripped than he did in his clothes. He was very tanned and his hair was faded and streaked from the sun. He carried no extra weight and the scales saw that he weighed 192 pounds" (*Islands*, 12). We learn a bit more about Richard Cantwell, most of it centered around his scars. Looking at himself in the mirror, he sees the welts and ridges on his head, the result of plastic surgery after head wounds, and determines that his tan mitigates some of the ugliness. The narrator then relates what the colonel doesn't notice, but the information is sketchy: "the old used steel of his eyes," "the small, long extending laugh wrinkles at the corners of his eyes," "his broken nose [that] was like a gladiator's in the oldest statues," and "his basically kind mouth which could be truly ruthless" (*Across the River*, 111–12). Later, when Richard looks in the mirror again, he decides that his "gut is flat" and his "chest is all right except where it contains the defective muscle. We are hung as we are hung, for better or worse, or something, or something awful" (180).

The Old Man, Santiago, is "thin and gaunt with deep wrinkles in the back of his neck. The brown blotches of the benevolent skin cancer the sun brings from its reflection on the tropic sea were on his cheeks. The blotches ran well down the sides of his face and his hands had deep-creased scars from handling heavy fish on the cords. Everything about him was old except his eyes and they were the same color as the sea and were cheerful and undefeated" (*Old Man*, 9–10). He also has "strange shoulders, still powerful although very old" and a strong neck whose "creases did not show so much when the old man was asleep and his head fallen forward" (19–20). Finally, Robert Jordan is portrayed as a young man, "who was tall and thin, with sun-streaked fair hair, and a wind- and sun-burned face," wearing a "sun-faded flannel shirt, a pair of peasant's trousers and rope-soled shoes" (*Bell*, 5). That's it. Although we learn a great deal about what these men do and, to a lesser extent, about how they feel, we don't receive further information about their looks.

The only Hemingway hero whose face and body are developed into a clear image is Harry Morgan, and how those features come into existence is instructive. Harry is as nondescript as his counterparts in other Hemingway fiction until his wife, Marie, watches him leave their house for what turns out to be the last time:

> She watched him go out of the house, tall, wide-shouldered, flat-backed, his hips narrow, moving, still, *she thought*, like some kind of animal, easy and swift and not old yet, he moves so light and smooth-like, *she thought*, and when he got in the car she saw him blonde, with the sunburned hair, his face with the broad mongol

cheek bones, and the narrow eyes, the nose broken at the bridge, the wide mouth and the round jaw, and getting in the car he grinned at her and she began to cry. "His goddamn face," *she thought*. "Everytime I see his goddamn face it makes me want to cry." (*Have*, 128; emphasis added)

The reiterated "she thought" is unnecessary yet purposeful. It reminds us, as if we might forget, that we are seeing Harry's body and face through the eyes of a woman. Harry's case is exceptional because Marie's reverie constitutes one of the few times a narrator in Hemingway's fiction looks at the world through a woman's eyes. Such an exception suggests that Hemingway resists lingering on the male hero's body because he worries that turning the narrator's male gaze on these men will not only feminize them but produce homosexual implications.

This suggestion is supported by the fact that, in contrast to Hemingway's heroes, his female protagonists are described frequently and specifically, albeit stereotypically. For instance, as we have already seen, Jake describes Brett as "damned good-looking. She wore a slipover jersey sweater and a tweed skirt, and her hair was brushed back like a boy's.... She was built with curves like the hull of a racing yacht, and you missed none of it with that wool jersey" (*Sun*, 22). We also view her white face and "the long line of her neck" (25), and later Jake tells us that she wears "a black, sleeveless evening dress. She looked quite beautiful" (146). In *A Farewell to Arms*, when Frederic Henry first sees Catherine Barkley, he relates that she "was quite tall. She wore what seemed to me to be a nurse's uniform, was blonde and had a tawny skin and gray eyes. I thought she was very beautiful" (18). After they become lovers, he tells us that she had "wonderfully beautiful hair, and I would lie sometimes and watch her twisting it up in the light.... She had a lovely face and body and lovely smooth skin too" (114).

Even more detail is provided about Maria in *For Whom the Bell Tolls*: "[Robert Jordan] noticed her handsome brown hands. Now she looked him full in the face and smiled. Her teeth were white in her brown face and her skin and her eyes were the same golden tawny brown. She had high cheekbones, merry eyes and a straight mouth with full lips. Her hair was the golden brown of a grain field that has been burned dark in the sun but it was cut short all over her head so that it was but little longer than the fur on a beaver pelt.... She has a beautiful face, Robert Jordan thought. She'd be beautiful if they hadn't cropped her hair" (*Bell*, 25–26). When Maria sits opposite him, Robert notices her legs "slanted long and clean from the open cuffs" of her trousers and "the shape of her small, up-tilted breasts under the gray shirt" (26). He looks at her face and body frequently, focusing on her "smooth skin," "the cup of her breasts," her "tawny brown face," full lips, "cropped sun-burned hair," and lovely body (48, 173–74, 176). In fact, one of Robert and Maria's last conversations before he bombs the bridge concerns her hair and body. She worries that he might prefer beautiful women of his own culture and determines to take care of her figure since Spanish women tend to gain weight easily. Robert allays these anxieties by telling Maria how to cut her hair to even out its choppy ends and reassuring her that her figure will maintain its fine shape for many years (371–76).

Specifics about Marie in *To Have and Have Not* are also plentiful. Despite her minimal role in the novel, Marie is described not only by her husband, Harry, but also by the visiting writer, Richard Gordon. When Marie gets into the car, Harry sees her as "a big woman, long legged, big handed, big hipped, still handsome, a hat pulled down over her bleached blonde hair" (116). In contrast, Richard is impressed by her ugliness. Passing her on the road after Harry is wounded, Richard observes "a heavy-set, big, blue-eyed woman, with bleached-blonde hair showing under her old man's felt hat, hurrying across the road, her eyes red from crying. Look at that big ox, he thought.... Wasn't she an appalling looking woman. Like a battleship. Terrific" (176). Although we are meant to understand that his impressions indicate his insensitivity and obtuseness, undesirable qualities in a writer, these details give extra weight and shape to Marie's face and body.

In *Across the River and Into the Trees*, Colonel Richard Cantwell watches Renata come into the room, "shining in her youth and tall striding beauty, and the carelessness the wind had made of her hair. She had pale, almost olive colored skin, a profile that could break your, or anyone else's heart, and her dark hair, of an alive texture, hung down over her shoulders" (80). Later when he kisses her, he feels "her wonderful, long, lithe and properly built body against his own body, which was hard and good, but beat-up" (109). Richard also sees her in the street "with the lovely long-legged stride and the wind doing anything it wants to her hair, and her true breasts under the sweater" (179). Like Robert Jordan, he presents himself as an expert on the preservation and deterioration of women's beauty and bodies, determining that Renata "could hold the pace and stay the course. The dark ones last the best, he thought, and look at the bony structure in that face" (247).

Two attractive white women come into Thomas Hudson's life during the course of his story, and his gaze moves over them both in similar ways. Like most female love interests in Hemingway's novels, Audrey Bruce has a beautiful face, smooth brown skin, tawny hair, good legs and breasts, and a lovely mouth. Thomas's first ex-wife (never named) is described similarly, although her features are more finely defined. "The high forehead, the magic rolling line of hair that was the same silvery ripe-wheat color as always, the high cheekbones with the hollows just below them, the hollows that could always break your heart, the slightly flattened nose, and the mouth he had just left that was disarranged by the kissing, and the lovely chin and throat line" (*Islands*, 306). And, finally, the two female protagonists in the published version of *The Garden of Eden* resemble their counterparts and, thus, each other as well. Catherine has "long brown legs," "a beautiful body tanned evenly," "laughing eyes," a "golden face with tiny freckles," and "breasts [that] show beautifully against the worn cloth" of her fisherman's shirt (12, 6). Readers are also privy to every intricacy regarding the color, shape, and length of her hair. The description of Marita is nearly a carbon copy, except that her skin is naturally dark—"almost Javanese," David thinks (236)—and her hair is dark as well (205).

This comparison between the descriptions of Hemingway's female and male protagonists suggests that in his fiction the body is identified as female (and simultaneously feminized) in part by the intensity of the male gaze, a pattern that mirrors a dynamic of the larger society. Equally important, the other way that Hemingway's female protagonists are marked as female is through the "perfection" of their bodies, the complete absence of physical scarring or wounds. Although these women might suffer psychological wounds—and, indeed, they have to suffer in some way in order to be worthy of the wounded men who love them—they rarely carry the physical scars of that suffering. The one exception to this rule is Maria of *For Whom the Bell Tolls*. Maria's chopped hair is a visible reminder of her imprisonment at Valladolid and her abusive treatment by the Falangists. Further, as Robert comes to know her more intimately, he speculates that her rapists might have scarred her genitals, causing her some pain (371). She also asks him to feel a small scar on her ear, the result of a razor cut made by the rapists. But except for her hair, which will grow to a "normal" length soon, Maria's physical scars are either too small to notice or hidden from view. Her body and skin are smooth; she has a perfect figure and no disabling or distracting disfigurements.

In Hemingway's fiction, then, the wound marks a body as white, male, masculine, and heterosexual, whereas the lack of the wound means that the body is most likely female, feminine, racialized, and/or homosexual. This arrangement reflects the cultural choreography of gender concisely described by John Berger: "men act and women appear" (quoted in Thomson, 110). But this is only half the story. For the wound to perform its classifying functions, it must be recorded, verified, *seen*. This requirement justifies turning the male gaze on the male body, a turn that places the body in the position traditionally occupied by the female, the feminized, the colonized, and/or the homosexual. An unresolvable tension arises wherein the wound that is supposed to preclude the gaze actually demands it. Further, the more the gaze lingers on the body, the more that body risks being re-marked as female, feminine, and homosexual.[60] This risk is heightened, rather than defused, by the hero's lack of distinct body imagery and features, for this ambiguity opens up that body to the re-marking of gender, sex, and sexuality. Other circumstances increase this risk, such as a female lover who wants to switch sexes or seeks to merge her identity with the hero's identity, as happens not just in *The Garden of Eden* but in almost every Hemingway novel,[61] or the fact that the male protagonist spends so much time with other men, or finally, the wound's implicit associations with castration, as in the associations with respect to Jake Barnes's injury.

A scene from *The Sun Also Rises* provides an excellent illustration of the dilemma I have just outlined. Undressing in his Paris hotel room, Jake looks at himself in the mirror, compelling the reader's gaze to follow his (30). Jake does not tell us what he sees, although his wry statements ("Of all the ways to be wounded. I suppose it was funny") and other evidence in the novel allow us to speculate that what he sees is, in fact, nothing: the penis is missing. Or, rather, Jake sees the lack which, in psychoanalytic terms, signifies the female and, in societal terms, indicates the diminishment of privilege and power. The wound is here revealed to be a castration, a revelation that is confirmed by the fact that, with the gaze turned on him, Jake occupies both the masculinized and the feminized position. He is not only the seer but the seen, spectator and spectacle.

Michael S. Kimmel reminds us that "masculine identity [which appears simultaneously with heterosexual identity] is born in the renunciation of the feminine, not in the direct affirmation of the masculine, which leaves masculine gender identity tenuous and fragile."[62] As I have argued in this section, the recurrence of the wound in Hemingway's fiction can be read not merely as a sign of heteromasculinity but, more crucially, as an attempt to stabilize that masculinity and to validate white hegemony. But, as I have also shown, the wound ultimately falters in that task. And it is in this faltering that I would propose one last meaning for the wound in Hemingway's work. The metonymic substitution of the wound for white heteromasculinity inevitably suggests that this particular form of masculinity is itself a wound, a disabling of the man who possesses it. That Hemingway himself carried the physical markings of many woundings, and that he required his heroes to pass the same test, simply emphasizes that he felt a constant need to prove his heteromasculinity. Yet because the wound in his fiction magnifies the very anxiety it is meant to deflect, it clarifies the logic of that need and supports the construction of Hemingway that I have been advancing here, a Hemingway who both rebuffed and desired the gaze of other men, whose desire never found a resting place on either side of the homo-hetero binary.[63]

NOTES

47. The facts of Hemingway's rescue of an Italian soldier during a shelling in World War I are widely disputed. Many critics and biographers argue that Hemingway could not possibly have performed such a feat given the seriousness of his own injuries. Nonetheless, the story persists, as can be seen most recently in the depiction of this rescue in the Hollywood film *In Love and War* (1997).

48. The term "body in pain" is borrowed from Elaine Scarry, whose work is quoted later in this section.

49. Lennard Davis, *Enforcing Normalcy: Disability, Deafness, and the Body* (London: Verso, 1995), 45.

50. Rosemarie Garland Thomson, *Extraordinary Bodies: Figuring Physical Disability in American Culture and Literature* (New York: Columbia University Press, 1997), 9.

51. Young's theory can be found in *Ernest Hemingway* (1952, 1965; revised reprint, London: Routledge, 1995). In brief, he argues that the Hemingway hero will be repeatedly barraged with physical and mental troubles but will never be able to recover completely from his wounds. Young is more interested in the psychic wound, whereas my argument dwells on the need for and function of the physical mark itself.

52. Peter Lehman, *Running Scared: Masculinity and the Representation of the Male Body* (Philadelphia: Temple University Press, 1993), 63.

53. Ernest Hemingway, *A Farewell to Arms* (New York: Charles Scribner's Sons, 1929), 59, 142, 299.

54. Ernest Hemingway, *Across the River and Into the Trees* (1950; reprint, New York: Collier Books, 1987), 10, 180.

55. Ernest Hemingway, *The Old Man and the Sea* (New York: Charles Scribner's Sons, 1953), 9–10, 114–15.

56. For reference to David Bourne's wound, see J. Gerald Kennedy, "Life as Fiction: The Lure of Hemingway's *Garden*," *The Southern Review* 24.2 (1988): 456.

57. Ernest Hemingway, *Islands in the Stream* (New York: Charles Scribner's Sons, 1970), 131.

58. Ernest Hemingway, *To Have and Have Not* (New York: Charles Scribner's Sons, 1937; Collier, 1987), 97.

59. Elaine Scarry, *The Body in Pain: The Making and Unmaking of the World* (New York: Oxford University Press, 1985), 118.

60. The risk of the hero's body being reclassified racially is minimal since the few identifying features that we do receive about Hemingway's heroes identify those heroes as white.

61. For instance, in *A Farewell to Arms*, Catherine determines that if Frederic will let his hair grow longer while she cuts hers, "we'd be just alike only one of us blonde and one

of us dark.... Oh, darling, I want you so much I want to be you too." Frederic replies, "We're the same one," to which Catherine states, "I know it. At night we are," 299. Maria expresses a similar urge to Robert Jordan, "I would have us exactly the same.... if thou should ever wish to change I would be glad to change. I would be thee because I love thee so," *For Whom the Bell Tolls*, 284. In *Across the River and Into the Trees*, the male hero seems even more receptive to this request for change and/or merger. When Renata tells the Colonel that she wants to be him, he replies, "That's awfully complicated. We could try of course," 156. Finally, in *Islands in the Stream*, Thomas Hudson has a dream in which his first wife asks, "Should I be you or you be me?" He says that she has first choice, so she decides that she'll be him. Thomas claims that he can't be her, but he'll try. Following her advice to "Try to lose everything and take everything too," he says he is doing it, and "It's wonderful," 344.

62. Michael S. Kimmel, "Masculinity as Homophobia: Fear, Shame, and Silence in the Construction of Gender Identity," in *Theorizing Masculinities*, ed. Harry Brod and Michael Kaufman (Thousand Oaks: Sage, 1994), 127.

63. Michael S. Kimmel states that "men prove their manhood in the eyes of other men," that masculinity is therefore a homosocial enactment, 129. Although Hemingway's masculinity surely fits this assessment, here I am asserting more than just a need for male approval; rather, I am focusing on Hemingway's desire for the male gaze, a homoerotic enactment.

SUSAN F. BEEGEL

Santiago and the Eternal Feminine: Gendering La Mar in The Old Man and the Sea

"Hemingway is always less embarrassing when he is not attempting to deal with women," Leslie A. Fiedler writes, with some smugness, of *The Old Man and the Sea*, "and he returns with relief (with what we as readers at least feel as relief) to that 'safe' American Romance of the boy and the old man" ("Adolescence" 108). Like Fiedler, most critics of this novella overlook the fact that *The Old Man and the Sea* has a powerful feminine persona in a title role. Hemingway tells us that Santiago "always thought of the sea as *la mar* which is what people call her in Spanish when they love her. Sometimes those who love her say bad things of her but they are always said as though she were a woman" (29). If the novella is an "American Romance," it is not the love story of Santiago and Manolin but of the old man and the sea, conjoined in the title like Hero and Leander, Troilus and Cressida, Antony and Cleopatra, Tristan and Isolde. Given the nature of the sea in Hemingway's novella, this is not a "safe" romance at all but a story about the tragic love of mortal man for capricious goddess.

I propose a reading of *The Old Man and the Sea* that abandons the anthropocentric critical practice of relegating nature to the role of setting— of thinking like the novella's young fishermen, who consider the sea to be "a place" rather than a living being (30). When we recognize that the sea, as the novella's title suggests, is a protagonist on an equal footing with Santiago, we see how Hemingway—using a rich tapestry of images drawn from

From *Hemingway and Women: Female Critics and the Female Voice.* © 2003 by the University of Alabama Press.

mythology, folklore, religion, marine natural history, and literature—genders the sea as feminine throughout the text, thereby raising key questions about the right relationship of man and nature.[1] Although one strand of ecofeminist thought argues that men characteristically gender nature as female to justify treating the land in a dominating, exploitative way (virgin land), while expecting unending forgiveness (Mother Earth), Hemingway argues that the true sin is masculinizing nature, treating nature as an enemy or contestant to be met in combat. Examining the role played by the feminine sea in this story may reveal that *The Old Man and the Sea* has a stronger ecological ethic than previously supposed.

Santiago genders the sea early in the novella as he rows out to fish in the early morning darkness. He begins by "feeling sorry for the birds, especially the small delicate dark terns that were always flying and looking and almost never finding" (29). Then he wonders, "Why did they make birds so delicate and fine as those sea swallows when the ocean can be so cruel? She is kind and very beautiful. But she can be so cruel and it comes so suddenly." This is the moment when we learn that Santiago "always thought of the sea as *la mar*, which is what people call her in Spanish when they love her." We learn further that

> [T]he old man always thought of her as feminine and as something that gave or withheld great favours, and if she did wild or wicked things, it was because she could not help them. The moon affects her as it does a woman, he thought. (30)

These few sentences propose a complex persona for the sea that resonates throughout the novella. I want to begin by examining how they suggest the sea's connection to a spiritual and biological principle of the Eternal Feminine. The sea's kindness, beauty, and generosity—the zenith of the natural cycle involving fecundity, copulation, birth, and nurture—offer important suggestions about right relationship to nature. Next, I want to look at the sin of masculinizing the sea instead of honoring her feminine nature, then examine the "bad things" said about the sea as though she were a woman—that she is cruel, wild, and wicked, and represents the nadir of the natural cycle—the inexorability of the death and decomposition that nourishes life. Throughout, I want to refer not only to published criticism on *The Old Man and the Sea* but also to the voices of those women students who seem less culturally conditioned than men to accept this as a story of contest and who are more likely to question the novella's violence. Finally, I will consider how gendering the sea relates to the tragedy of Santiago and its redemptive message.

Those, like Santiago, who gender what is supremely dangerous in nature as feminine (hurricanes, for instance, were traditionally called by women's names before the National Hurricane Center decided this folkloric practice was "sexist") and especially as maternal (the Tibetan name for Everest is Jomolungma, Mother Goddess of the World) do so in part as a form of appeasement. They hope if they approach with love, understanding, and respect, nature will treat them with feminine gentleness and especially with the unconditional love of a mother. Walt Whitman provides an example in "As I Ebbed with the Ocean of Life" that illuminates Santiago's professions of love for *la mar:*

> Ebb, ocean of life, (the flow will return,)
> Cease not your moaning you fierce old mother,
> Endlessly cry for your castaways, but fear not, deny not me,
> Rustle not up so hoarse and angry against my feet as I touch you
> or gather from you.
> I mean tenderly by you and all,
> I gather for myself. (186)

Santiago's hope that the sea will not rise up angry against him as he gathers for himself explains in part his need to gender the "cruel" sea as feminine.

Santiago begins his consideration of *la mar* from a pagan or "primitive" viewpoint. The words "why did *they* make" imply his belief in a pantheon of gods responsible for natural creation. At once kind and beautiful, cruel and capricious, the sea is goddess and member of that pantheon—"they" know this "she"; "they" should have considered "her" cruelty when they made terns. Associated with the creative and destructive forces in nature, the sea in this novella represents the Eternal Feminine. She might remind us of a figure from Greek or Roman mythology—Tethys, wife of Oceanus and daughter of Uranus and Gaia, or Aphrodite, daughter of Zeus and Dione. Santiago, however, knows her as *"la mar."*

The novella also draws from Catholic imagery in representing the sea as the Eternal Feminine. A devotional picture of the Virgin of Cobre, the patroness of Cuba, hangs next to an image of the Sacred Heart of Jesus on the wall of Santiago's shack.[2] The Virgin is a feminine icon, relic of his dead wife (16). During his agon at sea, he promises to make a pilgrimage to the Virgin of Cobre's shrine if he should catch his fish, and the prayers that he offers are "Hail Marys," which he finds "easier to say" than "Our Fathers" (65). She too is a sea goddess. Santiago acknowledges this when he prays to

her for a great favor—"the death of this fish" (65). Bickford Sylvester
recounts the Cuban legend of how this small statue of the Virgin, now
enshrined in a sanctuary at Cobre, arrived from the sea. She was "floating on
a wooden board off the coast ... in 1628, when ... found by two Indians and
a Creole in a rowboat" ("Cuban Context" 252).

The Virgin Mother of Christ is most familiar to us in her medieval
roles as Mater Dolorosa and mediatrix: kind and beautiful, meek and mild,
sorrowing for the suffering of man, compassionately interceding for him,
offering clemency "at the hour of our death," in the words of the Ave. But
mariologists remind us that she is also the descendant of the pagan Magna
Mater and Eternal Feminine (Katainen) and of Old Testament figures
including Eve and the bride of the erotic "Song of Songs" (Johnson). Her
biblical foremothers are tricksters Tamar and Ruth, the prostitute Rahab,
and the adultress Bathsheba—brave and holy women, to be sure, but scarcely
meek and mild (Shroer). Mary functions "as a bridge between cultures and
traditions" (Johnson), linking both paganism and Judaism to Christianity.
Ben Stolzfus notes that "the effect of the christological imagery" in *The Old
Man and the Sea* "is essentially non-Christian," that the novel is less
"Christian parable" than "pagan poem," and this is certainly true of the
Virgin of Cobre (42–43).

Insofar as she represents the Eternal Feminine and *la mar*, the Virgin
of Cobre's origins reside deep in humanity's primitive past. In *The Log from
the Sea of Cortez*,[3] John Steinbeck and Edward F. Ricketts suggest how the
Virgin may be more pagan than Christian as they describe the Virgin of
Loreto. Patroness of a Mexican fishing village on the Sea of Cortez, she is a
sister to Hemingway's Virgin of Cobre:

> This Lady, of plaster and wood and paint, is one of the strong
> ecological factors of the town of Loreto, and not to know her and
> her strength is to fail to know Loreto. One could not ignore a
> granite monolith in the path of the waves. Such a rock, breaking
> the rushing waters, would have an effect on animal distribution
> radiating in circles like a dropped stone in a pool. So has this
> plaster Lady a powerful effect on the deep black water of the
> human spirit. She may disappear, and her name be lost, as the
> Magna Mater, as Isis have disappeared. But something very like
> her will take her place, and the longings which created her will
> find somewhere in the world a similar altar on which to pour
> their force. No matter what her name is, Artemis or Venus, or a
> girl behind a Woolworth counter dimly remembered, she is as

eternal as our species, and we will continue to manufacture her as long as we survive. (207–08)

In the *la mar* passage, Santiago continues to gender the sea in a pagan vein when he considers that "The moon affects her as it does a woman" (30). Now he invokes the ancient personification of the moon as a feminine principle in nature, the monthly lunar changes affecting both the tides of the sea and woman's cycle of ovulation and fecundity, her provision of "the nutriment, the catamenia, or menstrual blood" (Merchant 13, 18–19), the nourishing matrix from which life grows. "[M]oon and sea and tide are one," write Steinbeck and Ricketts, and:

> The imprint [of tidal forces] is in us and in Sparky and in the ship's master, in the palolo worm, in mussel worms, in chitons, and in the menstrual cycle of women. The imprint lies heavily on our dreams and on the delicate threads of our nerves.... (37,39)

The disciplines of oceanography and marine biology both supply a scientific basis for Santiago's mythologizing the sea-as-matrix, a Mother Goddess obeying the cycles of the moon, with "changing woman" her acolyte. In *The Sea Around Us*,[4] Rachel Carson explains in a chapter titled "Mother Sea" how all life evolved from the sea and how the development of the human embryo recapitulates this evolutionary history.

> Fish, amphibian, and reptile, warm-blooded bird and mammal— each of us carries in our veins a salty stream in which the elements sodium, potassium, and calcium are combined in almost the same proportions as sea water.... [O]ur lime-hardened skeletons are a heritage from the calcium-rich ocean of Cambrian time. Even the protoplasm that streams within each cell of our bodies has the chemical structure impressed upon all living matter when the first simple creatures were brought forth in the ancient sea. And as life itself began in the sea, so each of us begins his individual life within his mother's womb, and in the stages of his embryonic development repeats the steps by which his race evolved, from gill-breathing inhabitants of a water world to creatures able to live on land. (*The Sea Around Us* 28–29)

Carson postulates that man's love for and desire to return to "mother sea," his mythologizing and gendering of the sea as female, springs from his evolutionary history and longing for "a world that, in the deepest part of his subconscious mind, he ha[s] never wholly forgotten" (29).

Santiago knows the maternal, womblike space the fishermen call "the great well," a sudden deep hole teeming with life, where the current stirs a nutrient upwelling and brings "all the wandering fish" to feed on "shrimp and bait fish and sometimes schools of squid" (28). He also experiences the sea-as-matrix when he looks at plankton and feels happy because it means fish:

> The water was a dark blue now, so dark that it was almost purple. As he looked down into it he saw the red sifting of the plankton in the dark water and the strange light the sun made now. He watched his lines to see them go straight down out of sight into the water and he was happy to see so much plankton because it meant fish. (35)

"Plankton," Thor Heyerdahl explains in *Kon-Tiki*,[5] "is a general name for thousands of species of visible and invisible small organisms which drift about near the surface of the sea. Some are plants (phyto-plankton), while others are loose fish ova and tiny living creatures (zoo-plankton)" (138). Where there is plankton, Steinbeck and Ricketts write, the sea "swarms with life." Plankton water is "tuna water—life water. It is complete from plankton to gray porpoises" (54). "These little animals, in their incalculable numbers, are probably the base food supply of the world"—their disappearance would "eliminate every living thing in the sea" if not "all life on the globe" (256).

Hemingway's sparing lines hint at all of this when Santiago experiences the plankton as a "red sifting" in the water (35). It's a "strange light" that makes translucent zooplankton and greenish phytoplankton appear red. But this coloring aligns the plankton with all of the blood of life spilled in the sea throughout the novella, and especially with the nutritive blood of the womb. Heyerdahl calls it "plankton porridge ... the squashy mess ... magic gruel" (140). From it, Mother Sea brings forth life.

The sea, Herman Melville reminds us in *Moby-Dick*, has its "submarine bridal-chambers" as well as its nurseries (400), and of this, Santiago is well aware. To him, "a great island of Sargasso weed that heaved and swung in the light sea" looks "as though the ocean were making love with something under a blanket" (72). In the night, two porpoises come around his boat, and Santiago "could tell the difference between the blowing noise the male made and the sighing blow of the female." He identifies with and values the porpoises for their mated love: "They are good.... They play and make jokes and love one another. They are our brothers ..." (48). Later, he dreams of "a vast school of porpoises that stretched for eight or ten miles and it was in the time of their mating and they would leap high in the air and return into the same hole they had made when they had leaped" (81).

Asked in class how Hemingway's seemingly simple and objective prose could achieve such poetic quality in *The Old Man and the Sea*, a woman student gave this explanation: "It's the difference between a man taking a photograph of a woman and a man taking a photograph of a woman he loves." Throughout the novella, the images selected to represent *la mar* establish that she is indeed "very beautiful," and that Santiago is a lover, engaged in what Terry Tempest Williams has called an "erotics of place," a "pagan" and "primal affair" (84). The sea itself is sublimely beautiful, with its deep blue waters and shafts of sunlight, as is the sky with its canyons of clouds. All of the sea's creatures except the *galano* sharks are beautiful, even the mako and the poisonous jelly fish, and some are exceptionally so, like the dorado that takes Santiago's bait from beneath the erotically heaving blanket of Sargasso weed: "He saw it first when it jumped in the air, true gold in the last of the sun and bending and flapping wildly in the air" (72).

Always the prose seeks what Hemingway called "the action that makes the emotion" ("Monologue" 219), and the emotion is love: "In the dark the old man could feel the morning coming and as he rowed he heard the trembling sound as the flying fish left the water and the hissing that their stiff wings made as they soared away in the darkness" (29). Or, "as the old man watched, a small tuna rose in the air, turned and dropped head first into the water. The tuna shone silver in the sun and after he had dropped back into the water another and another rose and they were jumping in all directions, churning the water and leaping in long jumps after the bait" (38). "Listen to Hemingway write!" responds another woman student. "Gorgeous!" (Gensler). Most "gorgeous" of all is the giant marlin that is the sea's great gift to Santiago:

> The line rose slowly and steadily and then the surface of the ocean bulged ahead of the boat and the fish came out. He came out unendingly and water poured from his sides. He was bright in the sun and his head and back were dark purple and in the sun the stripes on his sides showed wide and a light lavender. (62)

Although *The Old Man and the Sea* may seem to be about "men without women," the figure of a man *wedded* to a feminine sea is omnipresent in our culture, from ancient myths of Venus rising from the foam of the sea to be given as bride to Vulcan, to a contemporary rock ballad such as E. Lurie's "Brandy," where a sailor tells his human lover, "[Y]ou're a fine girl. What a good wife you would be. But my life, my lover, my lady is the sea." Santiago is no exception. He is a widower and feels his loss—"[T]here had been a tinted photograph of his wife on the wall but he had taken it down because it made him too lonely to see it" (16)—and his loss gives him empathy and compassion for the marlin. "The saddest thing [he] ever saw with them" was the reaction of a male to the capture of his mate. "He was beautiful, the old man remembered, and he had stayed" (50). But now the beauty of the sea assuages Santiago's loneliness for his flesh-and-blood wife: "[H]e looked ahead and saw a flight of wild ducks etching themselves against the sky over the water, then etching again and he knew no man was ever alone on the sea" (61).

In the course of the story, Santiago becomes wedded to the marlin. His angling uses the language of seduction: "'Yes', he said. 'Yes.'" (41). "Come on ... Aren't they lovely? Eat them good now and then there is the tuna. Hard and cold and lovely. Don't be shy, fish" (42). "Then he felt the gentle touch on the line and he was happy" (43). Even after the marlin is firmly hooked and Santiago's ordeal begins, his developing sense of connectedness with the fish is expressed in language from the sacrament of marriage: "Now we are joined together" (50) and "Fish ... I'll stay with you until I am dead" (52).

This sense of the sea-as-wife is not incompatible with Santiago's calling the marlin his "brother." Porpoises and flying fish of both sexes are Santiago's "brothers," too (48), and the word "brother" is neither gender-specific nor used only of humans in Hemingway's work. In "The Last Good Country," Nick's sister Littless looks like a "small wild animal" (SS 101), and wants to be both his "brother" (95) and his "wife" (104). In *The Garden of Eden*, Catherine Bourne tells David that he is "my good lovely husband and my brother too" (29), and David comes to understand that the elephant also is his "brother" (197).

Brothers are children of the same mother, living together in an implied state of equality and fraternity, depending on one another for mutual support. In *To Have and Have Not* Captain Willie says, of the human community at sea, "Most everybody goes in boats calls each other brother" (83). In *The Old Man and the Sea*, that marine community expands to include sea creatures. The man o'war bird is "a great help" to Santiago in locating fish (38), and Santiago in his turn aids the exhausted migrating warbler, "Take a good rest, small bird" (55). Hemingway's signature use of the word "brother" reflects longing for an Eden where men and women, husbands and wives, as well as birds, beasts, and fish might live together on such terms.

Such an Eden would bring male and female principles, as well as man and nature, into harmony and balance.

How then may Santiago ethically "live on the sea and kill [his] true brothers" (75)? To render sea creatures as children of the same mother raises vital questions about right relationship to nature. Hunter-philosopher Ted Kerasote proposes some answers. "Hunting," he writes, should be a "disciplined, mindful, sacred activity.... hav[ing] much to do with kindness, compassion, and sympathy for those other species with whom we share the web of life.... based on the pre-Christian belief that other life-forms, indeed the very plants and earth and air themselves, are invested with soul and spirit" (191). Here we recognize the "primitive" Santiago who fishes with unmatched physical and mental discipline and with prayers, the Santiago who hits the landed tuna on the head "for kindness" (42), who begs the female marlin's pardon and butchers her promptly (50), and who understands that the great marlin not only is his "brother," but suffers as Santiago himself suffers (92). In his introduction to *Atlantic Game Fishing*, Hemingway writes that "Anglers have a way of ... forgetting that the fish has a hook in his mouth, his gullet, or his belly, and is driven to the extremes of panic at which he runs, leaps, and pulls to get away until he dies" (qtd. in Farrington 11). Santiago never forgets the "fish's agony" (93).

Ethical killing, Kerasote tells us, is not for "the cruel delight that comes at another's demise," but for "the celebratory joy inherent in well-performed hunting that produces a gift of food" (190). The blood of life may only be spilled to nourish life. Here we recognize the Santiago who sacramentally partakes of the flesh of every fish he kills—dolphin, tuna, marlin, and even tiny shrimp from the floating blanket of Sargasso weed. This is the Santiago who seeks a fish to feed "many people," and who hopes to repay his indebtedness to his human community with "the belly meat of a big fish" (20). He is drawn in part from Hemingway's Cuban boat-handler, Carlos Gutiérrez, who unlike the trophy-hunting sport fishermen always calls the marlin "the bread of my children," relating it to the staff of life—and the continuity of life: "Oh look at the bread of my children! Joseph and Mary look at the bread of my children jump! There it goes the bread of my children! He'll never stop the bread the bread the bread of my children!" (Hemingway, "On the Blue Water" 242). "Everything kills everything else in some way" as Santiago observes (106), and is ethical so long as the killing is followed by eating, the act of communion, of sharing the blood of life.

Aldo Leopold writes that all ecological ethics "rest upon a single premise: that the individual is a member of a community with interdependent parts. His instincts prompt him to compete for his place in the community, but his ethics prompt him also to co-operate" (239). Glen A. Love feels that *The Old Man and the Sea* lacks a fully developed ecological ethic, because Santiago perceives some creatures of the sea, such as sharks and poisonous jellyfish, as "enemies." Hemingway, Love argues, does not understand that all of the sea's creatures "are members of a community which man is not privileged to exterminate for real or assumed self-benefits" (208). Yet Love's is an environmental sensibility that places man outside of the food web, forgetting, as Leopold does not, that survival demands an ethic that includes the necessity of competition as well as of cooperation.

Santiago, as a subsistence fisherman, knows that he is part of the web of life. His community is truly "the great sea with our friends and our enemies" (120). He loves to see big sea turtles eating the jellyfish, and then he in turn eats the eggs of the turtles that eat the jellyfish in order to be strong "for the truly big fish" he himself hunts (36–37).[6] Others do not like the taste, but Santiago drinks "a cup of shark liver oil each day from the big drum in the shack where the fishermen keep their gear" to sharpen his eyesight (37). Indeed, Santiago's eyes, "the same color as the sea ... cheerful and undefeated" emblematize that the sea and its creatures are the well-spring of his own life—"with his eyes closed there was no life in his face" (10, 19). He understands that the lives of his "enemies" too are part of the "celebratory gift," part of his fisherman's communion with life.

A woman student who does not accept the primitive hunter's communion of blood, the pagan appreciation of the intimate proximity of life and death, objects to Santiago's slaying of the marlin in gendered terms:

> Ultimately, while I pity Santiago and mourn his defeat, I can't relate to his struggle. I do not share his need to defeat the marlin, or his desire for conquest. This type of battle is common to Hemingway, I've come across the same one in *Islands in the Stream* and I know he's restaged it with bulls and matadors in other books. What I wonder is what form these epic battles would take if Hemingway had been a woman. How would she describe childbirth? Imagine, these arduous, protracted ordeals produce nothing but dead fish, but what magic, what power would be imparted to a two-day struggle to produce a screaming new human being? (Betancourt)

In one sense, *The Old Man and the Sea* may already fulfill this student's wish for a Hemingway who places the male values of strength and endurance in the service of the Eternal Feminine, of bringing forth rather than taking life.

To *la mar*, Santiago owes his disciple, the boy Manolin who is more to him than a son. Santiago has no child by his mortal wife, but has delivered Manolin from the sea in a violent birthing. "How old was I when you first took me in a boat?" the boy asks Santiago, in the manner of a child asking a parent for the legend of his birth. "Five and you were nearly killed when I brought the fish in too green and he nearly tore the boat to pieces. Can you remember?" (12). Manolin responds:

> I can remember the tail slapping and banging and the thwart breaking and the noise of clubbing. I can remember you throwing me into the bow where the wet coiled lines were and feeling the whole boat shiver and the noise of you clubbing him like chopping a tree down and the sweet blood smell all over me. (12)

Fish and boy are elided here, as man-midwife Santiago forcibly extracts the flapping, struggling fish from the sea and throws the child slicked in "sweet blood" into the bow. "Can you really remember that or did I just tell you?" asks Santiago. Manolin insists that he can, but the scene is so primal that readers may share Santiago's doubt, wondering whether the boy remembers it any more than he would remember the scene of his birth.

In an essay titled "Forceps" that is in part a history of masculine involvement in obstetrics, Hemingway's doctor father writes that for centuries men were not permitted to attend or witness normal births. "Men midwives," he mourns, "were not allowed at confinements ... except in cases where an extraction by *force* [his emphasis] of a dead fetus was required." He celebrates the eventual inclusion of men in the process of normal birthing: "to help and share the responsibility" of the "sacred trust" (C. Hemingway 3). In the "birthing" scene from *The Old Man and the Sea*, where Santiago acts as a man-midwife, we do see how his great strength and heroism might serve the cause of life.

On the positive side of the ledger, then, Santiago's gendering the sea as *la mar* underlies this novella's strong ecological ethic. To gender the sea as female or as a mother goddess implies reciprocal obligation. The man who approaches nature as his lover, wife, or mother, expecting "great favours" and kindness, must also, as Whitman phrases it, "mean tenderly" by her. The concept of the sea as a feminine, living being ought to serve, as Carolyn Merchant has pointed out on behalf of the earth, "as a cultural constraint restricting the actions of human beings. One does not readily slay a mother, dig into her entrails ... or mutilate her body.... As long as the earth [is] considered to be alive and sensitive, it could be considered a breach of human ethical behavior to carry out destructive acts against it" (3).

There is no more potent example in American literature of a book that genders the sea as masculine than Herman Melville's *Moby-Dick*, celebrating its centennial the year Hemingway composed *The Old Man and the Sea*.[7] "To and fro in the deeps, far down in the bottomless blue," Melville writes, "rushed mighty leviathans, sword-fish, and sharks, and these were the strong, troubled, murderous thinkings of the masculine sea" (543). No character more obviously treats the sea as masculine contestant and enemy than Captain Ahab, or is more closely associated with man's self-destructive technological assault on nature: "Swerve me? The path to my fixed purpose is laid with iron rails, whereon my soul is grooved to run. Over unsounded gorges, through the rifled hearts of mountains, under torrents' beds, unerringly I rush! Naught's an obstacle, naught's an angle to the iron way!" (172)

Santiago seems to uphold an ecological ethic diametrically opposed to Ahab's "iron way" when he recognizes that those who gender the sea as masculine treat the sea more violently than those who think of her as *la mar*:

> Some of the younger fishermen, those who used buoys as floats for their lines and had motorboats, bought when the shark livers had brought much money, spoke of her as *el mar* which is masculine. They spoke of her as a contestant or a place or even an enemy. (30)

These two sentences are dense with environmental history. Aligned with technology, Santiago's young fishermen are not only the workaday descendants of Captain Ahab, they are the ancestors of today's long-liners. Dr. Perry W. Gilbert, a shark expert familiar with the Cuban fishing village of Cojimar where Hemingway based *The Old Man and the Sea*, explains the fishing rig described above:

> [F]ishermen put out from Cojimar in their small boats, only eighteen to twenty-four feet over all, and head for the deep water. ... [T]wo men comprise the crew, and their boat carries ten to fifteen floating fishing rigs of three hooks each ... The hooks of one set hang at different intervals in the water, usually at twenty, fifty, and eighty fathoms.... The wooden buoys, spaced forty to fifty feet apart, are joined to each other by a three-quarter inch manila rope, attached at one end to a square wooden float bearing

the name of the boat ... and a four foot mast carrying a lantern and flag.... After the sets are all placed and the lanterns lit, they are patrolled until dawn. At daybreak the catch of dolphin, marlin, broadbill, and sharks is removed, and if the weather is fair, a set may be rebaited.... The 'Old Man,' of course, did not have this set. His lines were off his boat or in his hands. (qtd. in Farrington 28–30)

The young fishermen fish not so much for the "celebratory gift of food," Gilbert tells us, but for the "shark factory" mentioned at the beginning of *The Old Man and the Sea* (11), an industry processing their catch for the Oriental soup fin trade, for an Ocean Leather Company in New Jersey converting shark skin to wallets, belts, and shoes, and for the vitamin A in shark liver oil (in Farrington 30–31). Their motorboats are the fruits of war. "Shark livers had brought much money" during World War II, when German submarines in the North Atlantic cut off the Grand Banks and the world supply of cod liver oil for pharmaceuticals (R. Ellis 45); the Cojimar shark factory would remain profitable until 1958, when vitamin A was synthesized (Gilbert in Farrington 31).

Santiago sees in the young fishermen the death of his way of life, the end of putting to sea in small boats powered by oar and sail, of locating fish only with his own intimate knowledge of the sea and her creatures, and of catching them with the unaided strength of his body. In part, *The Old Man and the Sea* is Hemingway's elegy for the subsistence fisherman, and perhaps, as when Santiago wonders what it would be like to spot fish from airplanes (71), or to have a radio in the boat that would bring him the "baseball," but distract him from "thinking much" about the sea (105), a prophesy of things to come. Mary Hemingway recalled:

Our habit was to anchor *Pilar* in the little bay of Cojimar.... The town's population was almost entirely fishermen who went out as Santiago did in those days with their skiffs and were carried by the Gulf Stream, which flows from west to east across the northern part of Cuba's coast. They would then put their baits down and drift.... When they had their fish, or when the day was finished ... they'd stick up their sails and come sailing back against the Gulf Stream, the wind being stronger than the current.... [B]efore we left, the fishermen ... were able to add outboard motors to their boats. (qtd. in Bruccoli, "Interview" 193)

Neither Santiago nor Hemingway could predict the modern fleet of Atlantic swordboats—long-liners assisted by global positioning systems, weather fax, down temperature indicators, Doppler radar, color sounders, video plotters, radiofrequency beeper buoys, and hydraulic haulbacks for lines twenty-five to forty miles long, indiscriminately cleansing the sea of swordfish, sharks, sea turtles, tuna, and other deep oceanic fish (Greenlaw 137). Nor could they predict a generation whose most successful fishermen would be "fishing gear engineers and electronics wizards," ignoring birds and clouds to "study data and base decisions on statistics" (Greenlaw 137–38).

But Santiago does know that the fishermen of the future will follow the "el mar" ethos of treating the sea as a masculine enemy or contestant. Contemporary swordboat captain Linda Greenlaw, ironically a woman, bears him out when she describes her work as "Man vs. Nature." She uses words like "warrior," "relentless beast," "fight," "monstrous sword," "war," "forces," and "combat" to describe a losing contest with a commodified "$2,000 fish," and then, when the line snaps and the swordfish gets loose, leaps to the rail with her men to give the animal, perceived as "gloating" in "victory," the phallic upraised finger, and to scream "Fuck you" until her throat is raw (Greenlaw 173–75). If Carolyn Merchant is correct that gendering nature as female and as the mother-of-life acts as a cultural constraint against destructive acts, then the converse appears to be true, that gendering the sea as a masculine opponent enables destructive and violent behavior. Since the first swordfish took bait on an American longline in 1961, Santiago's "young fishermen" have swept the Atlantic of 75 percent of its bluefin tuna and 70 percent of its breeding-age swordfish (Safina, Chivers), carrying us ever closer to the "fishless desert" of Santiago's nightmare (2).

Santiago rejects those who masculinize the sea. But against his view of Mother Sea as a beautiful, kindly, and generous feminine provider—a belief that in many respects does temper his behavior toward her—he sets an opposing view of feminine nature as cruel and chaotic—spawning poisonous creatures, sudden storms, and hurricanes. Although early in the novella Hemingway tells us that Santiago "no longer dreamed of storms, nor of women, nor of great occurrences, nor of great fish, nor fights, nor contests of strength, nor of his wife," *The Old Man and the Sea* is a dream of all such things, and here we learn that Santiago includes the feminine principles of "women" and "wife" with "storms" and "great fish," natural things that might be fought or engaged in "contests of strength" (25). As Merchant points out, such views of nature as a disorderly female force call forth the male need for rationalistic or mechanistic power over her (127).

Critic Gerry Brenner labels the *la mar* passage "a litany of sexist aggressions" in part for Santiago's "metaphoric equation" of woman and the sea "as dependent on the moon or some power over which she has no control" (*Story* 84). However, the point of Santiago's "and if she did wild or wicked things it was because she could not help them," may be that women and the sea are not *under* control, but *beyond* control. Carson writes that man may approach "mother sea only on her terms.... He cannot control or change the ocean as ... he has subdued and plundered the continents" (*Sea Around Us* 29–30). When Santiago thinks "the moon affects her as it does a woman," he betrays male fear of female power, of the menstruous or monstrous woman, whose wildness and wickedness challenges his rationalism and control, and whose cruelty provokes his attempts at dominance. In *The Garden of Eden*, Catherine Bourne (who needs to "go up to the room" because "I'm a god damned woman"), speaks for menstruous woman, and perhaps for *la mar*, when she overrides David's effort to silence and control her: "Why should I hold it down? You want a girl, don't you? Don't you want everything that goes with it? Scenes, hysteria, false accusations, temperament, isn't that it?" (70).

Santiago believes that, in his great love for and understanding of *la mar*, he has accepted "everything that goes with" her femininity. He knows the months of the "sudden bad weather," and is not afraid to be out of sight of land in hurricane season, because he "can see the signs of [a hurricane] for days ahead" in the sky (61). He endures the painful sting of a ray hidden in the sand, and of the Portuguese man o'war jellyfish he genders as female and calls "Agua mala [evil water]" and "You whore." Although the jellyfish strike "like a whiplash," he loves to walk on them on the beach after a storm and "hear them pop when he step[s] on them with the horny soles of his feet" (82). While Brenner finds Santiago's "vilification of the jellyfish" the novella's most "blatant" example of "hostility or contempt towards things female" (82), Katharine T. Jobes believes the old man's epithet—"You whore"—is familiar, affectionate, a reflection of Santiago's "intimate at-homeness in nature" (16).

Yet despite Santiago's apparent acceptance of the sea's wild and wicked nature, ultimately he sins against her, and she bitches him. Gendering the sea as feminine does not resolve the problem of man's violence toward nature, but raises even more disturbing questions about right relationship than gendering the sea as *el mar*. Our culture generally accepts male-on-male violence—such as the cock-fighting and arm-wrestling in *Old Man*—provided it conforms to the rituals of warfare, chivalry, or sportsmanship. We perceive such violence as the "natural" outcome of male competition for territory and sexual prerogative, although neither instinct bodes well when directed against nature. Conversely, male-on-female violence is taboo, "unnatural" because the biological purpose of male-female relations is procreation, not competition.

As Melvin Backman has noted, *Death in the Afternoon* provides an interpretive key to the problem of sin in *The Old Man and the Sea:* "[W]hen a man is still in rebellion against death he has pleasure in taking to himself one of the Godlike attributes; that of giving it.... These things are done in pride and pride, of course, is a Christian sin and a pagan virtue ..." (233). The old man is surely in rebellion against death. His eighty-four days without a fish, the mockery of the young fishermen, the pity of the older fishermen, the charity of his village, the role reversal that sees his much-loved apprentice Manolin taking care of him ("You'll not fish without eating while I'm alive" [19]), and perhaps most of all the loss of Manolin, forced by his parents into a "luckier" boat, conspire to make Santiago feel his proximity to death. These things send him out to sea, beyond all other fishermen, to seek "a big one" (30), and the struggle with the marlin becomes in part a struggle with the "treachery of one's own body" (62), with his spells of faintness and blurred vision, with his cramped hand: "Pull, hands.... Hold up, legs. Last for me, head. Last for me" (91). Santiago's rebellion against death draws him first into sin, and then into an orgy of violence against the sea he loves.

In Christian iconography, both the sea and the Eternal Feminine are associated with death and resurrection. *The Book of Common Prayer* makes of the ocean a vast graveyard, and, strangely for a Christian text, feminizes the sea: "We therefore commit his body to the deep, to be turned into corruption, looking for the resurrection of the body, when the Sea shall give up *her* dead" (my emphasis, 552). The Virgin of Cobre places Santiago in this cycle of death and resurrection. Opus Dei scholar Dwight Duncan opines: "Christianity is the celebration of Christ as a man, one of us. So it is natural to approach it through the perspective of the mother. Mary is the guarantor of Christ's manhood" (Kennelly). Phrased somewhat differently, this means that the Virgin is the guarantor of Christ's suffering and death—and Santiago's. As his mortal progenitor, the Mother makes Christ subject—as all humanity is subject—to the immutable laws of biological nature.

Santiago kills the marlin with the most masculine of weapons, the harpoon, driving it deep into the fish's heart, the organ of love and the seat of life:

> The old man dropped the line and put his foot on it and lifted the harpoon as high as he could and drove it down with all his strength, and more strength he had just summoned, into the fish's

side just behind the great chest fin that rose high in the air to the
altitude of the man's chest. He felt the iron go in and he leaned
on it and drove it further and then pushed all his weight after it.
Then the fish came alive, with his death in him, and rose high out
of the water showing all his great length and width and all his
power and his beauty. (93–94)

Three times Hemingway tells us that the old man's target was the heart: "I
must try for the heart" (91); "the sea was discoloring with the red of the
blood from his heart" (94); "I think I felt his heart.... When I pushed on the
harpoon shaft the second time" (95).

The heart of the marlin recalls the Sacred Heart of Jesus, the other
devotional icon that hangs on the wall of Santiago's shack next to the Virgin
of Cobre (16). That heart symbolizes the love and suffering of Christ, and his
sacrifice—his death that man might live. By suggesting that the marlin too
might have a sacred heart, Hemingway asks us to contemplate the passion of
the natural cycle, or, as Kerasote puts it, to "fac[e] up to this basic and
poignant condition of biological life on this planet—people, animals, and
plants as fated cohorts, as both dependents and donors of life" (191).
Hemingway invites us to understand that the marlin, in the words of
Santiago's "Hail Mary," is the "fruit of the womb" of the Eternal Feminine
(65). Coming "alive with his death in him," the marlin conjoins the principles
of life and death implicit both in natural cycles and in the iconography of
resurrection that arises from them. Santiago sees the eye of the dead fish
looking "as detached as mirrors in a periscope or as a saint in a procession"
(96), suggesting that the marlin should remind us of our own mortality, and
our own mortality should remind us to have compassion for all living things.

Santiago's harpoon, probing the sacred heart, probes again the essential
question of male-on-female violence, of right relationship of man and
nature. When may man ethically kill the thing he loves? "If you love him, it
is not a sin to kill him," Santiago thinks of the great marlin. "Or is it more?"
(105). Santiago cannot bear to pursue the question&mash; "You think too
much, old man"—he tells himself, but the text would seem to argue "more."
Too late, he recognizes that "You did not kill him to keep alive and to sell for
food," the only allowable answers, "You killed him for pride and because you
are a fisherman" (105). Despite knowing that the marlin is "two feet longer
than the skiff" and cannot be landed (63), despite believing that it is "unjust"
and that he is doing it to show the marlin "what a man can do and what a
man endures" (66), despite feeling that "there is no one worthy of eating him
from the manner of his behaviour and his great dignity" (75), the old man

proceeds to kill the marlin anyway. When sharks attack the fish, as Santiago knows they must, his tragedy will be to recognize that he was wrong: "'Half fish,' he said. 'Fish that you were. I am sorry that I went out too far. I ruined us both'" (115).

Sylvester has argued that Santiago's "slaying of the marlin and his responsibility for its mutilation are sins," but "tragic precisely because they are a necessary result of his behavior as a champion of his species" ("Extended Vision" 136). Sylvester sees "opposition to nature as paradoxically necessary to vitality in the natural field" ("Extended Vision" 132), and perhaps it's true that a man "born to be a fisherman as the fish was born to be a fish" (105) could not conceive, as Hemingway himself could conceive, of releasing a marlin and "giv[ing] him his life back" (G. Hemingway 73). Perhaps a man who fishes for his living cannot say, as young David Hudson says in *Islands in the Stream* about a marlin that escapes him after a gruelling fight: "I loved him so much when I saw him coming up that I couldn't stand it.... All I wanted was to see him closer.... Now I don't give a shit I lost him.... I don't care about records. I just thought I did. I'm glad that he's all right" (143). Yet if Sylvester's concept of "necessary sin" is correct, then the text violates Santiago's own philosophy—that it is wrong to gender the sea as *el mar* and to treat it as a contestant or enemy. A woman student proposes instead that Santiago's sin is both unnecessary and the direct result of the "masculine" thinking he himself has deplored:

> The code of manhood that gives Santiago the strength for his battle and even the reason to begin it is completely foreign to me. He doesn't *have* to do this—a fisherman can make a living on the tuna and dolphin that Santiago uses only for bait and sustenance. ... When Santiago says he has not caught a fish in eighty-seven [*sic*] days, he does not mean fish, he means Krakens, sea monsters. The bravery involved in just wresting a living from the sea is nothing ... Santiago has to be a saint and fight dragons.... I guess what it comes down to is greatness.... Killing a 1500 lb. Marlin puts him on the same level with the magnificent fish, giving him a power as great as the ocean's. There is nothing about this that's hard to understand; a man wishes to be strong and so he tests himself against the strongest thing he can find (Betancourt).

Nature's punishment for the harpoon in the heart is swift and inexorable. The heart pumps the blood of the stricken fish into the sea—"First it was dark as a shoal in the blue water that was more than a mile deep.

Then it spread like a cloud" (94). The heart's blood summons the first shark, a mako, and Santiago recognizes the consequences of his own actions: "The shark was not an accident. He had come up from deep down in the water as the dark cloud of blood had settled and dispersed in the mile deep sea" (100). Indeed, the mako almost seems like the marlin's avenging ghost: "His back was as blue as a sword fish's and his belly was silver and his hide was smooth and handsome. He was built like a sword fish except for his huge jaws" (100). Like the marlin too, the mako is "beautiful and noble" (106). His teeth "shaped like a man's fingers when they are crisped like claws" (100–101), recall Santiago's left hand cramped "tight as the gripped claws of an eagle" (63). The mako comes as a grim reminder that marlin, shark, and man—all predators—are brothers, children of the same mother.

Yet "the shadow of sharks is the shadow of death," as Peter Matthiessen has observed (5), and when Santiago sees the mako, he curses the mother— "*Dentuso*, he thought, bad luck to your mother" (101)—and who is the Mother of Sharks if not *la mar?* Santiago assaults the shadow of death "without hope but with resolution and complete malignancy" (102). He harpoons the mako with a precision so reminiscent of the bullfight, one wonders whether Hemingway knew that the ancient Hawaiians built marine arenas in shallow water, where men armed with shark-tooth daggers fought sharks to honor Kama-Hoa-Lii, the shark god (Cousteau 205). Harpooning the mako, Santiago sins a second time, and explicitly partakes of the matador's sin from *Death in the Afternoon*. "You enjoyed killing the *dentuso*, he thought" (105), and this is both the Christian sin of pride in taking pleasure in the Godlike attribute of giving death, and the pagan sin identified by Kerasote, of taking "cruel delight" in another's demise (109). Again Santiago's sin sends a blood message of life wrongfully taken into the sea: "Now my fish bleeds again," he thinks after the dead mako sinks with his harpoon, "and there will be others" (103). Santiago's rebellion against death, which has, from the start of the novella, underlain his quest for the marlin, now assumes crisis proportions.

Sharks begin to arrive in numbers, and they are a different species— not the "beautiful and noble" mako, *Isurus oxyrinchus*, that like the marlin preys on tuna and dolphin (Bigelow 23–25), but *galanos*, probably oceanic whitetip sharks, *Carcharhinus longimanus*, but certainly—and significantly—members of the family *Carcharinidae*,[8] commonly known as the "Requiem sharks" (R. Ellis 130). These sharks are not only biologically apt (whitetips are well-known to whalemen and big game fishermen for feeding on their kills, and notorious for attacks on victims of shipwrecks and air disasters), but for a marine naturalist like Hemingway they also allude to the introit of the Roman Catholic mass for the dead. Santiago truly vilifies the *galanos* as

> hateful sharks, bad smelling, scavengers as well as killers, and when they were hungry they would bite at an oar or the rudder of a boat. It was these sharks that would cut the turtles' legs and flippers off when the turtles were asleep on the surface, and they would hit a man in the water, if they were hungry, even if the man had no smell of fish blood nor of fish slime on him. (108)

Rising from the sea as from the grave, their evil smell a reminder that the body is destined "to be turned into corruption," the scavenging *galanos* are the ultimate reminder of death as the reabsorption of the individual into the matrix of life. When Santiago sees them, he makes "a noise such as a man might make, involuntarily, feeling the nail go through his hands and into the wood" (107). "Old men should burn and rave at close of day," Dylan Thomas writes (942), and Santiago does indeed rage against the dying of the light, stabbing, hacking, and clubbing at the sharks with everything he has, although he knows that the fight is "useless" (118). "Fight them,' he said. 'I'll fight them until I die'" (115). Like the mako, the *galanos* too are sent by the mother, and Santiago seems to perceive himself as sending a message of defiance to her when he says to a shark he has killed: "Go on, *galano*. Slide down a mile deep. Go see your friend, or maybe it's your mother" (109).

The "evil" of the shark, emblematizing the inexorability of suffering and death in nature, has long constituted a theological problem, calling into question the benevolent intentions of God toward man, and suggesting instead cruelty and indifference. "Queequeg no care what god made him shark," pronounces Melville's savage, "wedder Fejee god or Nantucket god; but de god wat made shark must be one dam Ingin" (310). Even a marine ecologist such as Philippe Cousteau, who recognizes that it is risible to "qualif[y] one animal as 'good' and another as 'bad'" (133), can write of the same oceanic whitetip shark that Santiago finds hateful:

> [O]ne of the most formidable of the deep-sea sharks, a great *longimanus*.... this species is absolutely hideous. His yellow-brown color is not uniform, but streaked with irregular markings resembling a bad job of military camouflage.... He swims in a jerky, irregular manner, swinging his shortened, broad snout from side to side. His tiny eyes are hard and cruel-looking. (89)

Cousteau also recognizes that his fear of sharks is related to his fear of an indifferent, inhuman creator: "The shark moves through my universe like a marionette whose strings are controlled by someone other than the power manipulating mine" (70).

The Old Man and the Sea suggests, through its twice-repeated reference to the "mother" of sharks, that "de god wat made shark" must be one damn woman—cruel, wild, wicked, irrational, beyond control. Santiago's battle with the sharks, his rage and rebellion against *la mar*, is his most Melvillean moment. Like Ahab, Santiago seems to say:

> I now know thee ... and I now know thy right worship is defiance. To neither love nor reverence wilt thou be kind; and e'en for hate thou canst but kill; and all are killed.... I now own thy speechless, placeless power; but to the last gasp of my earthquake life will dispute its unconditional mastery in me. In the midst of the personified impersonal, a personality stands here. (512)

Santiago puts it more simply, spitting blood coughed up from his chest into the sea when the last of the shark pack leaves the ruined marlin, saying "Eat that, *galanos*, and make a dream you've killed a man" (119). The life that burns in him, the will to survive, is the source of his proud individualism and refusal to submit tamely to annihilation. Ahab proclaims "[O]f thy fire thou madest me, and like a true child of fire, I breathe it back" (512).

Ahab's defiance of a masculine god places him outside of nature and against nature, a crime for which he will be executed with a hempen cord of whale line around the neck. Santiago's defiance of the feminine "mother of sharks" places him inside nature and outside of nature. Like the turtle whose heart beats "for hours after he has been cut up and butchered" (37), like the great marlin who comes "alive, with his death in him" (94), and especially like the shark who is dead but "would not accept it" (102), Santiago is a true child of *la mar*. Her law proclaims that "all are killed," but her law also proclaims that all—turtle, marlin, shark, and man—will dispute their deaths. The sea punishes Santiago for the wrongful deaths of marlin and mako, but for the final battle with the sharks—for breathing back the fire of life—she forgives him.

When the battle with the sharks is finally and irretrievably lost, Santiago achieves a kind of serenity born of acceptance that Ahab never knows. Ahab neither repents nor relents—"for hate's sake I spit my last breath at thee" (574–75). Santiago does both, apologizing to the marlin and acknowledging that he has been "beaten now finally" by the sharks

(119). This the old man experiences as a lightening, a release from a great burden:

> He settled the sack around his shoulders and put the skiff on her course. He sailed lightly now and he had no thoughts nor any feelings of any kind. He was past everything now.... In the night sharks hit the carcass.... The old man paid no attention to them and did not pay attention to anything except steering. He only noticed how lightly and how well the skiff sailed now there was no great weight beside her. (119)

Eric Waggoner reads this passage as a restoration of harmony, citing the *Tao-te Ching:* "Return is the movement of the Way; / yielding is the function of the way" (102). Waggoner's Taoist perspective prompts us to understand that by yielding to the sea, by accepting his place in nature, "[Santiago] can re-place himself in the balance of his fishing life and sail his skiff 'well'" (102). Still more important, however, is the end of Santiago's rebellion against death, and the beginning of his acquiescence.

Now Santiago is "inside the current," and the text restores him to his original love and reverence for the sea with all her vagaries and caprices. In this key passage, *la mar* is aligned not with an enemy wind that sends great storms, but with the friendly wind that carries an exhausted fisherman lightly home. The sea is associated not with the cruelty of a watery grave and its scavenging sharks, but with bed, where a tired man may find rest:

> The wind is our friend, anyway, he thought. Then he added, sometimes. And the great sea with our friends and enemies. And bed, he thought. Bed is my friend. Just bed, he thought. Bed will be a great thing. It is easy when you are beaten, he thought. I never knew how easy it was. (120)

Now, in Whitmanian rather than Melvillean fashion, Santiago hears the word up from feminine rather than masculine waves, the word of "the sweetest song and all songs," the word "out of the cradle endlessly rocking," the word whispered by the sea—death (184).

Santiago's acquiescence is not Christian. Earlier, Santiago has confessed that he is "not religious" (64); there is no hint that he believes in resurrection. But if he believes in the sea as both friend and enemy, cradle and grave, life and death, and accepts her cycles, then he may partake in the "natural" consolation of Ecclesiastes slightly revised—"One generation passeth away and another generation cometh: but the [sea] abideth forever" (1.6). The pagan—and the naturalist—both draw spiritual comfort from material immortality in the Eternal Feminine. As Carson puts it in *Under the Sea Wind*: "[I]n the sea, nothing is lost. One dies, another lives, as the precious elements of life are passed on and on in endless chains" (105).[9]

A text that masculinized the sea might end with Santiago "destroyed but not defeated" (103), the existential hero with the trophy of his pyrrhic victory, "the great fish ... now just garbage waiting to go out with the tide" (126). But *The Old Man and the Sea* ends instead not only with Santiago's acceptance of death as natural as sleep—but with the cycle of life turning upwards once more. Hemingway reunites Santiago with Manolin, the boy who is more-than-son to him, the child of Santiago's man-midwifery, delivered from the sea. Theirs is what Claire Rosenfeld calls a "spiritual kinship" (43); the sea as wife-and-mother joins them as father-and-son. Manolin cares tenderly for the old man, allowing him to sleep undisturbed, bringing him coffee, food, newspapers, and a clean shirt, and making cheerful talk about the future. When Santiago cannot see him, the boy weeps for the old man's ordeal and shows his understanding: he weeps for Santiago's suffering when he sees the bloody stigmata of the rope on the old man's hands (122), he weeps for the ruin of the great fish when he sees the skeleton lashed to the skiff (122), and he weeps for his mentor's heartbreak and imminent death after Santiago tells him that "something in his chest [feels] broken" (125).

Manolin will carry Santiago's legacy forward, insuring the continuity of life in the face of destruction. The boy asks for and receives the spear of the great marlin from his mentor (124), a gift that represents not only Santiago's greatness as a fisherman, but the dignity and courage and beauty of the fish himself and the lesson of his loss. The spear is also a gift from the sea that binds man and boy and fish together, a true family heirloom, and a pagan devotional icon. Having received the bequest of the spear, Manolin promises in his turn to leave the boats of the young fishermen where his other "family" has placed him, to follow Santiago for "I still have much to learn" (125). If Santiago is dying, then Manolin's discipleship may be more metaphorical than literal, but the passage of the marlin's spear to him affirms the continuation of Santiago's values, the perpetuation of a line of fishermen who gender the sea as *la mar* because they love her. That Manolin is a worthy heir, we know. From the beginning of the text, when he tells Santiago—"If I cannot fish with you, I would like to serve in some way" (12)—this filial boy has met the test of love as defined by the priest in *A Farewell to Arms*: "When you love you wish to do things for. You wish to sacrifice for. You wish to serve." (72). We expect Manolin to honor both Santiago and the sea by fishing in the disciplined, mindful, sacred way.

Making his bequest, accomplishing this transition, brings Santiago final serenity and this text full circle. We leave him asleep, the boy keeping vigil beside him, dreaming the recurrent dream of lions that has been with him from the beginning of the story (25, 127). The dream lions, we know, come to a long yellow beach to play like young cats in the dusk, and Santiago "love[s] them as he love[s] the boy" (25). "Why are the lions the main thing that is left?" (66), Santiago has wondered, and we may wonder too. Perhaps his dream of innocent predators, allied with the boy and the continuity of life, carries him to a Peaceable Kingdom, an Eden unspoiled by sin where men no longer need to "live on the sea and kill our true brothers" (75), to a place where viewing nature as a contestant or an enemy is no longer possible, and love alone remains.

NOTES

1. This essay will refer to works Hemingway read (*Moby-Dick*, the poetry of Whitman, Thor Heyerdahl's *Kon-Tiki*) before composing *The Old Man and the Sea*, as well as books that he may have read during its composition (Carson's *The Sea Around Us* and *Under the Sea Wind*, Steinbeck and Ricketts's *The Log from the Sea of Cortez*). Hemingway drafted his novella in January and February 1951 (Baker, *Life* 489–90) but did not publish the story until 1 September 1952, in a single installment of *Life* magazine. The long lag between the initial composition of the story and its publication has interesting implications for understanding how Hemingway's reading might have influenced *The Old Man and the Sea* and its ecological ethics. During this period, Hemingway was reading Carson, Steinbeck, and Ricketts and was probably rereading *Moby-Dick*, celebrating its centennial year in 1951. The John F. Kennedy Library holds two typescripts of *The Old Man and the Sea* with corrections in ink; however, Mary Hemingway recalled that her husband "did the whole thing by hand and then I typed it" (qtd. in Bruccoli 191). No longhand draft of *The Old Man and the Sea* has yet been located, making a study of Hemingway's possible revisions based on his 1951 reading impossible.

2. When Hemingway won the Nobel Prize, in part for his achievement in *The Old Man and the Sea*, he gave his medal to the Virgin of Cobre, to be kept in her sanctuary at Santiago de Cuba (Baker, *Life* 528).

3. Originally published in 1941 as *Sea of Cortez: A Leisurely Journal of Travel and Research*, this book was reissued in 1951 as *The Log from the Sea of Cortez*, with its scientific apparatus (an appendix including a phyletic catalogue on the marine animals of the Panamic faunal province) removed.

4. Hemingway owned a copy of the 1951 edition (Brasch and Sigman).

5. Hemingway owned a copy of *Kon-Tiki*, a nonfiction bestseller of 1950, the year before he wrote *The Old Man and the Sea* (Brasch and Sigman).

6. Santiago also admires the loggerheads because they are "strange in their

lovemaking" (36), and in *To Have and Have Not*, Hemingway refers to the widely held belief that loggerheads copulate for three days—"Do they really do it three days? Coot for three days?" Marie asks Harry (113). For this reason, the loggerhead eggs that Santiago eats to "give himself strength" (37) are considered an aphrodisiac (Dennis), and some of this folklore may resonate in his three-day battle with the fish.

Hemingway's description of the loggerhead turtle eating jellyfish with its eyes closed is probably drawn from Thomas Barbour's *A Naturalist in Cuba*, a book in Hemingway's library (Brasch and Sigman). Barbour writes:

> I saw an enormous loggerhead ease up to a Portuguese man-of-war, close its eyes, and nip at the beast. Physalia is well provided with stinging cells and its tentacles are dangerous things to touch. It was amusing to see the old turtle close his eyes as he made his dab at the jellyfish. I have no doubt that the membranes surrounding his eyeballs were the only place where the stinging cells of the siphonophore's arms would have been effective. All other regions were protected by heavy armor. (76)

7. Malcolm Cowley notes that when *The Old Man and the Sea* was published, it was widely referred to as "the poor man's *Moby-Dick*" ("Hemingway's Novel" 106).

8. In Caribbean Spanish, the word *galano*, when applied to an animal, simply means having a dappled or mottled skin (Mandel, e-mail to Beegel). Hence, the Cuban common name for this shark helps with identification. Shark expert Dr. Perry Gilbert notes that near the village of Cojimar a "grande Galano" may be a bull shark (in Farrington 32), or *Carcharhinus leucas*. However, this species, which can inhabit fresh and brackish water as well as saltwater, is never found far from land (R. Ellis 139) and hence cannot be Santiago's deepwater *galano*. Miriam B. Mandel located among Hemingway's papers a 1936 list of commercially valuable fish published by the Cuban secretary of agriculture giving for a *galano* the scientific name of *Charcharias limbatus* (*Reading Hemingway* 352), probably an error for *Carcharhinus limbatus*. But the characteristic black-tipped fins of *C. limbatus* (R. Ellis 302) mean it cannot be Santiago's *galano*, which has "white-tipped wide pectoral fins" (107). Mandel's correspondence with Dr. José I. Castro, senior research scientist of the National Marine Fisheries Service, Miami Branch, identifies the *galano* as the occanic whitetip, *Carcharhinus longimanus* (*Reading Hemingway* 352, 522). In my opinion, this is the only identification that satisfactorily covers the shark's deepwater habitat, mottled skin, white-tipped fins, aggressive scavenging behavior, and notoriety as a man-eater.

9. Rachel Carson first published *Under the Sea Wind* in 1941. The book was republished in April 1952, when it joined *The Sea Around Us* on the *New York Times* bestseller list (Lear 226). Hemingway owned a copy of the 1952 edition (Brasch and Sigman).

Chronology

1899	Born Ernest Miller Hemingway on July 21 in Oak Park, Illinois
1917	Graduates from Oak Park and River Forest High School where he wrote for the school newspaper the *Trapeze*. After graduation he works as a reporter for the *Kansas City Star*.
1918	Enlists in the Red Cross Ambulance Corps and serves in Italy as an ambulance driver; on July 8 he is wounded near Fossalta di Piave; over 200 pieces of shrapnel need to be removed from his leg.
1920	Begins writing for the *Toronto Star* newspapers.
1921	Marries Elizabeth Hadley Richardson; moves to Paris, France on the advice of Sherwood Anderson.
1922	Hemingway meets Ezra Pound and Gertrude Stein.
1923	Attends first bullfight in Spain; publishes *Three Stories and Ten Poems*; moves to Toronto; son John (Bumby) is born in October.
1924	Returns to Paris; publishes *In Our Time* in Europe.
1925	Publishes *In Our Time* in America; meets F. Scott Fitzgerald.
1926	Publishes *The Torrents of Spring* and *The Sun Also Rises*.
1927	Divorces Hadley Richardson; marries Pauline Pfeiffer; publishes *Men Without Women*.

1928	Moves to Key West, Florida; son Patrick is born; father Clarence commits suicide.
1929	Publishes *A Farewell to Arms*.
1931	Hemingway's third son Gregory is born.
1932	Publishes *Death in the Afternoon*.
1933	Publishes *Winner Take Nothing*; begins first African safari.
1935	Publishes *Green Hills of Africa*.
1937	Begins covering Spanish Civil War for the North American Newspaper Alliance while contributing funds to the Loyalist cause; publishes *To Have and Have Not*.
1938	Publishes *The Fifth Column and the First Forty-nine Stories*.
1940	Publishes *For Whom the Bell Tolls*; divorces Pauline Pfeiffer; marries Martha Gellhorn; buys Finca Vigia estate in Cuba.
1942	Begins hunting for German submarines on his boat the *Pilar*.
1944	Serves as war correspondent in Europe and participates in the liberation of Paris; suffers concussion in serious auto accident.
1945	Divorces Martha Gellhorn.
1946	Marries Mary Welsh; they live in Cuba and Idaho.
1950	Publishes *Across the River and into the Trees*; survives a near-fatal plane crash.
1951	Hemingway's mother Grace dies.
1952	Publishes *The Old Man and the Sea*.
1953	Awarded Pulitzer Prize for fiction for 1952; begins second African safari.
1954	Suffers major injuries in two plane crashes in Africa; receives Nobel Prize in literature.
1960	Hemingway returns to the U.S. and is hospitalized for a number of ailments including depression, diabetes, and liver disease; undergoes shock therapy.
1961	Commits suicide in Ketchum, Idaho, on July 2.
1964	*A Moveable Feast* is published.
1970	*Islands in the Stream* is published.
1985	*The Dangerous Summer* is published.
1986	*The Garden of Eden* is published.
1999	*True at First Light* is published.

Contributors

HAROLD BLOOM is Sterling Professor of the Humanities at Yale University. He is the author of over 20 books, including *Shelley's Mythmaking* (1959), *The Visionary Company* (1961), *Blake's Apocalypse* (1963), *Yeats* (1970), *A Map of Misreading* (1975), *Kabbalah and Criticism* (1975), *Agon: Toward a Theory of Revisionism* (1982), *The American Religion* (1992), *The Western Canon* (1994), and *Omens of Millennium: The Gnosis of Angels, Dreams, and Resurrection* (1996). *The Anxiety of Influence* (1973) sets forth Professor Bloom's provocative theory of the literary relationships between the great writers and their predecessors. His most recent books include *Shakespeare: The Invention of the Human* (1998), a 1998 National Book Award finalist, *How to Read and Why* (2000), and *Genius: A Mosaic of One Hundred Exemplary Creative Minds* (2002). In 1999, Professor Bloom received the prestigious American Academy of Arts and Letters Gold Medal for Criticism, and in 2002 he received the Catalonia International Prize.

EDMUND WILSON was literary editor of *The New Republic* (1926–31), and his wide-ranging writing and criticism includes *Axel's Castle* (1931), *To the Finland Station* (1940), *Memoirs of Hecate County* (1946), *The Dead Sea Scrolls* (1969), and *Patriotic Gore* (1962).

ROBERT PENN WARREN is the author of *Promises* (1957), *The Cave* (1959), *Incarnations* (1968), *Audubon: A Vision* (1969), *Now and Then* (1978), *Chief Joseph of the Nez Perce* (1983), and the prose works *World Enough and Time* (1950), *Band of Angels* (1955), and *Democracy and Poetry* (1975). He taught at many institutions, primarily Yale (1961–73), and was named the first official Poet Laureate of the United States (1986). Based in Fairfield, CT, he worked as an editor, wrote critical essays, poetry, and novels, the most famous of which is *All the King's Men* (1946), based on the career of Huey Long. He was also a founder and editor of the *Southern Review* (1935–42) and an advisory editor of *Kenyon Review* (1938-68).

CARLOS BAKER, Hemingway's official biographer, has also written on Shelley, and is the author of the novels *A Friend in Power* (1958), *The Land of Rumbelow* (1963), and *The Gay Head Conspiracy* (1973).

JOHN HOLLANDER is Sterling Professor Emeritus of English at Yale University. Most recent among his seventeen books of poetry are *Figurehead* (1999), *Tesserae* (1993), *Selected Poetry* (1993) a reissue of his earlier *Reflections on Espionage* (2000). His critical books include *The Untuning of the Sky: Ideas of Music in English Poetry, 1500–1700* (1961), *Vision and Resonance* (1975), *The Figure of Echo* (1981), *Rhyme's Reason* (1981) [3rd expanded edition 2000], *Melodious Guile* (1988) *The Gazer's Spirit*, (1995) *The Work of Poetry* (1997),*The Poetry of Everyday Life* (1998).

EARL ROVIT, Professor of English at the City College of New York, is the author of *Herald to Chaos* (1960), a study of the novels of Elizabeth Madox Roberts, and *Saul Bellow* (1967). Along with many articles on American literature and culture, he has published three novels.

GERRY BRENNER, a member of the English department at the University of Montana, is the author of *Concealments in Hemingway's Works* (1983) and a number of articles on American and British literature.

EDWARD F. STANTON is Professor of Spanish at the University of Kentucky. He is the author of *The Tragic Myth: Lorca and "Cante Jondo"* and the coeditor of *The Uruguay* by José Basílío da Gama.

MARK SPILKA, a Professor of English and Comparative Literature at Brown University, is the editor of *Novel: A Forum on Fiction* and the author of *Virginia Woolf's Quarrel with Grieving* (1980).

HUBERT ZAPF is Professor of English and American Literature at the University of Paderborn, Germany, and the author of *Saul Bellow, Theory and Structure of Modern English Drama*, and other articles on English and American literature and literary theory.

DEBRA A. MODDELMOG is Professor, Director of Graduate Studies and coordinator of the interdisciplinary minor in sexuality studies in the Ohio State University department of English. Her areas of interest include twentieth-century American literatures, multiculturalism, and queer theory. She has published a number of articles in these areas, as well as two books: *Readers and Mythic Signs: The Oedipus Myth in Twentieth-Century Fiction* (1993) and *Reading Desire: In Pursuit of Ernest Hemingway* (1999).

SUSAN F. BEEGEL is a Professor in the Williams College-Mystic Seaport Maritime Studies Program, where she teaches "Literature of the Sea." She is editor of *The Ernest Hemingway Review*, and her books include *Hemingway's Craft of Omission* (1988), *Hemingway's Neglected Short Fiction* (1989), and *Steinbeck and the Environment: Interdisciplinary Approaches* (1997).

Bibliography

Aldridge, John. "*The Sun Also Rises*: Sixty Years Later." *Sewanee Review* 94.2 (1986): 337–45.

Astro, Richard and Jackson J. Benson. eds. *Hemingway in Our Time*. Corvallis: Oregon State UP 1974

Baker, Carlos. Ernest Hemingway: Critiques of Four Major Novels. New York: Scribner's, 1962.

———. *Ernest Hemingway: A Life Story*. New York: Scribner's, 1969.

———. *Hemingway, The Writer As Artist*. Princeton, NJ: Princeton University Press, 1972.

———, ed. Ernest Hemingway, Selected Letters. New York: Granda, 1981.

Balassi, William. "The Trail to *The Sun Also Rises*: The First Week of Writing." In *Hemingway: Essays of Reassessment*. Ed. Frank Scafella. Oxford: Oxford University Press, 1991.

Beegel, Susan. ed. *Hemingway's Neglected Short Fiction*. Tuscaloosa: University of Alabama Press, 1992.

Benson, Jackson J., ed. *The Short Stories of Ernest Hemingway: Critical Essays*. Durham, N.C.: Duke University Press, 1975.

———.*New Critical Approaches to the Short Stories of Ernest Hemingway*. Durham, North Carolina: Duke University Press, 1990.

Bloom, Harold, ed. *Bloom's BioCritiques: Ernest Hemingway*. Philadelphia: Chelsea House Publishers, 2002.

———. *Bloom's Major Novelists: Ernest Hemingway*. Philadelphia: Chelsea House Publishers, 2000.

———. *Bloom's Short Story Writers: Ernest Hemingway*. Philadelphia: Chelsea House Publishers, 1999.

Brenner, Gerry. *Concealments in Hemingway's Works*. Columbus: Ohio State University Press, 1983.

———. *The Old Man and the Sea: Story of a Common Man*. New York: Twayne Publishers, 1991.

Brasch, James D. and Joseph Sigman. *Hemingway's Library: A Composite Record*. New York: Garland, 1981.

Bruccoli, Matthew J. *Scott and Ernest: The Authority of Failure and the Authority of Success*. New York: Random House, 1978.

Burgess, Anthony. *Ernest Hemingway and His World*. New York: Scribner, 1978.

Burgess, Robert F. *Hemingway's Paris and Pamplona, Then, and Now: A Personal Memoir*. iUniverse.com, 2000.

Burwell, Rose Marie. *Hemingway: The Postwar Years and the Posthumous Novels*. NY: Cambridge University Press, 1996.

Comley, Nancy, and Robert Scholes. *Hemingway's Genders: Rereading the Hemingway Text*. New Haven: Yale University Press, 1994.

Davidson, Arnold E. and Cathy. "Decoding the Hemingway Hero in *The Sun Also Rises*." In *New Essays on the Sun Also Rises*. Ed. Linda Wagner-Martin. New York: Cambridge University Press, 1987.

Donaldson, Scott. *By Force of Will: The Life and Art of Ernest Hemingway*. New York: Viking P, 1977.

———, ed. *The Cambridge Companion to Ernest Hemingway*. New York: Cambridge University Press, 1996.

Eby, Carl P. *Hemingway's Fetishism: Psychoanalysis and the Mirror of Manhood*. Albany, NY: State University of NY Press, 1998.

Falco, Joseph M. *The Hero in Hemingway's Short Stories*. Pittsburgh: University of Pittsburgh Press, 1968.

Fenton, Charles Andrews. *The Apprenticeship of Ernest Hemingway: The Early Years*. New York: Farrar, Straus and Young, 1954.

Fleming, Robert E. *The Face in the Mirror: Hemingway's Writers*. University of Alabama Press, 1994.

Flora, Joseph M. *Hemingway's Nick Adams*. Baton Rouge: Louisiana State University Press, 1982.

———. *Ernest Hemingway: A Study of the Short Fiction*. Boston: Twayne, 1989.

Gurko, Leo. *Ernest Hemingway and The Pursuit of Heroism*. New York: Crowell, 1968.

Hatten, Charles. "The Crisis of Masculinity, Reified Desire, and Catherine Barkley in *A Farewell to Arms*." *Journal of the History of Sexuality* 4 (July 1993): 76–98.

Hays, Peter L. *Ernest Hemingway*. New York: Continuum, 1990.

Hemingway, Ernest. *Men Without Women*. New York: Scribner's, 1927.

———. *Death in the Afternoon*. New York: Scribner's, 1932.

———. *Green Hills of Africa*. New York: Scribner's, 1935.

———. *To Have and Have Not*. New York: Scribner's, 1937.

———. *The Fifth Column, and the First Forty-Nine Stories*. New York: Scribner's, 1938.

———. *For Whom the Bell Tolls*. New York: Scribner's, 1940.

———. *Across the River and Into the Trees*. New York: Scribner's, 1950.

———. *The Old Man and the Sea*. New York: Scribner's, 1952.

———. *The Sun Also Rises*. New York: Scribner's, 1954.

———. *A Farewell to Arms*. New York: Scribner's, 1957.

———. *In Our Time*. New York: Scribner's, 1958.

———. *A Moveable Feast*. New York: Scribner's, 1964.

———. *The Snows of Kilimanjaro, and Other Stories*. New York: Scribner's, 1970.

———. *Islands in the Stream*. New York: Scribner's, 1970.

———. *The Nick Adams Stories*. New York: Scribner's, 1972.

———. *Winner Take Nothing*. New York: Scribner's, 1983.

Hemingway, Gregory. *Papa: A Personal Memoir*. Boston: Houghton Mifflin, 1976.

Hemingway, Leicester. *My Brother Ernest Hemingway*. Cleveland: World Publishing, 1962.

Josephs, Allen. *For Whom the Bell Tolls: Ernest Hemingway's Undiscovered Country*. New York: Twayne Publishers, 1994.

Kert, Bernice. *The Hemingway Women*. NY: Norton, 1985.

Lamb, Robert P. "Hemingway and the Creation of Twentieth-Century Dialogue." *Twentieth Century literature* 42.4 (Wint 1996): 453–481.

Larson, Kelli A. *Ernest Hemingway: A Reference Guide, 1974–1989*. Boston: G.K. Hall, 1991.

Lee, A. Robert. *Ernest Hemingway: New Critical Essays* Totowa, N.J.: Barnes & Noble, 1983.

Lewis, Robert W. *A Farewell to Arms: The War of the Words*. New York: Twayne Publishers, 1992.

Meyers, Jeffrey, ed. *Hemingway, The Critical Heritage*. Boston: Routledge & Kegan Paul, 1982.

Monteiro, George, Ed. *Critical Essays on Ernest Hemingway's A Farewell to Arms*. New York: G. K. Hall, 1994.

Nagel, James, ed. *Ernest Hemingway, The Writer in Context*. Madison: University of Wisconsin Press, 1984.

Nahal, Chaman Lal. *The Narrative Pattern in Ernest Hemingway's Fiction*. Rutherford, N.J.: Fairleigh Dickinson University Press, 1971

Nelson, Raymond S. *Ernest Hemingway, Life, Work, and Criticism*. Fredericton, N.B.: York Press, 1984.

Raeburn, John. *Fame Became Him: Hemingway as a Public Writer.* Bloomington: Indiana University Press, 1984.

Reynolds, Michael S. *Hemingway's First War: The Making of "A Farewell to Arms."* Princeton: Princeton University Press, 1976.

———. *Critical Essays on Ernest Hemingway's "In Our Time."* Boston: G.K. Hall, 1983.

———. *Hemingway: The Paris Years*. Cambridge: Blackwell, 1989.

———. *Hemingway: The American Homecoming*. Cambridge: Blackwell, 1992.

———. *Hemingway: The 1930's*. NY: Norton, 1997.

———. *Hemingway: The Final Years*. NY: Norton, 1999.

Rovit, Earl H. *Ernest Hemingway*. Boston: Twayne , 1986.

Rudat, Wolfgang. *A Rotten Way To Be Wounded: The Tragicomedy of The Sun Also Rises.*. New York: Peter Lang, 1990.

———. "Hemingway's *The Sun Also Rises*:: Masculinity, Feminism, and Gender-Role Reversal." *American Imago* 47.1 (1990): 43–68.

Ryan, Frank L. *The Immediate Critical Reception of Ernest Hemingway*. Washington D.C., University Press of America, 1980.

Scafella, Frank, ed. *Hemingway: Essays of Reassessment*. Oxford: Oxford University Press, 1991.

Smith, Paul. *A Reader's Guide to the Short Stories of Ernest Hemingway*. NY: MacMillan, 1989.

———. ed. *New Essays on Hemingway's Short Fiction*. NY: Cambridge University Press, 1998.

Spilka, Mark. "The Death of Love in *The Sun Also Rises*." In *Ernest*

Hemingway: Critiques of Four Major Novels. Ed. Carlos Baker. New York: Charles Scribner's Sons, 1962.

———. *Hemingway's Quarrel with Androgyny.* Lincoln: University of Nebraska Press, 1990.

Stephens, Robert O., ed. *Ernest Hemingway: The Critical Reception.* New York: B. Franklin, 1977.

Strychacz, Thomas. "Dramatizations of Manhood in Hemingway's In Our Time and *The Sun Also Rises.*." *American Literature* 61.2 (1989): 245–60.

Wagner-Martin, Linda. *Hemingway and Faulkner: Inventors/Masters.* Metuchen, N.J.: Scarecrow P, 1975.

———. ed. *Ernest Hemingway: Five Decades of Criticism.* East Lansing: Michigan State University Press, 1974.

Weber, Ronald. *Hemingway's Art of Non-Fiction.* New York: St. Martin's Press, 1990.

White, William, ed. *By-Line: Hemingway, Selected Articles and Dispatches of Four Decades.* New York: Scribner's, 1967.

Acknowledgments

"Hemingway: Gauge of Morale" from *The Wound and the Bow: Seven Studies In The Literature* by Edmund Wilson. 214–242. © 1978 by Edmund Wilson. Reprinted by permission of Farrar, Straus and Giroux, LLC.

"Ernest Hemingway" from *Robert Penn Warren: Selected Essays*. 80–118. © 1935 by the Bookman Co. & 1951 by Random House. Reprinted by permission.

"The Way It Was" from *Hemingway: The Writer as Artist by Carlos Baker*. 48–74. © 1952 by Princeton University Press, 2nd Edition, 1980 renewed in author's name. Reprinted by permission of Princeton University Press.

"Hemingway's Extraordinary Actuality" by John Hollander. From *Ernest Hemingway* Harold Bloom, ed. 211–216. © 1985 by John Hollander. Reprinted by permission.

"Of Tyros and Tutors" from *Ernest Hemingway* by Earl Rovit and Gerry Brenner. 37–61. © 1986 by G.K. Hall & Co. Reprinted by permission of the Gale Group.

"Of Bulls and Men" From *Hemingway and Spain: A Pursuit* by Edward F. Stanton. 91–125. © 1989 by The University of Washington Press. Reprinted by permission.

"A Retrospective Epilogue: On the Importance of Being Androgynous" from *Hemingway's Quarrel With Androgyny* by Mark Spilka. 327–336. © 1990 by the University of Nebraska Press. Reprinted by permission of the University of Nebraska Press.

"Reflection vs. Daydream: Two Types of the Implied Reader in Hemingway's Fiction" by Hubert Zapf. From *New Critical Approaches to the Short Stories of Ernest Hemingway*, edited by Jackson J. Benson. 96–111. © 1990 by Duke University Press. All rights reserved. Used by permission of the publisher.

"On Psychic Retrenchment in Hemingway" by Earl Rovit from *Hemingway: Essays of Reassessment*, edited by Frank Scafella. 181–188. © 1991 by Oxford University Press, Inc. Used by permission of Oxford University Press.

"The Disabled Body and the White Heteromasculinity" from *Reading Desire: In Pursuit of Ernest Hemingway* by Debra A. Moddelmog. 119–130. © 1999 by Cornell University. Used by permission of Cornell University Press.

"Santiago and the Eternal Feminine Gendering La Mar in The Old Man and the Sea" by Susan F. Beegel. From *Hemingway and Women: Female Critics and the Female Voice*, edited by Lawrence R. Broer and Gloria Holland. 131–156. © 2003 The University of Alabama Press. Reprinted by permission.

Index

Characters in literary works are indexed by first name followed by the name of the work in parentheses.